KENNEDY, MACMILLAN AND NUCLEAR WEAPONS

COLD WAR HISTORY SERIES
General Editor: Saki Dockrill, Senior Lecturer in War Studies,
King's College, London

The new Cold War History Series aims to make available to scholars and students the results of advanced research on the origins and the development of the Cold War and its impact on nations, alliances and regions at various levels of statecraft, and in areas such as diplomacy, security, economy, military and society. Volumes in the series range from detailed and original specialised studies, proceedings of conferences, to broader and more comprehensive accounts. Each work deals with individual themes and periods of the Cold War and each author or editor approaches the Cold War with a variety of narrative, analysis, explanation, interpretation and reassessments of recent scholarship. These studies are designed to encourage investigation and debate on important themes and events in the Cold War, as seen from both East and West, in an effort to deepen our understanding of this phenomenon and place it in its context in world history.

Titles include:

Günter Bischof
AUSTRIA IN THE FIRST COLD WAR, 1945–55
The Leverage of the Weak

Donette Murray
KENNEDY, MACMILLAN AND NUCLEAR WEAPONS

Cold War History
Series Standing Order ISBN 0–333–79482–6
(*outside North America only*)

You can receive future titles in this series as they are published by placing a standing order. Please contact your bookseller or, in case of difficulty, write to us at the address below with your name and address, the title of the series and the ISBN quoted above.

Customer Services Department, Macmillan Distribution Ltd
Houndmills, Basingstoke, Hampshire RG21 6XS, England

Kennedy, Macmillan and Nuclear Weapons

Donette Murray

Lecturer in Modern and Contemporary History
University of Ulster at Coleraine
Northern Ireland

First published in Great Britain 2000 by
MACMILLAN PRESS LTD
Houndmills, Basingstoke, Hampshire RG21 6XS and London
Companies and representatives throughout the world

A catalogue record for this book is available from the British Library.

ISBN 0–333–75382–8

First published in the United States of America 2000 by
ST. MARTIN'S PRESS, INC.,
Scholarly and Reference Division,
175 Fifth Avenue, New York, N.Y. 10010

ISBN 0–312–22221–1

Library of Congress Cataloging-in-Publication Data
Murray, Donette, 1973–
Kennedy, Macmillan and nuclear weapons / Donette Murray.
p. cm. — (Cold War history)
Includes bibliographical references and index.
ISBN 0–312–22221–1 (cloth)
1. United States—Military relations—Great Britain. 2. Great
Britain—Military relations—United States. 3. Nuclear weapons.
I. Title. II. Series.
UA23.M928 1999
355'.031'09410973—dc21 99–21772
CIP

This book is printed on paper suitable for recycling and made from fully managed and
sustained forest sources.

10   9   8   7   6   5   4   3   2   1
09   08   07   06   05   04   03   02   01   00

Printed and bound in Great Britain by
Antony Rowe Ltd, Chippenham, Wiltshire

Contents

Acknowledgements   vii

Abbreviations   ix

Introduction   1

1 Special Relations?   13

2 The Origins of a Crisis   31

3 Chaos and Confusion – Allies in Trouble   45

4 A Crisis Explained   57

5 Finding a Solution – The Nassau Compromise   81

6 A New Foreign Policy Initiative – Are There Any
   Takers?   105

7 Do or Die – The Making and Breaking of the
   Multilateral Nuclear Force   122

Conclusion   144

Notes and References   159

Glossary of Names   198

Select Bibliography   203

Index   215

v

Acknowledgements

This work originally took the form of a DPhil thesis, awarded in 1997. I am deeply grateful for the help and advice of my doctoral supervisor, Tom Fraser, who deftly guided me through the bewildering and at times frustrating path of research with great patience and care. I owe a great debt both to him and to Michael Dockrill and Alan Sharp who examined the thesis. They, along with Saki Dockrill, were instrumental in helping me to transform it into this book. In particular, I would like to express my gratitude to Saki Dockrill, my editor, who provided guidance, encouragement and helpful criticism, which were both very much appreciated and extremely useful.

This work has benefited greatly from the comments and suggestions of the following who kindly and patiently took time to respond to the numerous questions posed by the author: Richard Neustadt, Arthur Schlesinger Jr, Carl Kaysen, Sir Frederick Bishop, Sir Arthur Henderson, Sir Edward Playfair, Eunan O'Halpin, Michael Cox, Simon Ball, Richard Aldous and Sabine Lee.

The research for this book was helped by a number of archivists and librarians at various institutions in both the UK and the United States. I wish to express my thanks to the archivists at the Public Record Office, Kew; the John F. Kennedy Library, Boston; the National Archives, Washington, DC; and the Bodleian Library, Oxford. They were all extremely courteous and kind. My thanks also to the library staff at the University of Ulster and in particular to Kay Ballantyne who provided invaluable assistance.

I would also like to thank the staff and graduate students at the University of Ulster, and in particular Alan Sharp, Ken Ward, Tony Emmerson, Bill Riches and Joanne Taggart. I gratefully acknowledge the financial assistance given to me by the University of Ulster.

Copyright material from the Public Record Office, Kew, appears by permission of Her Majesty's Stationery Office. Abridged portions of chapters 3, 4, 5, and 6 appeared in *Royal Irish Academy Conference Proceedings* in 1996 and in Sabine Lee and Richard Aldous (eds), *Harold Macmillan: Aspects of a Political Life* (Macmillan, forthcoming). Full citations appear in the bibliography.

I would also like to thank the Macmillan Trustees for their kind permission to examine and reproduce extracts from the Harold Macmillan diaries.

I wish to thank Tim Farmiloe, Publishing Director, and Annabelle Buckley, Senior Commissioning Editor, at Macmillan for their great help in preparing the manuscript for publication.

I owe a particular debt to Keith Kyle who gave not only of his time, but also of his vast knowledge and colourful recollections.

Finally, I express my gratitude and thanks to my parents, family and friends for their help and humour and to Martin for his support and encouragement throughout. His unshakable belief in me and uncompromising love mean more than he will ever know.

Donette Murray
Derry

Abbreviations

AEA	Atomic Energy Authority
AEC	Atomic Energy Committee
ALBM	air-launched ballistic missile
AWRE	Atomic Weapons Research Establishment
BOAR	British Army of the Rhine
BJSM	British Joint Staff Mission, Washington
BMEWS	Ballistic Missile Early Warning System
BNDSG	British Nuclear Deterrent Study Group
CAS	Chief of the Air Staff
CDS	Chief of the Defence Staff
CINCLANT	Commander in Chief, Atlantic
CND	Campaign for Nuclear Disarmament
COS	Chiefs of Staff
COSC	Chiefs of Staff Committee
DOD	Department of Defense
FO	Foreign Office
GNP	Gross National Product
ICBM	inter-continental ballistic missile
IRBM	intermediate-range ballistic missile
JCAE	Joint Committee on Atomic Energy
JCS	Joint Chiefs of Staff
JIC	Joint Intelligence Committee
JPS	Joint Planning Staff
KT	kiloton
MLF	multilateral nuclear force
MOD	Ministry of Defence
MRBM	medium-range ballistic missile
MT	megaton
MWDP	Mutual Weapons Development Weapon
NAC	North Atlantic Council
NATO	North Atlantic Treaty Organization
NSC	National Security Council
OR	operational requirement
PM	Prime Minister
PSAC	President's Science Advisory Committee
R & D	Research and Development

SAC	Strategic Air Command
SACEUR	Supreme Allied Commander, Europe
SACLANT	Supreme Allied Commander, Atlantic
SAGW	surface-to-air guided weapon
SHAPE	Supreme Headquarters Allied Powers Europe
SIOP	single-integrated operational plan
SLBM	submarine-launched ballistic missile
UKAEC	United Kingdom Atomic Energy Authority
USAEC	United States Atomic Energy Commission
USAF	United States Air Force
USJCAE	United States Joint Committee on Atomic Energy (US Congress)
USJCS	United States Joint Chiefs of Staff
USN	United States Navy

Introduction

Throughout this story most of what went wrong cast shadows in advance. There was no lack of clues; the lack was time, or thought, to pick them up and read them.[1]

Alliance diplomacy failed in late 1962 when Britain and the United States almost fell out over the cancellation of an experimental weapon – the Skybolt air-launched ballistic missile. The threatened breakdown in Anglo-American relations appeared to have been resolved at the December Nassau Conference, but the upset was deemed all the more disturbing since the two parties were thought to have been the closest of allies. If this could happen between Britain and the United States, observers on both sides of the Atlantic speculated, what disasters could arise out of disputes with an enemy? In this instance, cordial, even intimate relations between the two allies had not prevented a situation that had looked dangerously close to developing into a full-blown crisis with potentially highly damaging consequences. Even after the Skybolt crisis appeared to have been resolved, the heated debate over the Multilateral Nuclear Force envisaged for NATO (an idea that had been in circulation for some years but was resurrected with renewed vigour and importance as a result of the decisions reached between Britain and the United States at the Nassau Conference in December 1962) ensured that 1963 would be a year of continued conflict, tension and argument within Anglo-American and Atlantic Alliance relations. This study attempts to identify and explain these events, offering an analysis based on the reading of newly available material. In short, this is an examination of debate, disagreement and, ultimately, of crisis within Anglo-American relations.

The presidency of John F. Kennedy was a short-lived one and seemed to capture the hearts and minds of people all over the world. Early biographies by close Kennedy aides Arthur Schlesinger Jr and Theodore Sorenson established an image that created the Kennedy 'myth'. The late president was portrayed as a vigorous, dynamic and charismatic leader, whose style and passion marked a new era in political affairs in the United States. The Kennedy 'New Frontier' had promised to rejuvenate all aspects of American life after the sterile and uninspiring 1950s. But, the president did not

1

live long enough to fulfil many of the expectations demanded of him. His 1,000 days in office turned out to be a short, transitory period of hope. Lyndon Johnson, although getting through Congress many of the progressive pieces of legislation sponsored by the previous administration, soon became embroiled in a war that not only destroyed his political career, but caused disillusionment and despair to a generation of Americans. During the 1970s and 1980s, historiography attempted to dispel the Kennedy 'myth', with claims that Kennedy was a very average, even disappointing president when assessed by his legislative record. Now, a new decade has brought a new perspective on how the Kennedy presidency is perceived. The consensus is less harsh than that of the 1970s, but neither is it blinded by the wave of emotion and profound sense of loss that characterised the early analyses. American innocence and belief in the possibility of bright, good, new things died with Kennedy. Today, American presidents are still trying to recapture the spirit and the elusive charm of the Kennedy era.

The British Prime Minister Harold Macmillan had come to power some years before Kennedy, following the resignation of Anthony Eden. Macmillan had expected to remain in office for just six weeks, but once the general election had confirmed him for considerably longer, he had set about organising the Conservative Party and the country according to his very firm views. Probably his greatest objective in foreign policy was to restore close Anglo-American relations.

Historians and political scientists over the past two decades have produced a number of well-informed and generally accurate accounts of the crises that occurred in Anglo-American relations during the Kennedy administration. Most of these studies agree about the basic diplomacy of the events in question. The best of the early analyses can be found in the works of David Nunnerley and Andrew J. Pierre, both written in the early 1970s. Nunnerley's book, *President Kennedy and Britain*, analyses the so-called 'special Anglo-American relationship' and offers detailed accounts of the common interests and shared problems that occupied Britain and the United States in this period. This is a fairly concise account, based largely on dozens of lengthy interviews with top British and American officials, identifying a number of the themes central to the Skybolt crisis and the Multilateral Nuclear Force debate. For example, he highlights the breakdown of communication – so often cited as one of the main factors contributing to the crisis – and the different agendas pursued by both governments. Like Nunnerley's, Pierre's detailed account of Britain's experience with nuclear weapons, *Nuclear Politics: The British Experience with an Independent Strategic Force 1939–1970*, provides a valuable insight into events from an 'insider's' point of view. (Pierre was on the staff of the American Embassy in London during the Skybolt and MLF episodes.) More recent works have undoubtedly relied heavily on these two volumes. John Baylis's *Ambiguity and Deterrence: British Nuclear Strategy* and Ian Clark's *Nuclear Diplomacy and the Special Relationship* both offer excellent accounts of the period.[2] Making use of a great deal of recently released information and documents, they have largely fulfilled their claims of 'setting the record straight' by filling in the acknowledged gaps and correcting a number of fallacies and inaccuracies along the way. Their adjustments have gone some way to achieving a clearer and more detailed picture of the crises under examination. For example, Nunnerley's assertion that the British Ambassador, David Ormsby-Gore, and American Ambassador, David Bruce, failed to fulfil their potential as brokers of a settlement has been challenged. Likewise, in his account, Pierre suggested that there was no agreed US position before the Nassau Conference.[3] Baylis, however, has produced evidence to indicate that Kennedy and his team had indeed discussed and agreed that Polaris must be considered as a solution to the Skybolt problem at a meeting on 16 December.

Clark attempts to understand the domestic dilemmas of British nuclear strategy in the context of Anglo-American relations by concentrating on two parallel sets of developments – the evolution of British nuclear strategy itself and the quest for the hardware necessary to put such a strategy into effect. His account seeks to assess the degree of British accommodation to, or influence over, American policy.[4] Clark offers a systematic interpretation of the official rationales of British nuclear strategy and of the considerations and concerns which contributed to specific decisions about weapons and force levels. He sheds new light on the nature of the commitment given by Eisenhower to Macmillan, concerning Polaris at Camp David and the diplomacy of the Skybolt cancellation crisis, as well as the reasons for Kennedy's decision to sell Polaris.[5] In his work, Clark arrives at two main conclusions. First, he points out that it has become something of a fixture in the literature to pose the issue in 1960 as a clear choice between Skybolt and Polaris and offers an explanation as to why Polaris was not selected at that stage. Clark suggests that it was not so much a matter of choosing

Polaris as deferring the moment when the approach might best be made. He believes that even if the Admiralty had been a more energetic or skilful lobby on behalf of Polaris, no convincing evidence exists to suggest that a deal could have been struck in 1960 for the simple reason that the United States was not prepared to make Polaris available to Britain on terms acceptable to the government.[6] Clark's second point concerns the original Skybolt–Holy Loch 'deal' which, he claims, was more diverse than a straightforward quid pro quo. To the extent that there was a written linkage, it involved three elements and not those two alone. The third element was the proposal for a NATO MRBM force. Clark maintains that if the government was adamant, both at the beginning and at the end of the process, that there was indeed a formal linkage, it was being selective in its interpretation of the Camp David understandings by failing to take seriously the third element, which was some commitment to the MRBM proposal. This evidence dispels the false assumption that if Macmillan had taken Polaris and run in 1960, the traumatic experiences of the next two years might have been avoided. Moreover, the full extent of the discussion of Polaris in 1960 and its location in the MRBM context offers a better appreciation of the forces at work at Nassau in 1962 when the issue was suddenly projected to the forefront of the diplomatic stage.[7]

Baylis focuses on British nuclear strategy and aligns himself closely with Clark in his analysis of the Skybolt and MLF debates, sharing many of the latter's assumptions and observations. Baylis mirrors Clark in his comment that 'despite attempts in late 1961 to clear up some of the confusion over what was meant by "independence", British strategic planning continued to suffer from a lack of clear direction as contradictory pressures pulled in different directions and the service Chiefs continued to offer conflicting advice'.[8] In his account, he sheds new light on the mechanics of the Nassau agreement, dispelling the myths that there was a conspiracy on the British side to get Polaris, and that Kennedy had been persuaded by Macmillan at the conference to offer Britain Polaris.[9] Baylis also clears up some of the ambiguity surrounding the actual agreement, identifying prior confusion and slack staff work among American officials rather than British machinations as the cause of the contradictory references to multilateralism and multinationalism in the Nassau Communiqué.[10]

These interpretations, while highly accurate in many respects, are not fully representative and lack some of the depth and clarity now afforded by the release of newly declassified archival material. For example, it can now be shown that evidence exists to suggest that this propensity towards Polaris was established at an even earlier meeting, on 10 December – a crucial development because it *preceded* Secretary of Defense Robert McNamara's pivotal and combative meeting with his British counterpart, Peter Thorneycroft, the following day.

This study presents the most complete and up-to-date account and analysis of the Skybolt crisis and MLF controversy. Using the most recently available archival material it outlines and discusses the straining and breakdown of Alliance diplomacy and provides a reinterpretation of the difficult relations the problems created between the two countries.[11]

The period under examination was one of great change and upheaval. The United States was a mighty superpower and seemed to be expanding at a phenomenal rate economically, technologically and culturally. With the arrival of jet airliners, television, computers, interstate highways, direct long-distance telephone dialling, and mind-expanding drugs, the pace of life was speeding up at an unprecedented rate. These changes in society were reflected in popular music. The 'perky' love songs of the previous decade were replaced by more serious lyrics dealing with social injustice, protests against society and the government, and expressions of sexual freedom, peace and self-awareness.[12] Against this background of unprecedented wealth, personal freedom and opportunity lay the deep-rooted fear of nuclear annihilation in a war with the Soviet Union. Empowered to a greater extent than their forefathers, Americans still faced the chilling threat of destruction. These conflicting developments created a society supremely confident and forward-looking but which was also deeply paralysed by the fear of communism and obsessed with national defence.

Britain, in comparison, was something of a poor relation. Still suffering from the effects of the Second World War and Korea, it had neither the wealth nor optimism that inspired her powerful ally across the Atlantic. Although people were better off than they had been, the sheer volume of social and economic problems in Britain prevented the country from experiencing anything like the changes sweeping the United States. Everything happened first in America and then slowly made its way across the Atlantic. Britain looked to the United States for the latest fashions, innovations, gadgets, entertainment and technology. British leaders were aware that these momentous changes had serious implications for the country and its role in the world order. Britain could no longer expect to lead the world in scientific and technological innovation, nor could it expect to pursue the same foreign policy ambitions that had once made Britain 'Great'. In short, this was a time of change.

The aim of the study is to examine the relationship between the United States and Britain in the period 1961–3. The two countries had been the closest of allies for decades, weathering upsets and upheavals with a success that pointed to a deep bond. During the Kennedy presidency, the Anglo-American relationship again came under severe pressure, culminating in what has been described as the most serious crisis to rock the alliance since the Suez débâcle. Alliance relations were considered fundamental to the stability of world order by the United States, and the problems and difficulties besetting the alliance were a subject of deep concern. In consequence, the search for consensus and co-operation informed policy-making on both sides of the Atlantic. In the light of new evidence it is now possible to challenge even this assumption and ask if, indeed, this was really a crisis, and, if so, what implications the affair had on British strategic policy-making and Anglo-American relations in general. What lessons did each side take in order to prevent a similar occurrence at some point in the future? As Richard Neustadt, President Kennedy's adviser and author of the report into the Skybolt affair commented:

> From 'Skybolt' as an issue in our policy-making I draw a simple lesson: regardless of structures or procedures, much of what occurred here will occur again. How much depends upon the vigilance (and luck) of individuals.[13]

Chapter 1 is concerned with the 'special relationship' which has been both cherished and deplored by politicians and commentators on both sides of the Atlantic. Writing in the early 1970s, David Nunnerley thought it probable that the 'specialness' had all but disappeared from Anglo-American relations, enough at least for him to write dispassionately about what was regarded at one time as a unique bond that visited great prizes and burdens on the parties involved. Although the late 1960s and 1970s did see a marked deterioration in relations between the two countries, today it is difficult to share this certainty. Despite the changing international scene and momentous events, none greater than the unanticipated collapse of communism and the ending of the Cold War, relations between Britain and the United States would appear to retain an element of 'specialness'. Margaret Thatcher and Ronald Reagan shared a very public closeness. Bill Clinton and Tony Blair have apparently recaptured some of the warmth and intimacy attributed to the Kennedy–Macmillan relationship. In short, however it has been defined, to some degree a close and unique relationship must be said to have existed and continues to exist between the United States and Britain. Chapter 1 attempts to define and explain the nature of this ambiguous relationship in the period 1961–3 and to identify what impact this had on the difficulties the two allies faced. Was it 'special', and if so, for whom? Was the importance attached to the relationship disproportionate, and again, if so, why? What relevance did it have for the events and disputes under investigation? Did the 'special relationship' help overcome the difficulties experienced between the two countries, or did the intimacy of the relations hinder or exacerbate the problems? This chapter focuses on what have been traditionally regarded as the primary elements within the 'special relationship' – defence/military and intelligence – and traces the development of this unique relationship from its origins in the Second World War.

Co-operation and collaboration during the Second World War set a precedent for intimacy that was never fully abandoned. Military operations, jointly co-ordinated, planned and executed, established contacts between the Armed Services and the men who fought in them. Likewise, shared intelligence gathering and interpretation created links in the intelligence world unparalleled in relations between any other allied countries. Perhaps most significantly, however, were the contacts and relationships formed during the quest for atomic mastery. What had begun as a British-sponsored attempt to produce atomic power became transformed into an essentially Anglo-American concern with the creation of the Manhattan Project in 1942 in which Britain rapidly became the junior partner. After the successful development of an atomic bomb and the close of the war, the United States introduced legislation that effectively prevented Britain from continuing to pursue nuclear research in collaboration with America, thereby forcing Britain to begin an unaided native atomic weapons project. This policy of non-cooperation was gradually amended and, by 1960, full nuclear co-operation had been officially restored and the military collaboration that had never really ceased was given official approval.

The changes in the defence relations between Britain and the United States can be attributed to a number of factors and events from which they both benefited and, at times, suffered. The Suez Affair in 1956 was one confrontation that had enormous and far-reaching repercussions for the 'special relationship'. The confrontation stimulated two contradictory sentiments and policies: on the one hand, Suez encouraged a renewed push for the restoration of the close relations the two countries enjoyed; while on the other, it provoked a debate about the wisdom of increasing interdependence with the United States and questioned whether or not Britain – for reasons of influence, and prestige and in the case America, should decide at some later time to relinquish her commitments in and to Europe – should be independent. The interdependence vs. independence debate permeated British policy and decision-making. Without reaching any decision, the government attempted to keep both policies alive and viable. This came to a head in 1962 and 1963 when Macmillan and his colleagues faced two major areas of Anglo-American disagreement: confrontation and, ultimately, crisis.

Chapters 2 and 3 define and assess the factors and events leading up to the cancellation of the Skybolt weapons system in December 1962, while chapter 4 is devoted to an analysis of the crisis. The decision by the US Secretary of Defense took place against a backdrop of profound strategic doctrinal and technological changes, a change in the American presidency and reassessment of the British government's attitudes towards a number of policies. Moreover, the cancellation heightened tensions and uncertainties already in existence with implications that extended far beyond the confines of Anglo-American relations. The story of Skybolt is one that has been recounted many times and is generally well known. However, as is so often the case in historical debate, new evidence has made it possible to look back over this key event and offer a fresh assessment of the crisis and the implications it had for both Anglo-American relations and the NATO partners.

When a subject is familiar there is the danger that small and seemingly inconsequential details may be overlooked or ignored. This has been the case with the Skybolt crisis. A close reading of all the available documentation and accounts of the incident revealed inconsistencies and unanswered questions which have left many gaps in the conventional analysis. A number of questions can now be posed: what was the real nature of the linkage between the original 1960 Skybolt and Holy Loch agreements? This is still ambiguous and difficult to pinpoint. There would appear to be no *formal* link in the official documents. However, a great deal of negotiation took place in the months after Camp David in March 1960 in an effort to reach a formal agreement on the two matters. For a better understanding of the crisis, it is necessary to determine the exact linkage between the original 1960 Skybolt and Holy Loch agreements and what implications this had for the crisis in 1962.

Another aspect of the original negotiations for Skybolt that remains unclear is the extent to which the Polaris weapons system was discussed as a possible alternative to Skybolt in 1960. Previous accounts have been vague on this issue and have tended towards the assumption that Macmillan and his team chose Skybolt instead of Polaris and then regretted their choice as it became clear which was the better system. Recently, Clark and Baylis have achieved considerable clarity on this point. Was the British government offered Polaris at Camp David or at some point after, or did they believe that the weapons system would be made available to them at a later date? The perception of how Britain stood vis-à-vis Polaris is highly critical and of central importance to understanding the crisis.

The roles of the various players in the Skybolt story are another grey area that demands clarification. Conventional wisdom holds that Kennedy was not properly briefed about the true nature and proportions of the crisis, that Dean Rusk was disinterested and lax in his handling of the matter leaving the decisions and the consequences to his colleague the Secretary of Defense, and that the Ambassadors on both sides failed to become involved in the affair either because they were deliberately sidelined or through lack of initiative.

Previous accounts have also supposed that the cancellation may have been an attempt in some quarters to redefine the United States' special nuclear relationship with Britain, although it is unclear just how far this thinking was accepted in the administration. Detailed examination of the documentation has revealed these analyses to be incorrect. Now, questions about the roles of the individuals and their motivations can be asked and judgements made about the true extent of the part they played in the crisis.

In addition, much uncertainty surrounds the roles of Prime Minister Harold Macmillan and his Minister of Defence, Peter Thorneycroft. Were both men badly caught out, or were they following an agenda? Did Macmillan's priorities change as he faced up to the Anglo-American crisis? At what point did he decide that Britain's European venture was unlikely to succeed? There also remains confusion over a number of events leading up to the crisis including the 11 December meeting in London between Thorneycroft and McNamara. It has been said that they clashed because the British Minister expected to be offered Polaris as a substitute, and his American counterpart was waiting to be asked for the weapon, but in some multilateral context. In short, the two men clashed because neither understood nor had anticipated the other's position or problems. Could it be that some other factor was responsible for the apparent breakdown in communication? This question can now be answered in the light of new evidence.

In addition: why did Britain and the United States, which enjoyed seemingly good relations, find themselves so predisposed to crisis? Was intimacy a factor? Was there a clearly evident breakdown in communication? And if so, was it a natural occurrence or a manipulated strategy? Was the British government aware of the precarious nature of Skybolt's existence and when did Ministers realise that the missile was a likely candidate for cancellation? Why was nothing done in anticipation of this possibility/eventuality?

Finally, did the Cuban Missile Crisis of October 1962 exacerbate tensions, as has been claimed in earlier accounts, and lay the foundations for a subsequent crisis over Skybolt?

The resolution of the Skybolt crisis is the subject of chapter 5. The Nassau Conference in late December 1962 provided the setting for the most serious Anglo-American confrontation since the Suez Crisis of 1956. By the time Macmillan and Kennedy met, the stakes had been raised in both countries. For Britain, the meeting marked a potential turning point in the history of nuclear strategy when a decision had to be made concerning not only the nature and substance of the British nuclear deterrent, but its entire future. Indeed, the desirability of having such a force was in question. Moreover, the understanding reached at the Conference was responsible for creating further problems, disagreements and tensions between the two allies. The fact that Britain was left with a deterrent gap until Polaris was available and that much ambiguity still surrounded the Multilateral Nuclear Force proposal ensured that the controversy provoked by the decisions reached at Nassau would not easily fade away.

In order to gain a fuller understanding of what took place at Nassau, a number of queries not satisfactorily explained in previous accounts must be answered: what pressures were Macmillan and Kennedy under at the Conference? How far did these pressures and other considerations determine or influence their positions and the eventual outcome of the talks? Some confusion exists in the literature over when the decision was taken to offer Polaris as a replacement for Skybolt. Was this crucial decision taken before or during the crisis and therefore as a result of American planning or British persuasion? Why did Kennedy overrule his advisers and allow such a radical U-turn in American foreign policy? How serious was the offer that Kennedy formulated with the help of the British Ambassador, David Ormsby-Gore, en route to Nassau? What was the purpose of this proposal? The final agreement reached at Nassau was vague and open to differing interpretations. Was this a deliberate strategy in order to facilitate later defence of the agreement, or simply the result of poor preparatory staff work and lack of specialists present at the Conference? Finally, how did the various groups within the Kennedy administration view the Nassau Agreement? Did they believe that America had secured sufficient or attractive enough concessions from Britain?

The story of the Multilateral Nuclear Force proposal forwarded by the United States is a complicated one, not least because it was a policy that had originated under a previous administration and which managed to survive innumerable setbacks and obstacles before finally disappearing three presidents and several years later. The subject engages us here because of the problems that the proposal caused for Anglo-American relations during the Kennedy presidency. Britain and the United States, as it turned out, had very different views on the force and the need for it.

Chapter 6 begins by examining the proposal as it was conceived in January 1963 as opposed to what had been advanced in the years leading up to the Nassau Conference when it was adopted by the Kennedy administration. The chapter poses a number of questions: What was behind the proposal, i.e. what were the concerns and worries that prompted the initiative? Was the threat of West Germany becoming a nuclear power ever a credible concern? Did American efforts to curb this perceived slide towards nuclear proliferation encourage the very trends the Americans were desperate to control? Why did America's closest ally not share these fears about the future of Germany and Western Europe? Who was behind the MLF thrust in 1963? Did the whole administration support the proposal? How did Kennedy feel about the Multilateral Force idea – was he consistent in his approach or did his commitment vary? How crucial was the successful implementation of the proposal to the Kennedy administration? Finally, how did these new strains on Anglo-American relations affect the Alliance?

British reaction to the Multilateral Nuclear Force proposal was a matter of great concern to the Kennedy administration in 1963. The contentious issue of NATO and nuclear weapons had been thrust into the spotlight at the Nassau Conference when part of the settlement of the Skybolt crisis had been the creation of a multilateral force which would be part of the NATO deterrent. In the months after the agreement was reached, Britain and the United States engaged in a highly charged debate over the nature of Britain's commitment to participate in the force. The vagueness of the Nassau Agreement had ensured that the two sides were opposed in their interpretation of the settlement. This sparked months of wrangling, culminating in intense pressure from the US Department of State on the British government to agree to engage in discussions about the force. What is striking about the MLF debate is the fact that Britain and the United States directly opposed each other on an issue concerned with the defence of NATO. Britain, however, although in complete disagreement over the need and purpose of the force, ultimately agreed to participate in talks so as not to jeopardise the close relations with the United States. In order to reach a better understanding of the controversy over the MLF, it is necessary to examine the debate in greater detail.

Chapter 7 asks a number of questions: What did the British government think of the American MLF proposal? What did they believe they had signed up to at Nassau? Did the government's view change during the course of 1963? What influences or pressures contributed to the evolution of the British position? Where did Britain's other foreign policy interests fit into the American designs for Europe? Was American goodwill and the continuation of the 'special relationship' more important than financial or policy considerations? The chapter finishes with a brief look at what became of the proposal and the impact the policy of multilateralism had on NATO and Western defence.

1 Special Relations?

> In the post-war period the Anglo-American Alliance has become
> the most intimate international relationship which the United
> States maintains, and it is also unmatched on the British side by
> anything comparable . . . It is the product of an essential similar-
> ity of views concerning the dangers inherent in a world situation
> threatened by a militantly aggressive ideology allied with the So-
> viet Union.[1]

This paper was prepared by the American Embassy in London for
consideration by the new Kennedy administration which had just
taken office. Identifying the 'special relationship' as a highly significant one, it stressed the need to maintain the close links that
had been carefully nurtured in the two countries. The document
acknowledged the existence of something that many would call into
question, increasingly so as the decade wore on. Although few could
deny that Britain and the United States were linked in a unique
way, tied by bonds of culture, shared history, ideology and language, some would claim that the 'specialness' of the relationship
was more of an aspiration than a reality by the 1960s. Moreover, it
was a sentiment, sceptics suggested, nursed by British politicians
eager to preserve some tangible influence over her powerful ally.[2]
   The origins of the so-called 'special relationship' arguably lie
beyond the twentieth century, but for the purposes of this discussion, we will begin our examination of Anglo-American relations
with the Second World War. The involvement of the United States
in the affairs of Europe signalled a major change in policy after
the isolationist 1930s to which many attributed the breakdown of
democratic politics. The Second World War brought changes to
relationships and all aspects of life. The great upheaval and need
for innovation and co-operation prompted alliances that might not
have been necessary or even possible before. The changes that it
heralded were portents of the great changes that were to occur in
the years to come. In two areas, a unique co-operation began between
the United States and Britain. These were in military/defence and
intelligence. Together they formed the dominant and key elements

of what became thought of as the 'special relationship'. Some have tried to argue that the 'special relationship' never really existed; that it was an emotional 'ploy' engineered by successive British governments to snare and compel the United States to follow foreign policy, military and defence goals that suited Britain and complemented her needs and desires. This argument lacks substance simply because successive governments, politicians, journalists and writers have expended considerable efforts in pursuing an explanation of this 'non-existent' relationship. The substance and nature of the 'special relationship' is almost certainly as difficult to pin down as people's perception of it. But the very fact that for a great many individuals and groups, politicians and diplomats a relationship that was both 'crucial' and unique existed, and influenced government policy at all levels of decision-making, is enough to warrant examination.[3]

In the estimation of Henry Kissinger, who both participated and observed Anglo-American co-operation:

it was an extraordinary relationship because it rested on no legal claim; it was formalized by no document; it was carried forward by succeeding British governments as if no alternative were conceivable. Britain's influence was great precisely because it never insisted on it; the 'special relationship' demonstrated the value of intangibles . . .[4]

Anglo-American co-operation began during the Second World War when the two countries embarked upon an endeavour that would both bind them together and separate them for many years. The outbreak of war had coincided with a discovery of momentous proportions. In 1938 two German scientists discovered how to split an atom of uranium.[5] Not only had they discovered a source of unimaginable heat and power, but there also existed a remote possibility that the new discovery might provide the mechanism for producing an explosion of inconceivable destructiveness. Soon it became apparent that fission was more likely to occur in uranium 235 than uranium 238. In order to create enough uranium 235 to produce the necessary reaction, separation of the atoms was necessary. The difficulty lay in the fact that the atoms were virtually identical, the only difference being that uranium 235 was slightly lighter in weight. Thus it became apparent that much work was needed before scientists could successfully produce an explosive device. In the spring of 1940 two refugee physicists at Birmingham

University, Rudolf Peierls and Otto Frisch, produced a paper that explained how a bomb could be built utilising the fission process. This development prompted the British to set up the Maud Committee whose report in 1940 explained how an atomic bomb was possible using U-235 and possibly with the man-made element plutonium. With the tide of war seemingly surging in Germany's favour, it was concluded that Germany must not be the first to profit from this deadly discovery.[6] Until 1941 development of this technology had proceeded separately in the United States and Britain.[7] A pooling of resources and research had been suggested by the Americans on a number of occasions, only to be rejected by Britain who still enjoyed a long lead in atomic energy research.[8] As the war effort began to take its toll, however, Britain began to find it increasingly difficult to devote the necessary time and resources to the project[9] and eventually came round to the idea of collaboration with the United States, whose own project had been galvanised by the findings of the Maud Committee.[10] Ironically, by this time, the positions had become reversed and American politicians were now reluctant to share the work done in the United States. When the two programmes were eventually pooled in mid-1942, Britain was clearly a junior partner in the huge American Manhattan Project. Thus the British allowed the work which they had pioneered to become absorbed into the American project, although their scientists remained intimately involved. Their contribution was of crucial importance.[11]

By 1944, however, the balance of the relationship had shifted away from Britain to the United States. With the full mobilisation of that country's massive economic and technological resources the United States quickly dwarfed her struggling ally, and was now without doubt the most powerful country in the world and the undisputed senior partner in the Anglo-American relationship. After the successful development of the first atomic weapons at the close of the war, relations began to deteriorate. While America had come out of the war more powerful than it had been before the conflict, Britain faced hard times. In spite of this, politicians were determined to continue with Britain's nuclear programme. Many in the United States, however, were fearful of the implications of nuclear proliferation and argued that they should retain complete control of atomic energy. In 1946 Congress passed the McMahon Act which forbade any and all co-operation in nuclear matters, thus preserving the American monopoly on nuclear weaponry and technology.[12] This came as a great shock to Britain, whose government and scientists

had expected to continue playing an integral role in the development of the technology that they had begun.[13] Although the formal
decision was not taken until January 1947, work on the construction of a British bomb began almost immediately without the aid
or intervention of the United States, resulting in the successful
explosion of the first British atomic device in 1952.[14] During these
four years, however, not all collaboration ceased. Although the Anglo-
American nuclear collaboration had abruptly ended with the passage
of the McMahon Act, co-operation continued in other fields. In
1948 the *modus vivendi* agreement allowed for the sharing of commercial and industrial nuclear information.[15] The British government,
whilst pursuing a nuclear policy, had also decided to work towards
the restoration of special relations with the United States. One of
the areas in which co-operation had been preserved was in the
military.

The extensive military relations built up during the Second World
War provided the basis for a continuing relationship between Britain
and the United States with the onset of the Cold War.[16] The outbreak of the Korean War in 1950 came as a profound shock to the
West and immediate measures were taken to build up the depleted
postwar forces necessary to meet the Soviet threat. Under the aegis
of the United Nations, the United States and Britain fought along-
side forces from the Republic of Korea in what was seen as the
first major Cold War confrontation. Korea underlined the need for
Western cohesion, co-operation and stability. Joint planning, co-
ordination and often execution of missions and goals brought the
three services in Britain into regular contact with their opposite
numbers in the United States, developing a diverse range of personal
and professional contacts and friendships.[17] Sharing common interests,
the services tended to back each other up in disputes against 'outside' attempts to force through budget cuts or strategic changes
even when the 'outside' agencies happened to be from their own
government. As Simon Ball notes:

> one of the main conduits for working out the nuclear relationship
> flowed between the military establishments of the two countries.
> The utility of this relationship was considerable . . .[18]

These contacts were 'institutionalised' by the maintenance of a high-
level British mission in Washington replaced in 1949 with the formal
military alliance under the North Atlantic Treaty.

RAF–USAF links were largely responsible for the establishment of US airforce bases in Britain from 1948 onwards. No formal agreement or official invitation precipitated the arrival of the first B-29 squadrons in July/August of that year and Britain had no real say over the control of the bases or American military planning in connection with the bombers. The USAF commander remarked on the circumstances surrounding the agreement saying:

> never before in history has one first-class power gone into another first-class power's country without any agreement. We were just told to come over and 'we should be pleased to have you'...[19]

The presence of the aircraft was based on a relationship of trust, tenaciously held on to by the military. Under the Military Assistance Program, 70 B-29s were made available to Britain in order to bridge the gap until her V-bombers became operational in the mid-1950s.[20] Another agreement made in June 1956 enabled the transfer of information on submarine nuclear propulsion systems to be given to the Royal Navy, whose officers were invited to participate in US missile development programme for a solid-fuelled rocket designed to be fired from submarines.[21]

In 1953 East–West relations were at an all-time low. Stalemate in Korea reinforced deep-seated fears about the West's ability to stand firm against the threat of communism. One priority of the new Eisenhower administration was to develop a closer nuclear and defence relationship with Britain. The first steps towards this came when Congress passed the Atomic Energy Act which amended the McMahon Act to allow bilateral agreements with countries that had made significant independent advances in the field on nuclear energy.[22] This was followed by two further agreements which facilitated civil and military atomic co-operation.[23] In December 1955, as Simon Ball recently discovered, two highly secret projects, E and X, were set up. Project E was designed to convert British planes to carry US atomic bombs, while Project X prepared the RAF to carry US hydrogen bombs. Britain received 20 dummy bombs and details of their advanced low-altitude bombing system so that the Canberra bombers could be modified to carry American nuclear weapons.[24] In 1956 the US agreed on a joint RAF–USAF targeting plan. It was in this area of strategic targeting, according to Peter Malone, that the 'special Anglo-American relationships – nuclear and intelligence collaboration – commingled'.[25]

In October 1956, the Eden government, without consulting the United States, arranged during secret discussions with France and

Israel to attack Egypt in order to overthrow the government of Colonel Nasser, prompted by the latter's nationalisation of the Suez Canal in July.[26] The Israeli invasion of the Sinai Peninsula provided the excuse for British and French troops to 'intervene' as peace-keepers in a thinly veiled attempt to oust the Egyptian leader. President Eisenhower was enraged and, less than 24 hours after the main assault began, American diplomatic and economic pressures forced Britain to halt the invasion.[27] After the 1956 Suez Crisis there followed a period of introspection largely centring on the meaning of the independent national deterrent, the British role in world affairs and her relationship vis-à-vis the United States. The confrontation had clearly indicated that Britain could not engage in any military activity that was contrary to the interests of the United States. It also highlighted the fact that Britain could not always rely on the United States.

Two paradoxical decisions came out of the crisis. First, Britain would continue to construct an independent nuclear deterrent to defend the interest of the United Kingdom, and second, a reaffirmation of the need to have close ties led to vigorous efforts to restore or re-establish the 'special relationship'. The Suez Crisis should have made relations between the two countries difficult and strained. While this was a natural legacy of the affair and did contaminate relations and create deeply felt suspicions, the post-Suez period represented a remarkable high-point in the Anglo-American relationship. As Admiral Sir James Eberle, formerly Director of the Royal Institute of International Affairs, stated 'Suez should have been the end of the US–British tie . . . in fact it was the amphitheatre of its rebirth . . .'[28]

The closer nuclear co-operation discussed at the military level for many years now became the official recommendation of the president. The 1957 Bermuda meeting between Eisenhower and the new prime minister, Harold Macmillan signalled the beginning of the nuclear thaw. Macmillan was determined to preside over invigorated and strengthened relations between the two countries and made this aspiration a central element of his policy platform. As Ambassador David Bruce said of the prime minister in a memorandum to the Department of State:

[he] picked up after Suez, and, Churchillian tradition, made [the] touchstone [of] his own decisions in [the] field [of] foreign policy accommodation with ultimate US positions . . .[29]

Macmillan was continuing to advance a policy of seeking American rather than continental co-operation. France had requested Britain's help in building a gaseous diffusion plant in 1955, but was ultimately turned down. Although the debate about whether or not to amend this policy of non-cooperation with France on nuclear/defence matters occupied some considerable discussion time, it remained essentially unchanged.[30] In contrast, Anglo-American co-operation was reaffirmed by the instillation of 60 Thor liquid-fuelled Intermediate Range Ballistic Missiles (IRBMs) under a two-key system.[31] Macmillan had several reasons for adopting this strategy. In May of that year, to the great surprise of American officials, Britain exploded its first hydrogen device. This remarkable feat was soon surpassed by the news that the Soviet Union had successfully launched *Sputnik* – the world's first orbiting satellite. This, among other considerations, prompted the Eisenhower administration to seek the repeal of the McMahon Act by amending the 1954 Atomic Energy Act and then signing two bilateral agreements with Britain in July 1958 and in May 1959. Recent evidence suggests that even before these agreements were signed the United States had started to supply Britain with nuclear weapons.[32] Again, military ties, loyalties and considerations came into play. The restoration of the nuclear element of the 'special relationship' was almost complete with the 1958 and 1959 amendments.[33] They paved the way for an exchange of nuclear weapons and targeting information as well as an opportunity to implement joint strategy planning and assessment which was restricted to the two countries only. Soon after, the interdependence extended to delivery systems with the American decision to sell Skybolt missiles to Britain. No other ally (until the Nassau offer of Polaris to France) was offered or enjoyed a similar level of nuclear intimacy or the benefits that accompanied it.

The only other aspect of Anglo-American relations that was regarded as similarly close was intelligence. During the Second World War, American and British cryptanalysts had worked closely together. After the war, they had agreed to pool resources in the financially constrained 1940s. The British Government Communications Headquarters (GCHQ) and the American National Security Agency (NSA) habitually exchanged personnel and shared facilities in Britain and elsewhere around the world. In the area of human intelligence gathering and analysis, co-operation founded in wartime continued in the years when resources were limited and into the Cold War.

Both sides possessed highly valuable assets. The British were regarded as having a greater number of agents and generally more experienced case officers and handlers, as well as a vast colonial base for potential intelligence gathering. The Americans, on the other hand, had better relations with surviving German intelligence officers and better interrogation facilities.[34] Substantial collaboration also took place in the field of photographic intelligence. USAF and RAF analysts shared the results of slant photography, predominantly from illegal incursions into the Soviet Union, and data recovered from border surveillance. Wartime contacts and cooperation had proved to both sides that the exchange of raw and processed intelligence was most successful when as much information as possible was shared. The effective communications networks established to facilitate this exchange remained a crucial element in cementing the relations between Britain and the United States.[35]

The 'special relationship' was not so much a sentimental attachment for Britain (although many regarded it as such) as it was a hugely practical and necessary aspect of British foreign and defence policy. Britain needed the United States because it was glaringly obvious that it could not keep up with the nuclear and technological developments which were occurring with increasing rapidity throughout the 1950s. Britain needed financial and technological help in order to retain a credible deterrent and a sense that it still had an important and valued role to play in world affairs. This was only possible by calling upon the Americans to honour the 'special relationship'. Throughout the period in question British politicians and diplomats spoke often and with emotion about the bonds of the 'special relationship'. They created an image or perception of something tangible and yet elusive – something that could not be broken or cast aside.[36]

The American view of the 'special relationship' was very different. A British planning document outlined what officials believed to be the American perception of Britain:

> The sense of Association between the British and Americans goes so deep, is felt at so many levels and yet is so intangible that neither are fully conscious of it ... seen from the US, Britain looks fairly small in the world and will look smaller as her capability to influence events declines. None the less, though the Americans may often doubt our capacities and sometimes question our judgement *they still pay more attention to us than they do to any other of their allies* ... (emphasis added).[37]

There were many areas where they did not see eye to eye and
which caused problems: détente and summitry, NATO and conventional goals, communist China, colonialism, the European Sixes
and Sevs divide.[38] America was much less impressed with the
relationship and, as the years progressed, it was deemed less important and even detrimental to the furthering and achievement of
America's other foreign policy ambitions. America initially had some
need for Britain – as in the early years after the war, when it needed
bases from which to launch a nuclear attack against the Soviet Union.
US governments were also keen to have as much control over the
British nuclear programme as possible. But as the years passed and
weapons changed from bombers to missiles, Britain's appeal diminished perceptively, minimising any practical benefits she might
have offered. What was left was the concept or perception of an
old ally, America's oldest friend. As *The Times* commented:

> the sincere regard which many Americans feel for Britain is largely
> instinctive and emotional . . . For America, powerful allies are
> desirable; for Britain they are indispensable . . .[39]

Increasingly, administrations found themselves struggling with a
deeply rooted sense of obligation and sentimental attachment to
Britain which conflicted with current foreign policy directives.[40]

Much depended on personalities – the ability to work together,
common perceptions of aims and needs, and shared understandings
on how these could be achieved. John F. Kennedy and Harold
Macmillan had a remarkable relationship that presided over a high
point followed by the decline of the old-style 'special relationship'.

KENNEDY AND MACMILLAN: THE PERSONAL TOUCH

As Harold Macmillan awaited the election of a new American leader, he
wrote dejectedly to his old friend, the outgoing President Eisenhower:

> As I think over the history of our collaboration which has now
> lasted some eighteen years . . . one thing stands out. Whether we
> agreed or disagreed on particular policies we had I think a deep
> unity of purpose and, I like to feel, a frank and honest appreciation
> of each other's good faith . . . this was something which one does
> not, alas, often find between Heads of Government even of Allied
> countries; personal friendship and trust cannot be manufactured,
> they just grow.[41]

Macmillan was at times deeply despondent about the outcome of the election and unimpressed with both candidates. When Eisenhower had asked him for his personal assessment of the two candidates, Kennedy and Richard Nixon, the prime minister had replied (ironically as it later turned out) that Nixon (Eisenhower's Republican nominee) was 'beat', explaining that 'one looked like a convicted criminal and the other looked like a rather engaging young undergraduate'.[42] Keenly following the campaigning, Macmillan had rapidly concluded that the 'engaging young undergraduate' was likely to become the next President of the United States.[43] Nevertheless his confidence in the electoral prospects of the Democratic Senator from Massachusetts did not extend to optimism about Kennedy's ability to lead the country and indeed the free world, or the possibility of establishing a close and productive relationship with him. About this he was extremely pessimistic. Some time after seeing his prediction come true, Macmillan wrote in his diary:

> I feel in my bones that President Kennedy is going to fail to produce any real leadership. The American press and public are beginning to feel the same. In a few weeks they may turn to us. We must be ready. Otherwise we may drift to disaster over Berlin – a terrible diplomatic defeat or (out of sheer incompetence) a nuclear war.[44]

The comparisons made between the men, Macmillan knew, would be frequent and predictable. At first glance they appeared remarkably, perhaps impossibly, dissimilar. Not only did age separate them – Kennedy was 43, Macmillan 67, but more than this, observers often pointed out, was the fact that the young president and the patriarchal prime minister seemed to hail not simply from different generations, but from different centuries. The 'languid Edwardian', as he was often called, was deeply anxious about the obstacles that might prevent him from establishing a close rapport with Kennedy. His reservations stemmed largely from a limited knowledge of the character and policies of the man as opposed to what he saw clearly as his own style of politics and leadership skills. The 'young cocky Irishman', as he initially viewed him, presented a formidable challenge to the ageing prime minister.[45] To begin with, Kennedy was the son of Joseph Kennedy, the infamous wartime US Ambassador to London. The elder Kennedy had succeeded in becoming one of the most disliked and distrusted Americans in Britain during his appointment thanks to his arrogance and frequently articulated anti-

British feelings. The new president, Macmillan feared, could not have escaped being influenced by his domineering father. Moreover, Kennedy came from an extremely wealthy background which arguably left him out of touch with the vast majority of the people he now proposed to lead. Well known in society circles, and married to an acclaimed society beauty, Kennedy did not appear to be a particularly good choice. The president-elect had also surrounded himself with an unusual team of advisers and staff. Choosing people on the basis of intellectual merit and suitability for the job, Kennedy's team consisted of a hitherto unprecedented number of bright, young (and, in Macmillan's judgement, untested) intellectuals, unfamiliar with the governing of a country, but enthusiastic and confident. The prime minister was concerned that the new administration was not sufficiently experienced to deal with the complex and difficult art of diplomacy and politicking – something he was sure was his own finest political quality. This worried Macmillan, especially, as the new president was presenting himself as a dynamic leader of vision who intended to make strong, imaginative foreign policy decisions. Kennedy's lack of experience and understanding of international affairs might adversely affect Macmillan's ability or freedom to influence matters. Certainly, if the new president was unwilling or incapable of taking good advice from an elder statesman, the prime minister could find it difficult to maintain close and advantageous relations with the United States.

Macmillan was also aware of the absence of common experience, which had proved a strong bond in his relationship with Kennedy's predecessor and which had cemented relations between Roosevelt and Churchill. This common denominator did not and could not have applied to Kennedy. While he could always 'appeal to memories' with Eisenhower, with this younger man, he wrote:

we have nothing of the kind to draw on. We must therefore, I think make our contacts in the realm of ideas. I must somehow convince him that I am worth consulting not as an old friend (as Eisenhower felt) but as a man who, although of advancing years, has young and fresh thought . . .[46]

Intensely curious about Kennedy, Macmillan set about questioning anyone who knew the president or who could provide any information about him. One of the first people to whom Macmillan turned was Kennedy's old friend, David Ormsby-Gore, a distant relation and a Foreign Office minister. Harold Caccia, the British

Ambassador in Washington, was asked for his personal assessment along with numerous journalists, businessmen and acquaintances of the Kennedys. What emerged was a mass of contradictions. As Arthur Schlesinger, a Kennedy adviser and close associate put it:

> He was a Harvard man, a naval hero, an Irishman, a politician, a bon vivant, a man of unusual intelligence, charm, wit and ambition . . .[47]

American Ambassador Jock Whitney described Kennedy to Macmillan as a 'strange character . . . obstinate, sensitive, ruthless and highly sexed'.[48] Macmillan soon discovered that Kennedy had a deep interest in, and admiration for, British political society of the eighteenth and early nineteenth centuries and the political characters who populated that period. William Pitt's subtlety and Charles James Fox's conciliatory talents were reportedly much admired by the American president who sought, it was said, to imitate these qualities in his own style of government.[49] According to Schlesinger:

> [he was] enchanted by the Whig zest, versatility and nonchalance; he liked the idea of a society where politics invigorated but did not monopolise life. But Whiggism . . . was too passive for Kennedy, [he] hoped to guide and anticipate it.[50]

History captivated and fed the ferocious curiosity and appetite for knowledge that Kennedy was said to possess. He was widely regarded as a prolific reader whose favourite subjects included history and political biographies such as David Cecil's *The Young Melbourne*, an account of the life of the young British prime minister – an interest, incidentally, that he shared with Macmillan.[51] History and knowledge for its own sake, however, had little purpose for Kennedy unless used as a yardstick or lesson for the present or the future. Above all, Macmillan learned, the president was a man of action. Ideas were of little value if they could not be implemented or used to produce tangible results. As Walt Rostow observed, Kennedy's most common statement was: 'All right, I've got the idea. But what do you want me to do about it today?'[52] As a dynamic, pragmatic realist, politics was a means to an end and not simply an exercise to be pursued for its own sake. Kennedy deeply felt the need (as did Macmillan) to achieve something positive during his term of office, although he recognised what he regarded as the fatalistic nature of history, which was largely shaped by forces beyond man's control.[53] Macmillan also discovered that Kennedy, though initially barred from active service in the war due to chronic back problems, had nevertheless managed to become involved and was later responsible for the rescue of crew members from his destroyed PT-boat.[54] Kennedy's heroism and the war wounds that he sustained as a result were things Macmillan, himself a veteran of two world wars, could understand. Despite frequently suffering from considerable pain, the president, it appeared, was a man of great humour and wit that tended toward the 'black', and was strongly imbued with a touch of irony.[55] He delighted, his friends said, in the irreverent and the ridiculous, and frequently displayed a charmingly 'puckish' sense of mischief.[56]

FIRST IMPRESSIONS

The first encounter between the two premiers had been scheduled for 4 April in Washington. Although they had corresponded since Kennedy's coming to office, Macmillan was nevertheless anxious about his first personal contact. He was more than a little surprised and somewhat gratified when, taking a break in the Bahamas, he received an urgent communication from Kennedy asking him to fly 'without delay' to Key West, Florida for an ad hoc meeting to discuss the deteriorating political situation in Laos.[57] Apprehensive about the meeting and worried Kennedy might think him a 'stuff shirt', or 'square',[58] Macmillan embarked on the five-hour flight deeply curious about how Kennedy was going to handle his first major foreign policy problem. Moreover, he was keen to see what kind of role he was expected to play by the new president. Macmillan's first impression of Kennedy was of 'a curious mixture of qualities – courteous, quiet, quick, decisive and tough'.[59] He was impressed by the way in which Kennedy had held back, listening to the proposals being presented by his advisers for dealing with the Laotian crisis. In a letter to Jacqueline Kennedy some time later, Macmillan recalled this meeting:

> the very first time we met to talk – I felt something had happened. Naturally I 'fell' for him. But (much more unexpectedly) he seemed to warm to me . . .[60]

Others recall that it was not until the two men met later in the year that a friendship began to blossom, for the meeting on Laos was neither an easy nor a particularly productive one.[61] The Laotian situation had been deteriorating rapidly since the late 1950s, so much so that President Eisenhower had warned his successor that it was going to be one of his most difficult and immediate problems. By 1960 American and Soviet Union intervention on opposite sides had escalated the civil war conflict to dangerous proportions.[62] British government policy had been to resist strongly any military intervention, although there was great concern about the fate of the rest of South East Asia if Laos were to fall into Communist hands. Macmillan, however, did not want Britain embroiled in a war there either as part of South East Asia Treaty Organisation (SEATO), as the Americans had been urging for some time, or bilaterally, in direct support of unilateral action by the United States. When Kennedy asked Macmillan for his opinion on the plan for a possible military solution the prime minister was unimpressed and outlined the problems and dangers associated with such a course of action. Nevertheless, knowing that he could not afford to be seen to break with the new administration, he conceded, with 'deepest despondency', the need to present a united front to the Soviet Union and reluctantly agreed to ask for Cabinet approval for British support if this proved necessary.[63] Having made his point as forcefully as he could under the circumstances, Macmillan hoped that his warning against military action would mean he would not have to make good his promise.[64]

The scheduled Washington meeting that took place a few days later saw a more relaxed Macmillan. It was at this encounter he noted in his diary that the two men discovered a deep and genuine fondness and mutual respect. They soon found, as Schlesinger recalls, 'a considerable temperamental rapport'.[65]

The two leaders found that beneath the superficial differences, much emphasised by the media, they were more alike than any might have guessed.[66] As Macmillan himself confided to his diary after Kennedy's visit to London:

> the President's visit was a success from the point of view of our personal relations. He was kind, intelligent, and *very* friendly. I find my *personal* friendship beginning to grow into something like that which I got with Eisenhower after a few months at Algiers . . .[67]

A few months later, David Ormsby-Gore spoke of the special relationship that was continuing to flourish between the two countries saying:

our two governments . . . are cooperating today more closely than
at any time in history, probably more closely than any two free
and sovereign governments have ever cooperated before . . . only
because they can draw upon a vast reservoir of understanding
and goodwill which has been built up over the years by individuals
and institutions dedicated to Anglo-American friendship . . .[68]

The new British Ambassador was himself a key factor in the establishment of a close personal relationship between Kennedy and
Macmillan.[69] Friendly with the president since the 1930s, Ormsby-
Gore was related to both the Devonshires and Cavendishes, being
cousin of and best friend to Kennedy's sister Kathleen's husband,
the Marquis of Hartington. He had virtually unlimited, rapid and
informal access to Kennedy and frequently discussed with the president matters unrelated to his role as Ambassador. Their friendship
was so close that they could enjoy warm personal and professional
relations without one impinging upon the other. In the course of
their discussions Ormsby-Gore always seemed to know what information or position Kennedy wanted passed on to Macmillan, while
Kennedy was aware of occasions in which Ormsby-Gore spoke
unofficially about his government's position. As Bundy remarked:

> I think it is true that the British Government's position and David's
> position were not always identical and that we knew him well
> enough, and were on sufficiently intimate terms to know when
> they were not identical . . .[70]

Their relationship was, perhaps, unparalleled in modern times and
facilitated a virtually unbroken period of smooth and untroubled
relations.

Kennedy and Macmillan also shared a degree of fascination with
the aristocracy and aristocratic life. Although not born into it,
Macmillan was related through marriage to the Devonshire family.
Kennedy, on the other hand, while similarly linked through the
marriage of his sister Kathleen, had spent some of his formative
years among the aristocracy of pre-war England, and counted among
his closest friends Sir David Ormsby-Gore (later Lord Harlech).
In spite of their social status both possessed a strong sense of duty
to the electorate, especially with regard to the problems of social
inequality and injustice. Macmillan had proved that he had the
political courage and will to pursue radical and unpopular policies
during his long career when he believed change was necessary.

Kennedy seemed to promise the same. Both shared a deep horror of nuclear war and the dangers that proliferation and war by miscalculation or misjudgement threatened to unleash. Kennedy agreed with Macmillan that the Soviet Union must be encouraged to sign up to a proposal to end nuclear testing and thus prevent any further escalation of the dangerous and costly arms race. Like David Ormsby-Gore, Macmillan offered Kennedy a commodity that he came to greatly value – wise counsel. As Macmillan confided to his diary:

> the President likes these private and confidential talks. He seems to want advice – or at least comfort . . .[71]

The Prime Minister prided himself on his image of 'unflappability'[72] and shared with Kennedy the ability to deal with dramatic issues in a calm, pragmatic and intelligent way.[73] Macmillan easily assumed the role of sage counsellor and loyal ally, playing a 'father' to Kennedy's 'son'. As Ormsby-Gore recalled, 'it was almost like a family discussion when we all met'.[74] Macmillan was in no doubt about the depth of the relationship. Writing to Jacqueline Kennedy some years after the president's death, he recalled:

> he seemed to *trust* me, and (as you well know) for those of us who have had to play the so-called game of politics – national and international – this is something very rare but very precious . . .[75]

The deep need for someone to talk to and 'touch base' with underpinned Kennedy's relationship with the British prime minister.[76] He once remarked:

> I feel at home with Macmillan because I can share my loneliness with him. The others are all foreigners to me . . .[77]

The two leaders were bound together by a powerful sense of isolation fuelled by the knowledge that they were ultimately responsible for the well-being of their respective countries. Kennedy, according to Carl Kaysen, 'liked and admired' Macmillan while regarding him as 'a successful politician with whose general political attitudes he was sympathetic and with whom he could talk easily, informally, and directly'. 'No other European figures, nor indeed foreign politician', he believed, 'filled a similar position'.[78]

The Cuban Missile Crisis of 16–28 October 1962 tested the strength of the relationship and undoubtedly brought the two men closer together.[79] The small group of men trusted by Kennedy to deal with the crisis included David Ormsby-Gore, who played a pivotal role advising the president. During the crisis, Kennedy kept in close touch with Macmillan, whom he telephoned on a regular basis to discuss developments and strategy.[80] Afterwards, although the British press severely criticised the British leader for the perceived lack of consultation during the crisis, Macmillan kept his counsel informing his Cabinet:

> in fact we had played an active and helpful part in bringing matters to their present conclusion, but in public little had been said and the impression had been created that we had been playing a purely passive role. It would not be easy to correct this without revealing the degree of informal consultation which had taken place; but this might be embarrassing to President Kennedy . . .[81]

On the seven occasions that Kennedy and Macmillan met it was often the case that they disagreed on matters of policy and strategy although they were always, Lord Home recalls, 'intimate affairs with a spicing of fun'.[82] As Macmillan wrote to Kennedy, 'it is of the greatest value to me to have the opportunity for private talk which these meetings provide'.[83]

Issues such as China's admission to the UN, summit meetings, national nuclear deterrents, the dismantling of the old colonial empires, conventional force levels and arms control were often controversial and occasions for much heated discussion.[84] Increasingly, Kennedy found himself beset by advisers on one side telling him that the relationship with Britain was a paradox and ultimately damaging to American's other interests, while others stressed the importance of maintaining close links:

> in the careful consideration of diplomatic parry and riposte . . . it is important that the desirability of acknowledging the special friendship that characterises the US–UK relationship not be overlooked . . .[85]

Within the administration a debate raged about the relative advantages of having a 'special relationship' with Britain. While certain policy documents like the April 1961 NSC Memorandum[86] clearly identified official policy moving away from preserving these special links, Macmillan's relationship with Kennedy muddied these waters and often caused problems for those trying to enforce a policy of non-favouritism. Ultimately, Kennedy recognised that the easy intimacy he had with Macmillan reinforced and strengthened their ability to work together on issues of common interest such as a nuclear test ban treaty, NATO, Britain's Common Market aspirations and Berlin.[87] In addition, one of his aides recalls, Kennedy found Britain 'more reliable than any of our other major allies'.[88] More often than not, the extraordinarily solid relationship shared by the two men frequently enabled disagreements to be dealt with in a frank, open and, more often than not, friendly way.

A letter from Kennedy after de Gaulle's blunt rejection of Britain's bid to enter the EEC reveals the depth of the relationship:

> you will know without my saying so that we are with you in feeling and in purpose in this time of de Gaulle's great effort to test the chances for his dream world. Neither of us must forget for a moment that reality is what rules and the central reality is that he is wrong and Europe knows he is wrong ... We are doing everything we can at this end, as our people will be telling yours *And if this is an unmentionable special relationship, so much the better* ...[89]

The focus of this study is the difficulties that occurred in Anglo-American nuclear relations during this period. Against the backdrop of the visibly restored 'special relationship', two problems emerged: one that threatened to disrupt the relationship in a sudden burst of crisis, and another that managed to drag on for some considerable time, contributing to a slow but dangerous poisoning of relations.

2 The Origins of a Crisis

Anglo-American relations were never so starkly and publicly in disarray as during the controversial Skybolt crisis. The American decision to cancel what had always been perceived as a highly complex and technically ambitious project sent shockwaves through the so-called 'special relationship', causing accusations of betrayal and voiced fears of secret hidden agendas to resonate in the corridors of Whitehall and the White House. Complacent trust was quickly replaced by suspicion, easy communication by silence, and co-operation by bewilderment and unchecked confusion. In the space of a few days, the Anglo-American alliance, characterised since 1941 by its unrivalled closeness, even intimacy, looked fragile and precarious. Much more than the future of a nuclear weapons system was at stake – for a short time, it seemed everything hinged on it.

It is interesting that the decision to proceed with Skybolt, an American-designed and manufactured weapon, at the expense of Britain's home-grown Blue Streak, did not provoke an outcry similar to the furore that surrounded the Skybolt affair just over two years later. In fact, the decision to opt for an American-designed and manufactured weapon caused little comment. Macmillan, after all, stressed his plans for Anglo-American interdependence and cited Skybolt as the perfect vehicle for and symbol of this policy. Blue Streak was simply not a viable project and thus had to be dropped.[1] Few observers felt strongly enough about the development to make a fuss. Why did this quite radical departure pass off with so little controversy? The seemingly effortless switch from Blue Streak to Skybolt was unchallenged largely due to the fact that it was perceived as the cancellation of a useless weapon by the government building it, which had secured a better weapon from its closest ally. There was no cry of betrayal or moribund suspicions. The cancellation of Skybolt, it seems, was another story altogether.

After successfully collaborating in the first nuclear energy project American legislation, in the shape of the McMahon Act after the close of the Second World War, effectively put an end to this shared undertaking and prevented Britain from continuing to pursue this field in conjunction with the United States.[2] Fearing security leaks and large-scale proliferation, and desirous of a nuclear monopoly,

31

the United States abruptly and decisively moved to cut its former partner out of the business. Furious protestations from across the Atlantic did nothing to alter the situation.

Forced to strike out alone, Britain had to make a fundamental decision: should the country pursue a national nuclear policy of developing an independent nuclear deterrent, or was this the time to bow out and accept the accompanying reduction in status to a second-class world power? For the government of the day, the choice was not difficult. Having 'won' the war, Britain could not accept such public humiliation. Besides, the tremendous drain of resources as a result of the war effort had left all the allies (except America) weak and vulnerable. Nuclear weapons promised a relatively simple and proportionately cheaper way of constructing a defence without having immediately to begin rebuilding costly conventional forces and equipment. As Martin Navias points out:

> British policy-makers viewed nuclear weapons as necessary accessories to world power status and Britain, which still perceived itself as such a power, could not be without them.[3]

Furthermore, for the government, an independent British nuclear deterrent had two additional advantages: it provided an insurance against the admittedly unlikely possibility of America withdrawing her protective strength,[4] while also giving Britain a degree of leverage with which it hoped to influence decisions its ally might make,[5] thus paving the way to the greater good of interdependence with the United States.[6] Which was more important is difficult to say. What stands out, however, is the obvious linking of the British deterrent to American deterrence. Britain did not take the decision to develop an independent force for the sole reason of British defence. The gaze of British politicians extended far beyond the borders of Great Britain – more important, almost from the beginning, was the need to secure a close and reciprocal defence relationship with America.[7] There was an acceptance of the role that nuclear weapons had to play in this strategy. As the bills mounted any thoughts of complete independence that still lingered got short shift. Britain needed to make savings in defence spending. If interdependence with the United States could be made effective, duplication of defence research cost could result in substantial savings.[8]

Having made the decision to develop nuclear weapons for an independent national deterrent, Britain had to continue to work unaided and without any co-operation or collaboration with its erstwhile partner. This was both a slow and expensive business, hampered by scientific and technological shortcomings and all the time frustrated by American unwillingness to share information that could save Britain crucial time and money. This forced alienation was deeply resented and contributed in no small part to the souring of relations.

The explosion of the first Soviet atomic bomb followed by what was perceived as a rapid expansion of Soviet missile technology ended America's monopoly of nuclear weapons and created a hitherto unknown sense of vulnerability in the Western world.[9] British and American strategies progressed on similar lines, both pursuing 'nuclear' as opposed to 'conventional' policies. The decision of the Eisenhower administration in 1953 to use nuclear weapons to justify dramatic cutbacks in the costly conventional capabilities was the beginning of a new direction in military strategic planning. According to one historian, the 'relatively low financial cost of nuclear weapons permitted Eisenhower to pursue a modified strategy of containment, avoiding both isolationism and overspending'.[10] This 'New Look' represented a determined hardening of American attitudes to perceived Soviet aggression.[11] John Foster Dulles, Eisenhower's Secretary of State, summed up the policy, declaring that the United States had abandoned the 'traditional' policy of meeting aggression by direct or local opposition, and would from now on depend 'primarily upon a great capacity to retaliate, instantly, by means and places of our choosing'.[12]

The concept of this doctrine of 'massive retaliation' remained the currency in the defence and policy planning communities until key members of the administration, including Thomas Gates and Dulles himself, influenced by a rash of independent and government-commissioned studies such as the 1957 Gaither Report, began to move away from the policy whose rigidity and preoccupation with 'Mutual Assured Destruction' effectively restricted the options available to those in charge at the beginning of a conflict situation.[13] Although some degree of nuclear retaliation was still considered the only conceivable response, planners were increasingly thinking in terms of a structure of graduated response, allowing for less 'total' retaliatory acts to be employed in circumstances where the aggression or incident was more limited. This shift in policy was accompanied by a renewed interest in conventional force levels and questioning of the role of NATO and nuclear weapons. By the late 1950s, President Eisenhower was becoming increasingly conscious of the need to improve relations in the defence field. Believing that Britain was perhaps America's most important ally in this period of Cold War instability, he made it his goal to repair relations. In Britain the new prime minister, Harold Macmillan, was of a similar disposition. He had decided that one of the central planks of his foreign policy platform would be the restoration of the 'special relationship'. Circumstances compelled the two leaders to act. Several factors had coalesced to make this important. The Suez Crisis of 1956 was nothing short of disastrous for Britain – humiliated and embarrassingly exposed as weak and dependent upon the acquiescence of the US – the whole affair left a bitter taste in the mouths of many. Eisenhower was concerned that the issue might impact on other foreign policy areas and perhaps upset the status quo in East–West relations.[14] It appeared that the Soviet Union was adopting a more confident and aggressive line in its relations with the West, supported by increased military strength.[15] The president was also concerned that the United States would be able to count on firm backing from Britain in the forthcoming nuclear test ban negotiations he was initiating, but knew this would be difficult unless Britain were given substantial access to nuclear technology in order to remove their need to test.[16]

In addition, the revelation on 4 October 1957 that the Soviet Union had successfully launched the first earth-orbiting satellite contributed to a re-evaluation of the question of nuclear sharing.[17] In the United States 'the overwhelming public feeling was a deeply felt sense of national crisis'.[18] Suddenly there was renewed urgency to reassure American public opinion and the anxious Allies by demonstrating both American technological prowess and a determination to unite NATO.[19] The United States was anxious to increase the ability to co-ordinate nuclear strategy and targeting within the alliance necessitated by the deployment, for the first time, of tactical nuclear weapons demanding increased scientific and technological co-operation in order to function optimally. There was a need to strengthen Western defences as a whole and to avoid, where possible, duplication and wastage in the military field.[20] Eisenhower was also encouraged by the discovery that Britain was not as technologically backward as had been previously thought – Britain had successfully exploded its first thermonuclear bomb on Christmas Island in May 1957 to the surprise of American officials, who had been 'amazed to learn the full extent of British knowledge and expertise'.[21] It seemed that the gap between the British and American atomic energy programmes had suddenly been narrowed.[22]

Thus, troubled by the repercussions of Suez and *Sputnik*, anxious to see test ban negotiations progress and impressed by Britain's apparent progress in nuclear technological terms, Eisenhower felt the time was right to consider relaxing the restrictive and resented legislation that had prevented Britain from intimate nuclear collaboration with the United States. Underpinning all this was a deep belief on Eisenhower's part that these restrictive measures were morally reprehensible and should never have been allowed to become law. He felt that Britain had been wronged and did not deserve to be penalised indefinitely in the nuclear field. According to Macmillan, the president described the Act as 'one of the most deplorable incidents in American history, of which he personally felt ashamed'.[23] Eisenhower himself later commented, 'When many of our former secrets were known to our enemies, it made no sense to keep them from our friends.'[24]

The beginning of Britain's promotion to a special nuclear status was in the mutually beneficial Thor agreement with the United States.[25] With the dawning of the missile age, America needed bases to house its Intermediate Range Ballistic Missiles (IRBMs) for targeting against the Soviet Union. Accepting Eisenhower's request for basing facilities was a calculated risk, like the Holy Loch Agreement some months later. Having American Thors on British soil had the undesirable consequence of making Britain a pre-emptive or first-strike target. To its advantage, however, was the close cooperative interaction with the Americans that such a venture would require. When Macmillan agreed, it was to a joint-control, two-key formula that signified a degree of interdependence.

Later that year, Macmillan made another attempt to press for increased co-operation. Shortly after the *Sputnik* shock he wrote to Eisenhower outlining his thoughts on how the Anglo-American alliance should meet this new challenge:

> in view of the extent of Russian power and technical capacity . . . couldn't we now pool all *our* resources to fight them – financial, military, technical, propaganda etc. This would involve getting rid of the McMahon Act. This act was to make sure that America's secrets were not sold or betrayed to Russia. But, it was intended for the situation in 1950. It's quite absurd now . . . [26]

The prime minister flew to Washington a few weeks later to discuss these and other matters. The two men talked of many things,

but topping the agenda was the delicate problem of how to redress
the perceived imbalance in East–West power relations following
the launch of the Russian satellite. For Britain, this was a unique
diplomatic opportunity to reopen discussions with the Americans
on matters of nuclear co-operation.[27] As Macmillan recorded in
his diary, almost anything was possible:

> the Russian success in launching the satellite has been some-
> thing equivalent to Pearl Harbor. The cock-sure-ness is shaken . . .
> the President is under severe attack for the first time . . . the
> administration realises that their attitude over the canal issue
> was fatal and led necessarily to the Suez situation . . . The at-
> mosphere is now such that almost anything might be decided,
> however revolutionary . . .[28]

What emerged from the October talks was a 'Declaration of Common Purpose' which committed Eisenhower to request Congress
to amend the Atomic Energy Act of 1954 'as may be necessary
and desirable to permit close and fruitful collaboration of scientists and engineers of Great Britain, the United States and other
friendly countries'.[29] This request in turn led to legislation that
permitted the signing of an 'Agreement for Cooperation on the
uses of Atomic Energy for Mutual Defense Purposes', which enabled
Britain to make important scientific and technological breakthroughs
needed to design and produce nuclear warheads. As a result, Britain
was able to design and produce smaller, more sophisticated warheads needed for Blue Streak and later for Polaris. These agreements
paved the way for the Amendments to the McMahon Act in August 1958. The changes permitted the release of weapons design
information to an ally that had made 'substantial progress' toward
a nuclear capability – wording implicitly excluding from this agreement any nation other than Britain. May 1959 saw a further relaxation
of legislation allowing Britain to buy component parts of nuclear
weapons from American weapon systems as well as the crucial
exchange of British plutonium for much needed American enriched
uranium. Thanks to these changes Britain was able to buy a ma-
rine nuclear propulsion plant from the US allowing the construction
of the first British nuclear submarine.[30] Although this agreement
virtually removed the legal impediments to Anglo-American nuclear
collaboration, this understanding in particular was obscure and open
to reinterpretation, something which was to cause some confusion
and resentment later.

As the 1950s drew to a close, the 'special relationship' appeared to have been restored. The amendments to the McMahon Act and the installation of the American Thors in Britain appeared to signal a new, close collaborative relationship. Problems, none the less, were not far from the surface of the still waters of the Anglo-American alliance. The 'New Look' policy of the Eisenhower administration had been warmly received, mirroring the policy of Churchill's government from 1951 which had decided to commit Britain to a nuclear as opposed to a conventional defence strategy, cutting the defence budget, ending compulsory national service and reducing conventional troop levels in the process. Now, however, two fundamental problems were beginning to emerge: first, in the space of just one decade, technological and scientific developments in the field of ICBMs and weapon delivery systems had augmented and escalated at such a frenetic pace that Britain, without a great deal of increased co-operation with the United States, would simply be left behind. One fundamental problem was that the British nuclear capability was becoming increasingly tied to the United States.[31]

A second problem was the fact that, just as Britain was moving on to a position where it could make real progress in nuclear weapons technology thanks to the relaxation of American restrictions on the sharing of nuclear information, American policy was itself beginning to move in a different, even contradictory direction, away from total reliance on nuclear strategy towards a more graduated, flexible response, placing renewed emphasis on a conventional role.[32] The British government was now being told that total nuclear dependence was outdated. Strategists, scientists and planners had come up with a more credible and effective doctrine – 'Flexible Response'.[33] This new thinking, however, was something the Americans believed Britain and the rest of the NATO allies would have to accept on trust. Unprecedented levels of security prevented allied access to data, results from analysis and interpretation techniques, not to mention the vital experience of war-gaming activities. Without these the allies could not hope to understand or assimilate this shift in policy. As this doctrine crystallised, American attitudes increasingly hardened against nuclear proliferation until the Kennedy administration made it one of the key policies in its defence package. It was against this background of profound policy changes that Macmillan and Eisenhower met for one of their periodic informal talks at Camp David in March 1960.

CAMP DAVID 1960

> It is an intriguing story, full of forbodings and uncertainties, of high political stakes dependent on technological progress, of a chain of errors of judgement carefully kept from the public gaze and, finally, at Nassau, one of the great confrontations in the history of Anglo-American relations.[34]

This is how Henry Brandon of *The Times* described the Skybolt crisis – the story of a controversial Air-Launched Ballistic Missile that threatened, for a time, to unbalance the Anglo-American relationship. The 'special relationship' was of vital importance to the Conservative government and, while not as important, it retained considerable significance for the Americans also. Macmillan had made the restoration of the relationship a priority after the damaging Suez débâcle.[35] Having succeeded beyond both their expectations, barely five years later, a repeat performance seemed a horrifying possibility. The fact that the cause of this crisis was a not uncommon change of heart by the US government concerning a piece of highly sophisticated and complex military hardware made the crisis seem even more bizarre.

The story begins at an Anglo-American Conference at Camp David in March 1960. The opening scenes of the drama gave no indication as to what lay ahead. A light-hearted and friendly meeting between Macmillan and Eisenhower in the tranquil surroundings of the president's Maryland retreat was typical of the good relations the two leaders had re-established. Co-operation in the field of defence had been at the top of Macmillan's agenda since becoming prime minister. As the two men now talked about this, Macmillan confided in his counterpart some of the problems facing his government.[36] The British were experiencing difficulties in keeping up with the increasingly sophisticated and complex development in weapons design. The shift from bombers to missile system delivery systems involved a leap in technology that was proving to be beyond their national capability. In order to preserve the British-designed V-bomber force as a credible deterrent by enabling them to penetrate Soviet air defences, a new weapon was needed. Largely thanks to assistance from the American 'Atlas' programme, Britain had been able to develop the Blue Streak (IRBM).[37] Unfortunately, time was against this venture. All indications pointed to the fact that the missile would enter its operational phase obsolete. Moreover, the cost was proving to be prohibitively high.[38] Macmillan's government had made an independent deterrent a high-profile policy. To abandon what had become the visible embodiment of that doctrine without having secured an acceptable replacement would have been highly contentious for the Conservatives.[39]

Fortunately, Eisenhower was sympathetic to Macmillan's dilemma and offered an attractive way out. The United States had a number of weapons currently under development. Of these, two in particular might be of interest to the British – Polaris, a sea-launched ballistic missile, and Skybolt, an air-launched missile being developed for use by the United States Air Force.[40] If Macmillan was interested, he could buy into one of these projects. The prime minister was delighted and agreed to further discussion in order to thrash out the details of the agreement in the coming months. He could now return home confident that whilst reaffirming the policy of interdependence, he had managed to preserve the national deterrent. Soon after he confided to his diary his thoughts on how the news of Blue Streak's imminent demise would be received; 'there will be a terrible row – but it's clearly the right decision . . .'[41] Shortly after his return, he announced the cancellation of Blue Streak.[42] With this, Skybolt became Britain's last hope.[43]

But why did Macmillan and his government decide to opt for Skybolt instead of Polaris? When Macmillan and Eisenhower met at Camp David in March 1960 it was for a routine conference. The British government had already taken the decision to cancel Blue Streak because it was proving to be too expensive and would add little or nothing to the credibility of the national deterrent.[44] Polaris had been discussed as a possible option for some time before the talks[45] and a strong US Navy lobby tried in vain to convince the British at Camp David that this was the better choice. But Macmillan and Watkinson, the Minister of Defence, were not to be persuaded.[46] Polaris was an attractive proposition (that much was undisputed), being a sea-launched ballistic missile that was relatively invulnerable with a second-strike capability and an effectiveness that assured it would be operational until well into the 1970s.[47] As early as January 1958 the Office of the Deputy Chief of the Naval Staff wrote to the First Sea Lord saying:

> I am very anxious to percolate slowly but gradually into the minds of our colleagues the future possibilities of submarines equipped with the I.R.B.M. POLARIS which is being developed in the

United States . . . I do not want to go too fast because nobody is as yet ready [but] I am sure that by 1967 or so missile sites will be out of this island and at sea in submarines . . .[48]

The British delegation, however, were not persuaded by the missile's merits. Polaris was deemed unsuitable for a number of reasons: it would change the traditional role of the armed services making the Navy and not the Air Force the carrier of the nuclear deterrent; such a move would almost certainly have the effect of creating unnecessary inter-service rivalry. In addition, while the RAF was vehemently opposed to any such move, the Royal Navy appeared unenthusiastic.[49] Recognising that, if Polaris was chosen, there was a strong possibility that it would absorb their entire budget at the expense of the much cherished surface fleet plans, the Navy was unconvinced of both the substance and the timing. Mindful of the tremendous expenditure and the complications involved in training crews and building submarines to house the missiles, the Navy decided it was better to hold back from such a massive commitment until it had become clearer just what exactly it would entail. If the US Navy's experience was anything to go by, their British counterpart would have to foot the bill from the existing budget and find money for additional costs as well.[50] Finally, the fact that Polaris had been mentioned in a multilateral context as part of a NATO MRBM force did little to improve the attractiveness of the weapon system.[51] Lord Mountbatten, the First Sea Lord, although convinced of the desirability of the weapon as a future British deterrent, did not feel that the time was right to seek Polaris.[52]

Skybolt, on the other hand, appeared to be just what was needed.[53] Cheaper than Polaris, it enabled the government to re-coup its investment on the ageing British V-bomber force (the mainstay of the national deterrent) which was expected to become obsolete by the mid-1960s, by promising to extend the force's life, while also reaffirming the position of the RAF, and all at a bargain price. There would be no need to set about building a vehicle to carry the missile, and using manned bombers offered an operational flexibility which, it was argued, a missile did not possess. Unlike a Polaris deal, the offer of Skybolt did not come with a huge price tag attached and it would come into service around 1965 instead of some five years later.[54] The United States would undertake and pay for all the research and development costs (which incidentally had only been given the go-ahead one month earlier), leaving Britain simply to pay for the number of missiles it decided to buy.[55] To the British, it seemed to be the perfect choice. Skybolt would fill the gap left by the Blue Streak cancellation, preserving the independent deterrent by propping up the V-bomber force without incurring a great deal of cost. It was a 'stop gap', quick-fix solution. Even so, Polaris was not ruled out completely;[56] nor had it been before the Camp David conference. Although obviously unsuitable for Britain's immediate needs, the benefits of such a weapon had not been ignored and it was thought prudent to reserve the option to acquire Polaris at a later date – possibly for the period after 1970.[57] As Clark commented, Skybolt represented only a short to medium-term solution.[58]

In short, Skybolt and Polaris were regarded not as alternatives but as successive weapons which, if handled correctly, would provide the country with a credible and effective national deterrent well into the 1970s and possibly beyond.[59] The Minister of Defence, Harold Watkinson, was under no illusions about the role of Polaris. In a letter to the prime minister in July 1960, he wrote, somewhat prophetically, that Polaris was 'by far the best, if not the only insurance against the failure of SKYBOLT', adding that the weapon was likely to be the basis for the next generation.[60]

Eisenhower was happy to be able to assist his counterpart with the offer of Skybolt. But he also needed something from Macmillan. While Britain could offer little by way of scientific or technological aid to the United States, it did possess something that was quite valuable – proximity to the Soviet Union. America badly needed docking and service facilities for its Polaris submarines within striking distance of Soviet territory. At Camp David, the price to which Macmillan had agreed in principle was the provision of these facilities.[61] A memorandum for the record stated:

> We welcome the assurance that, in the same spirit of cooperation, the United Kingdom would be agreeable in principle to making the necessary arrangements for United States POLARIS tenders in Scottish ports.[62]

Macmillan had found it very difficult to say no to the president's request. After all, he had just accepted an undeniably generous offer of Skybolt and could hardly be seen to refuse Eisenhower his ports.[63] But the Gareloch/Holy Loch agreement never did rest easy with the prime minister or the Cabinet. Presenting such a deal to the British public was a chief concern. In agreeing to let US submarines dock in Scotland, the British government had made Britain the target of a possible Soviet first strike.[64] Macmillan ran the risk of appearing as a weak lackey of the United States who was unable to assert his will in the face of US domination. For these reasons Macmillan engaged in much foot-dragging in an effort to stall Eisenhower and hopefully manoeuvre himself into a better position, while perhaps getting a better deal out of the Americans.[65]

Eisenhower had been too quick off the mark for Macmillan's liking. When the president wrote to the prime minister shortly after the two had met, thanking him for agreeing to let the Clyde be used as a dock,[66] Macmillan was not pleased, writing in the margin of the letter 'I did *not*, repeat *not* agree to this . . .'.[67] Increasingly the government worried about the impact on public opinion and rapidly agreed that:

> the best means of selling the scheme to the British Public would be to say that our agreement to the American project was tied up with this future (POLARIS) partnership . . .

and pressed a case in the discussions which followed the agreement for 'an option to buy or obtain the know-how to build, plus the purchase of missiles and components, facilities for training and servicing . . .'.[68]

Having secured the Skybolt deal in June,[69] the British government now explored the possibility of changing the parameters of the original agreement where Polaris base facilities were seen as an unofficial and informal exchange for Skybolt. It was not altogether clear, however, what the American position was. In one communication to the government it was pointed out that:

> it does not appear appropriate to consider a bilateral understanding on POLARIS until the problem of SACEUR's requirements has been satisfactorily been disposed of in NATO.[70]

On another occasion, Thomas Gates promised Watkinson, when the two met to formalise the Skybolt agreement, that he would consider 'further possible methods of making Polaris submarines and missiles available to the UK'.[71]

Owing to the great difficulties this arrangement was causing at home, the British now attempted to broker a new deal – Holy Loch for Polaris.[72] This way they could assure the public that this was a joint venture that the country was directly benefiting from, rather than a concession bullied out of them by the United States. The

Cabinet had agreed to the need for Polaris anyway. If they could secure it now, all the better. The government now moved to disassociate the Skybolt/Holy Loch deals with a view to bargaining Holy Loch for Polaris, with Skybolt safely 'in the bag'.[73] This attempt to exert moral pressure on the Americans met with a sharp closing of ranks and a flat refusal to countenance any such arrangement. Increasingly, Polaris was linked to a MRBM NATO force, so ruling out any possibility of a bilateral deal.[74] Fearing that the Holy Loch deal might not be sufficiently strong to entice the Americans to rethink their decision, the government decided to call a halt to attempts to exact further concessions.[75] If they pressed too hard they ran the risk of alienating the United States, which might then look elsewhere for the necessary docking facilities.[76] In the end, an unspoken assumption took the place of an official Polaris deal. As the *New York Times* reported, while the British had made it clear they would like the weapon at some time in the future, they were 'content to wait' for the time being.[77] Safe in the knowledge that Eisenhower had discussed the possibility of a Polaris arrangement, and fearing possible refusal at this time, Macmillan and his colleagues let it be known that Polaris had not been asked for. Underpinning this approach was the confidence, on Macmillan's part at least, that he had already received a verbal commitment from Eisenhower to provide the weapon – when the time was right.[78] By not pressing the matter, the British government calculated that they were giving the US administration and their own services time to assume the appropriate positions in order to facilitate this shift in policy.[79] This firm belief that the Skybolt and Holy Loch deals were reciprocal and morally although not legally binding, and that Polaris had been virtually promised, would prove of great importance when negotiations began to resolve the Skybolt crisis less than three years later. However, as later developments will show, divergent interpretations were already causing great gaps to appear in the understandings between the two countries. Not only did the British government believe that Polaris had been on the table, but the linking in a document of the Skybolt and Holy Loch agreements which they had agreed to also included a second paragraph dealing with the NATO MRBM force.[80] In British eyes, the negotiations for a Polaris force to succeed the Skybolt/V-bombers combination could take place after the NATO problems and SACEUR's demands had been resolved.[81] From the other side of the Atlantic things looked very different. In the estimation of the

United States, when the NATO issues had been settled the way would be open for the assignment to NATO of a British Polaris force. Where the Americans were thinking in terms of some sort of a multinational arrangement, the British government was dreaming in bilateral colours. Already in the story, misconceptions were trampling on the toes of reality.

3 Chaos and Confusion – Allies in Trouble

SKYBOLT UNDER EISENHOWER

The agreement reached in principle by Macmillan and Eisenhower at Camp David was finalised soon after when Watkinson went to Washington to thrash out the details in June. The basic terms agreed at Camp David stated that:

> In a desire to be of assistance in improving and extending the effective life of the V-bomber force, the United States, subject only to United States priorities, is prepared to provide SKYBOLT missiles – minus warheads – to the United Kingdom on a reimbursable basis in 1965 or thereafter. Since SKYBOLT is still in the early stages of development, this offer is necessarily dependent on the successful completion of its development program.[1]

A cheap, no-strings-attached deal, at first glance Skybolt seemed the perfect solution.[2] Upon closer inspection, complications began to appear. To begin with, the rationale for such a weapon was dubious, for the future of this particular mode of delivery was regarded by many as increasingly compromised by its inability to evade enemy air defences.[3] The missile was an ambitious project by any standards, requiring the development and application of highly advanced and, as yet, experimental technology needed to improve the credibility of the manned strategic bomber.[4] Also called the GAM-87A, Skybolt was an air-launched, two stage solid-propellant hypersonic ballistic missile with astro-inertial guidance and a range of approximately 1,000 miles.[5] It was, as Henry Brandon reported:

> the most complex ballistic missile the United States had yet undertaken – more so than MINUTEMAN or POLARIS. The missile had to be launched over an altitude of several thousand feet, to be able at high speed to resist shock, vibration and noise from a hostile environment and to be integrated in a unique way with the mother ship which, with its computer parts, contains about 130,000 parts.[6]

Unfortunately, however, the development of Skybolt was to coincide with the dawning of the missile age.[7] Whereas in the 1950s the weapon would have been ideal for use by the strategic bomber, by the beginning of the 1960s anti-aircraft innovations were thought to reduce its effectiveness radically. As it became clear that the Soviet Union was building increasingly sophisticated missile technology,[8] Skybolt's supporters sought to redefine the weapon's role, arguing the need for a kind of 'tin opener' that would knock out enemy air defences, thus clearing the way for other bombers and missiles.[9] Of course, this 'defence suppression' mission against enemy airfields and early-warning radar systems was also an attractive proposition for the British, whose ageing V-bomber fleet was becoming increasingly incapable of high-confidence penetration of anything. Skybolt would give these bombers a 'stand-off' capability, enabling them to perform the difficult task of targeting strategic locations within the heart of enemy territory without running the risk of, and succumbing to, interception. Skybolt was also being considered by the RAF as a possible addition to the 'Polaris of the Sky' (a nuclear-powered aircraft with enormous endurance) although military analyists considered satellites as a more likely platform for such a mission.[10]

Despite the unsurprising confidence of the USAF and the Douglas Corporation (Skybolt's prime contractor), Thomas Gates, the US Secretary of Defense under Eisenhower, was never happy with the project, believing among other things that it was badly run.[11] The USAF, claiming substantial British interest had pressed it upon him.[12] In June, just three months after the initial agreement had been reached, preparations were made for the insertion of a detailed termination clause providing that 'either party might terminate its interest at any time', although it was stressed that this must not happen without 'prior consultation with the other'.[13]

Gates and his deputy, James Douglas, unimpressed by the 'drawing board proposition' as they called it, nevertheless decided to approve the missile's development. They took this decision against the recommendation of a Pentagon report presented by the Fletcher Committee in 1959 which strongly suggested termination.[14] The reason? It would appear that the decision was influenced by the knowledge that although the United States had several missiles in development, so far, only the Atlas was operational. As for the others, it was nearly impossible to judge how quickly these weapons would clear their problem-prone infancies and how effective they would be once ready.[15]

Despite their decision, Gates and Douglas made no secret of their concern and frequently attempted to impress upon their British counterparts the problems facing the programme and the doubts surrounding its continuation to a successful conclusion.[16] Barely one month after the Technical Agreement had been signed, Douglas informed Watkinson that Skybolt was 'in real trouble'.[17] On another occasion Gates urged Sir Solly Zuckerman, the British government's Chief Scientific Adviser, to warn the Minister of Defence that 'nobody would gain from making a political issue out of it', adding that attention was now shifting noticeably in favour of the USN's *wunderkind* – the Polaris SLBM.[18] In December 1960 Watkinson wrote to the Prime Minister about the status of the project telling him:

> my talk about Skybolt with Gates was not all that encouraging. The technical difficulties . . . remain high; expenditure is going up very rapidly . . . From my point of view, all this is a strong confirmation of the doubts, which have always existed, whether we shall get Skybolt at all . . .[19]

Eventually, while not cancelling the project, a decision to reduce its funding radically in the last budget of the Eisenhower term ended effective development and the future of Skybolt hung in the balance as American politics moved into limbo pending the outcome of the 1960 presidential election.[20] In Britain, ministers in Whitehall held their breath and waited for some indication about the fate of the weapon.[21]

A NEW PRESIDENT AND A NEW POLICY

The Kennedy administration, which came into office in January 1961, initially backed Skybolt. The decision to maintain it was very much a 'stop-gap' measure designed to delay real consideration of the matter until Kennedy had established himself in the White House. An unsigned memorandum to Kennedy illustrates the doubts articulated about the wisdom of continuing with Skybolt even at this early stage:

> Although we have a moral commitment to the British on this, will equipping more bombers with still more missiles be necessary when this doubtful weapon (supposedly why Ike released B-70 funds) only replaces similar shorter-range Hound Dog missiles . . .[22]

Secretary of Defense Robert McNamara, however, was both worried about the current (and as yet undebunked) missile gap theory, and conscious of the fact that he was already contemplating scrapping another star in the Air Force's firmament – the B-70 bomber. Any attempt to cancel both programmes at once, the Secretary knew, would be tantamount to committing political suicide.[23]

McNamara brought to the job a very different perspective and set of experiences from his predecessors. Head of the Ford Motor Company before taking up his post as Kennedy's Defense Secretary, he was a highly successful and capable industrial manager – skills that were to have an enormous impact on his handling of the Department. Almost immediately, McNamara set about a radical review of the entire defence establishment with a view to identifying and removing wastage, inefficiency and outdated thinking and practices. Often criticised, he was a man with strong opinions and both the determination and ability to ensure they were put into practice. Under McNamara, the virulent inter-service rivalry, played out in an endless round of internal intrigues and lobbyist assaults, was forced to take a back seat as he initiated his review. While this was under way, McNamara was in no position to make any final decisions on individual projects.

Under McNamara's rationalisation of the Defense Department, Skybolt came under intense scrutiny. In US–UK defence talks in March 1961, the American team announced that, although the scheduled operational date had been delayed for a few months because of the funding problem now resolved, they were happy that the October 1964 date for operational deployment should be met. They also revealed that the whole system had been 'scrubbed down' in an effort to combat some of the complications associated with the guidance system. The British team returned to London reasonably content that all was progressing as planned.[24] Ignoring a confidential report from a panel of experts recommending cancellation, McNamara instead allocated more funds to the emaciated project in the belief that Gates' reduction would not prove either way if the missile was to be a success or failure. He explained to the Senate Subcommittee for Appropriations of his intent:

> In our judgement, the remaining 1961 funds cannot support a reasonable level of effort over the next 15 months. Either the project should be dropped entirely or it should be pursued in an orderly and efficient manner. On balance, we feel that the advantages of this weapon system warrant an effective development

effort, and we have requested $50 million for this purpose in 1962.[25]

'The master of the slide-rule' as he was often called, needed some breathing space. As Henry Brandon stated:

[McNamara] gave Skybolt time: he himself needed time to decide which fights within the services and Congress he would take on. Having introduced the so-called 'cost efficiency' system to establish criteria on weapons to keep and those to cut, he had some hard fights ahead of him . . .[26]

In the autumn of 1961 an impressive group of scientists led by Harold Brown, Director of Defense Research and Engineering, Jerome Weisner, the president's Scientific Adviser, and David Bell, the Budget Director, approached McNamara with a recommendation to terminate the project.[27] Their argument was a simple one: the only function that Skybolt could have performed for the United States was as a tactical weapon for 'defence suppression' and this would only have been valuable if cheap to do so. Unfortunately, Skybolt was proving anything but. The complicated guidance system was proving very costly to develop.[28] Although McNamara by now tended to agree with their assessment, he still felt unable to make a move against the project. A major factor counselling restraint was his recent brutal clash with Congress and the USAF over his B-70 cancellation. This fight had developed into an ugly and damaging confrontation which left McNamara badly bruised and wary of attempting a repeat performance again so soon.[29] More aware than ever of the importance of timing, he offered Skybolt a reprieve of sorts, a compromise deal that saw funding on the project capped, guaranteeing cancellation until he was better placed to engage the weapon's supporters.[30] Instead of making a firm decision, this deal made with Eugene Zuckert, the Secretary of the Air Force, effectively imposed a ceiling on the net spending of the project, restricting it to no more than $500 million in the next fiscal year.[31] In real terms this compromise allowed for a margin of less than $10 million for any further revision in the estimates for the whole of one year. This figure was to prove wildly unrealistic and far from representative of the actual state of the project's affairs. However, for those supporters of the programme, it was noted as proof of continuing government commitment.

In early December 1961, after reviewing the project, Kennedy approved continuation, proving that 'Douglas can perform'.[32] Just over six months later, little had changed, except for the fact that Minuteman – one of Skybolt's competitors – having tested successfully, was now a mere six months from leaving its production phase.[33] This, compounded by the progress made by both Polaris and Titan and the revelation that the missile gap was, if anything, a gap in the West's favour, did little to bolster the fortunes of Skybolt. By now the weapon was consistently experiencing costly and time-consuming setbacks. Not only was the monthly rate of expenditure now being regularly exceeded, but the development time lag was also markedly increasing. This made attempts to predict when it would enter its operational phase difficult. It was now clear that the missile would not be the first out of the American stables. All in all, it would be a considerable time, and a lot of money after both Polaris, Titan and Minuteman. This was certainly not what McNamara wanted to hear.

Not surprisingly, before the summer ended, McNamara's technical and budgetary aides were again urging him to close the project down.[34] Hitch and Brown presented the Secretary with the conclusions of the reports he had requested them to prepare. Though separate studies, both came to essentially the same conclusion:

> The . . . Skybolt force, as part . . . of a . . . B-52 force is inferior to the force which could be bought for a somewhat smaller amount of money by filling out the B-52 squadrons with Hound Dog missiles and buying a certain number of additional MINUTEMEN . . .[35]

The safest way, they recommended, would be to drop it from the next budget, thus hopefully avoiding a fight with Congress and the Air Force similar to the B-70 confrontation. McNamara concurred and ordered that funds for the programme be released on a monthly basis so as not to arouse suspicions that it was facing termination. The Secretary told his aides to reveal nothing of what had transpired until the time was right.[36] Hitch and Brown informed their respective aides, Alain Enthoven and John Rubel, about the decision and left it at that.

SKYBOLT'S LAST DAYS

Although McNamara was by now committed to cancellation, he could not reveal this when he was visited by the new British Minister of Defence, Peter Thorneycroft, in September. Instead, he informed him that the weapon had already failed four successive tests and, in terms of cost-effectiveness, was becoming an increasingly poor investment. Fearing that if he made his intentions too explicit Thorneycroft might alert the Royal Air Force and thus the USAF, McNamara went no further than to warn the Minister not to rest too easy on Skybolt's laurels.[37] Thorneycroft had offered the Secretary a routine warning that failure to deliver Skybolt would be detrimental not only to the British government, but to Anglo-American relations.[38] McNamara's mention of a routine release of production funds, however, reached Thorneycroft where his warnings did not. The British Minister returned home dismissive of McNamara's pessimistic account of Skybolt's problems and happy that all was progressing as expected. Having been reassured by excellent reports from the USAF and the Douglas Corporation, he was confident that the turbulence highlighted by McNamara would not impede a successful landing.[39] Not long after Thorneycroft's departure, the Kennedy administration was plunged into the all-consuming Cuban Missile Crisis. Hopelessly distracted, McNamara postponed taking action on the decision to cancel until he could devote his energies exclusively to the problem.

Meanwhile, word slowly began to filter through the administration. Paul Nitze, McNamara's Assistant Secretary of Defense, was informed in late September. From his International Security Affairs office, Jerome Weisner was able to extract the first solid hint of what was going on. By 15 October, Roswell Gilpatric, the deputy Secretary of State, confirmed to the Budget Bureau staff, under pledge of secrecy, that cancellation was imminent.[40]

As the Cuban Missile Crisis occupied the senior officials in the administration, Budget Director Bell's office was mulling over the Skybolt news and prepared a memorandum which, originally intended for the president, was sent instead to Bundy. Bell was concerned that the potential for crisis may have been overlooked:

> cancellation is likely to create internal political problems for the British . . . our actions up to now, while not actually committing us, have clearly implied an intention to proceed . . . It would seem important that suitable arrangements be made for advance notification . . . and consultation prior to the time that a decision becomes known publicly or through Air Force channels . . .[41]

Bundy was tied up with Cuba, but his deputy, Carl Kaysen, saw the memorandum and was sufficiently worried to approach both

Nitze and Tyler, asking the latter for an appraisal of the problem. Tyler passed the task to the BNA, the British desk in the State Department. Two days later, he sent their reply to Kaysen. The men who were traditionally consulted least in the Department had pulled out all the stops. The memorandum was blunt: 'cancellation of Skybolt', they declared, 'would put in jeopardy not only bomber command but a vital element of British defence philosophy . . . the independent nuclear deterrent'.

Two of the Conservative Party's talking points are that they have special and superior qualifications, as compared to Labour, for dealing with a) defense and b) the Americans . . . cancellation . . . could be an unmitigated political blow to the Conservatives . . . [they] would certainly feel let down hard . . . we still rely heavily on British real estate all over the world from Christmas Island to Holy Loch. We should carefully consider the consequences of the estrangement.

Their final recommendation was for time. The British, they advised, should be given ample time to prepare for the announcement. This would ensure that they were ready for consultation and a smooth resolution of the issue.[42] The facts of the matter were apparent for all to see. But somehow, the obvious reaction was ignored in preference for how the American officials imagined the British would react. The logic of the BNA's strong recommendations was not followed through.

Meanwhile in London, while Thorneycroft appeared confident in public, in private he was beginning to sense trouble. Rumours about the weapon's future were reaching Whitehall in greater numbers than ever. Speculation was rife that the project was earmarked for cancellation in the next budget. These concerns prompted the Minister to seek out some corroborative information about what was happening in Washington. His chance came when he discovered that John Rubel, the Deputy Director of Defense Research and Engineering, was in London for meetings. Over dinner, Thorneycroft grilled his guest about Skybolt's fate, asking him direct if his government intended to scrap the missile. Brandon is inaccurate in asserting that Rubel could only answer truthfully that he had no certain knowledge of this being the case. Sworn to secrecy by his superior, he could only reply that normal reviews were taking place. Having gained little information from Rubel, Thorneycroft decided to tackle McNamara himself. Two days after his unsatisfactory talk with Rubel, on 5 November Thorneycroft made his move. In an oddly worded telegram, he congratulated the Secretary on Skybolt having reached its production phase, stressing the importance of the project for the British government, which he called 'a central feature both of our defence policy and of our collaboration with you'.[43]

This 'piece of English understatement', as Neustadt calls it, reached the Pentagon the day that McNamara sent to the Joint Chiefs of Staff his draft budget proposals on strategic retaliatory forces, including the recommendation that Skybolt should be cancelled.[44] If Thorneycroft had hoped to sting McNamara into revealing his true intentions the telegram was a partial success. Reasoning that a written reply along the lines of one Paul Nitze had drawn up would not be appropriate under the circumstances, McNamara instead requested a meeting with Rusk and the president to discuss what steps to take. Thorneycroft had made it clear that he desired immediate clarification. Action was needed now.

On 7 November, McNamara met Kennedy and Rusk to plan the cancellation of Skybolt. The Secretary's argument seemed reasonable. Termination of the project would save $2.5 billion over several fiscal years, a fifth of it in the following year alone. McNamara's plan was to warn the British now, giving them time to consider their options so that consultation could take place once the decision-making process in the administration had taken place in about three weeks' time. Both men agreed with the Secretary of Defense's logic and stressed only the importance of letting the British down gently, urging consultation at the earliest possible opportunity. McNamara listened to their concerns and volunteered to handle the matter himself, promising to contact the British Ambassador, David Ormsby-Gore, and Peter Thorneycroft in person as soon as possible.[45] Kennedy and Rusk, content that the matter was under control, turned their attention to other matters.

The next day McNamara met Ormsby-Gore to brief him on Skybolt. This was not an easy task in itself as the Secretary could not tell the Ambassador that Skybolt was to be scrapped. As Neustadt stated:

He could not tell them Skybolt was about to die, no matter that he had decided so, for this was not yet an Administration decision. He was just then sending to our Joint Chiefs for comment, the conclusions of his own civilian staff in which he shared. The Joint Chiefs of Staff's response would be forthcoming in two weeks.

No doubt it would be favourable to SKYBOLT. The J.C.S.'s opinions and his own, on the whole defense budget, were to be submitted for decision by the President in conference with his Chief White House and Budget Bureau aides. The conference was tentatively set for Thanksgiving, three weeks hence. The President might opt for McNamara's view but he could not do so in form until Thanksgiving, lest referral to the Chiefs appear a mockery.[46]

However, his negative remarks about the project proved sufficient to alert the British Ambassador, who took the news very badly. Startled and appalled, he had sufficient composure to tell McNamara that such a move would be 'political dynamite' in London.[47] At Ormsby-Gore's request, McNamara agreed not to telephone Thorneycroft with this information until the Ambassador had briefed him. When McNamara did contact Thorneycroft, he was surprised at his calmness. He had expected a reaction similar to Ormsby-Gore's, but instead found him sounding reasonable, even open to discussion, prompting McNamara to conclude that matters were well under control in London. Encouraged, he told his counterpart that a final decision would be made by Kennedy between 23 November and 10 December, after which he would make it his business to come to London as soon as was expedient to discuss possible alternatives should the decision be to cancel.

After dealing with the British end, McNamara set about preparing his side. On 12 November he sent a rather unusual telegram to Ambassador Bruce to explain the impending developments. This 'eyes only' communication, sent not through the normal State Department channels but through military channels, was the first of its kind Bruce remembered having received.[48] McNamara then waited for the recommendation from the Joint Chiefs of Staff (which came on 20 November and not surprisingly recommended continuation) and the report he had requested from Nitze on alternatives to the system. This reached him on 23 November. By now, however, the Secretary was in Hyannis Port with Kennedy and the administration's budget aides to finalise the budget details. The meeting did not dwell long on the matter. Kennedy officially approved the plan 'subject to consultation with the British on alternatives'.[49] Since this aspect had already been discussed at the 7 November meeting, little more was said.[50]

For McNamara, everything was progressing according to plan.

Content that the British had been given ample time to prepare for a probable cancellation, he then became immersed in difficult budget details which were to occupy him until early December.[51] McNamara finally extracted himself from the budget difficulties in early December. Before he left for London and Paris he had one last meeting with the president to discuss the Skybolt problem. He made it clear that he was unconvinced about the likelihood of the British accepting any of the proposals forwarded by the State Department and suggested that an option of making Polaris available 'on the condition that the venture become multilateral if and when a multilateral force should be developed' should be regarded as a possible compromise.[52] When McNamara eventually did arrive in Britain, more than four weeks later, it was after the date he had predicted some time before would be the last day before the story leaked. He had been correct in his assessment, the story emerging in Washington on 7 December. On 11 December the British press was in an uproar. As Dean Rusk later commented, 'it hit like a thunderclap in London'.[53] As McNamara stepped off the plane, he issued a statement that clearly hinted at cancellation.[54] If there was a way to add fuel to the fire, the Secretary of Defense had just found it. Amazed at the hostility that seemed to greet him from all sides, McNamara retreated with his team to the sanctuary of the American Embassy. Surely this was contrived, he thought. Had not Thorneycroft seemed reasonable and in control when he had spoken to him not long before? McNamara, Neustadt remarked, 'had been surprised and lambasted'.[55]

The meeting was tense and uncomfortable. McNamara offered the British a document underlining the American approach to the problem and proceeded to read it to the gathering.[56] Thorneycroft, expecting an American offer of a replacement weapon, was appalled to find that all that was on offer was a missile vaguely similar to Skybolt called 'Hound Dog'. Other than that, McNamara was apparently suggesting that the British continue with Skybolt's development by themselves. The Secretary of Defense, for his part, was thoroughly confused. Did Thorneycroft expect him to offer Polaris as a replacement? Surely the Minister knew that this was beyond McNamara's mandate at this time. But if he were to ask for the weapon, a solid request could stand a much better chance in Washington. The Secretary wanted to help his counterpart with this problem, but Thorneycroft's attitude was combative at best.[57] In a final effort to make some headway, McNamara exceeded his brief by implying that there could be consideration of a Polaris deal, if the British would agree to pledge the force to NATO. This only exacerbated the situation, with Thorneycroft claiming that Polaris without this condition had been discussed during the telephone conversation the two men had had in November. Denying this, McNamara tried, and failed, to grasp what Thorneycroft and his team were expecting. Not surprisingly, the meeting concluded without anything having been resolved. The two men parted to prepare for the NATO ministers meeting the following day in Paris. The newspaper reports that appeared that evening confirmed McNamara's suspicions that Thorneycroft had staged the meeting in order to heighten the already tense atmosphere.[58] The resolution of the crisis was left to Kennedy and Macmillan, who were scheduled to meet in Nassau in a few days' time. It was here that the Skybolt crisis would be defused.

4 A Crisis Explained

The Skybolt crisis arose out of a mêlée of confusion, muddled perceptions, misunderstandings, overestimation of some elements and underestimation of others, compounded and exacerbated by feelings of mistrust, suspicion and betrayal. Much of the shock, it would seem, came from the fact that two close allies should so easily find themselves dramatically opposed. Perhaps, as Neustadt later remarked, no one bothers to take much notice when enemies fight, but when friends fall out everyone wants to know the reason why.

Many documents pertaining to the episode still remain classified in both Britain and the United States. But several key pieces, including Neustadt's report to Kennedy and transcripts of crucial meetings, have now been released. Questions that have never been adequately answered can now be asked again, inconsistencies explained and fallacies corrected. Several factors must collectively bear responsibility for the complex Skybolt crisis. Although it would be easy to point to an American agenda to remove Britain from the highly prestigious nuclear club, this would be a misleading oversimplification of the affair. Appealing though a conspiracy theory might be, one single factor cannot adequately explain why a weapons system decision by the US government caused such a crisis. In order to gain some insight into the affair a number of factors must be examined.

COMPLACENT INTIMACY – THE 'SPECIAL RELATIONSHIP' IN TROUBLE

Why did close allies have such a public and dramatic falling out? Was the scale of the crisis in proportion to the intimacy of the relationship enjoyed by the two countries? In short, was intimacy a contributing factor or a mediating influence that prevented the crisis from having an even more brutal and profound effect on the alliance? Was the relationship so close that it prevented the key characters from recognising that a problem existed? Did the intimacy cloud perceptions, distort views and generally restrict rational analysis of the situation?

Harold Macmillan had decided very early in his premiership on the importance of restoring a close relationship with the United States. To a large extent, by 1962 he had managed to achieve this quite successfully. Although he and Eisenhower had clashed on several occasions, the latter retained a considerable measure of respect, and indeed friendship, for his British counterpart which lasted long after he left office. This closeness was equalled, if not surpassed, when Kennedy took over the presidency. To the undisguised surprise of onlookers, the two men formed an unlikely, but warm friendship. As Theodore Sorenson was to remark: 'Macmillan was the leader Kennedy saw first, liked best and saw most often.'[1] The good relations Kennedy and Macmillan enjoyed went beyond the personal. In general the Kennedy administration and the Macmillan government got on quite well. Wartime friendships easily translated into good inter-governmental working relationships. Normally one would assume that the closer the relationship, the less chance there would be of misunderstandings occurring. This, however, soon proved to be flawed. As Richard Neustadt correctly noted:

> Misperceptions evidently make for crisis in proportion to the intimacy of relations. Hazards are proportionate to the degree of friendship. Indifference and hostility may not breed paranoia; friendship does.[2]

The problem was two-fold. First, the 'special relationship' was viewed very differently in Washington and London. While the British government continued to stress the importance of the relationship, Washington was moving perceptibly in the opposite direction. Anxious that the policy of aiding the British in nuclear matters was having a detrimental effect on relations with the other NATO allies, a substantial and influential body of opinion in the Kennedy administration was advocating the removal of this particular bone of contention. Increasingly, from the American point of view, the 'special relationship' was becoming something of a liability. The stark reality of the situation was that Britain needed America more than America needed Britain.[3] Unfortunately, this difference in perspective was not readily understood in London. From the beginning, the Skybolt deal was perceived in Britain as a symbol of the 'specialness' of the Anglo-American relationship – an example of the intimacy now enjoyed in the field of defence. For the Eisenhower administration it was a weapons deal which, whilst generous in nature, was no more than a technical agreement.

The second problem was the precise nature of the closeness fostered by the two leaders and their staff. Friendly and reciprocal working relations meant a complex warren of channels of communication which extended far beyond Kennedy and Macmillan. Of great importance was the appointment of David Ormsby-Gore as British Ambassador to Washington. Much respected and liked by the president's staff, Ormsby-Gore was a vital link who facilitated fluid and unhindered circulation of information and opinions.[4] Likewise, the American Ambassador in London, David Bruce, was a well-known and deeply respected diplomat who had established many friendships in Britain long before his appointment to the Court of St. James. The cordial relations enjoyed by Rusk and Home, McNamara and Watkinson, and later, Thorneycroft, were mirrored further down the chain of command. Many of their deputies and more junior staff managed to keep in regular contact with their counterparts about a great variety of different matters. For their part, the American Services and their British counterparts had long enjoyed close and supportive relations. The USAF and the RAF had been in contact about Skybolt even before the American Defense Department was informed of its development.[5] Similarly, the US and British Navies kept each other closely informed on a wide range of matters, including weapons development.[6] Close links also existed between academic and scientific communities. In Britain, the government's Chief Scientific Adviser, Sir Solly Zuckerman, conferred regularly with his American counterparts. Well known and liked, Zuckerman had easy access to the highest echelons of the Kennedy administration. Finally, Britain had a number of scientists and technical experts, as well as RAF and naval officers, working on several of the American missile projects.[7] Similarly, 20 RAF officers and 48 airmen, scientists and technical staff were involved in the Skybolt programme.[8] Their observations and contributions were filtered back through liaison officers.[9] Finally, the two countries had a powerful tie in the form of the total collaboration between their intelligence services. This was a unique element in the Anglo-American relationship which remained closed to all other countries, including France.

What is surprising is how so many apparent channels of communication suddenly became so few. When McNamara informed Ormsby-Gore and Thorneycroft about the likely fate of Skybolt, he believed he was giving Britain ample warning in order to consult and prepare alternatives for negotiation. Instead, he soon discovered that little discussion and virtually no detailed planning had taken place. During the weeks between McNamara's warning and his arrival in London the abundant channels of communication had become too few. Silence fell as conversation dried up. As Newhouse observed, 'for the people in Whitehall, it was often difficult to know where and how best to proceed with the Americans'.[10] The crisis grew more complicated and untenable in proportion to the number of people involved; many felt left out or even betrayed by colleagues and counterparts as the situation deteriorated. It appeared that the Anglo-American alliance had experienced a debilitating breakdown in communication.

WAS THERE A BREAKDOWN IN COMMUNICATION?

Some questions must be put. At what point did the British know of the Americans' intention to cancel the weapon? How much did they know? What action was taken in response? Why was the affair so handled? It has been suggested that a key factor in the crisis was the US administration's failure to initiate adequate consultation. This accusation gained high currency in Britain as the crisis unfolded. As we shall see, the strategy had its uses, but was it an accurate assessment of the situation or a manipulation designed for a specific purpose?

The Skybolt programme had never enjoyed a particularly smooth or untroubled path. From the earliest days of its development senior figures in the Eisenhower administration made little effort to disguise their scepticism and general lack of enthusiasm for the project. Harold Watkinson, the British Minister of Defence, was left under no illusions about the difficulties associated with the missile and the doubts, openly expressed within the administration, about the system ever seeing the light of day.[11] Watkinson never overcame his concern that, for one reason or another, the Americans would fail to deliver the weapon.[12] In June 1960 he warned the prime minister that the British weapon Blue Steel should be retained as 'a measure of reinsurance against the failure of Skybolt which must remain a possibility for at least a further twelve months...'.[13]

Watkinson was well aware that while Skybolt had its supporters in the USAF and Congress, powerful counterforces existed that could upset the precarious position the ill-fated weapons system seemed to occupy.[14] Watkinson was certainly in a position to know.

He had access to both projects through a large number of British personnel who had been assigned to liaise and work with their American counterparts.[15] Reports were frequent and procedures for reporting were, according to the minister, most satisfactory.[16] Watkinson and the prime minister kept in close touch, the former expressing on a regular basis his concerns about the project. In November 1960 he wrote to Macmillan:

> I think we should be ready now with a plan for what we should say in public if it began to leak out that the Americans have doubts over Skybolt . . . I am sure that we should take this calmly and be seen to be doing so from the start. We have foreseen it as a possibility and, for that reason, you and I have been at pains never to say that we were certain of Skybolt. I have purposely talked in public about other possibilities and shall continue to do so . . .[17]

The prime minister concurred. He had always known, as Watkinson had reminded him, that the project had never been touted as a 'sure thing'. Indeed, as early as December 1960, he had written in his diary that he doubted whether or not the Americans would actually honour the agreement.[18] He now responded to Watkinson:

> if Skybolt should fail we shall have, on the basis of our present arrangements, no way of maintaining an effective means of delivery of the nuclear deterrent in the period 1965–70 . . . if you think there is a real risk of Skybolt being abandoned soon, we must consider urgently what alternatives are open to us . . .[19]

Watkinson did not need to be told twice. He immediately set about preparing a detailed memorandum about the weapons system along with a list of alternatives.[20] In his report, Watkinson concluded:

> if we start asking questions about this, we shall give the impression that we are resigning ourselves to the loss of Skybolt. In any case, there would be little to learn because the USAF do not expect to lose Skybolt and have made no detailed studies of alternatives . . .[21]

Macmillan advised that nothing should be volunteered to indicate either total dependence on the project or that Britain feared cancellation. The danger, recognised and duly noted for the record, prompted no more action for the time being.

Aside from the liaison staff in the United States, Watkinson was kept informed of Skybolt's progress through another channel: Sir Solly Zuckerman. Zuckerman was in close contact with the scientific and technical experts in the US administration. His contacts left him in little doubt as to what he should expect from the weapon.[22] John Rubel, who was responsible for monitoring the programme for the US Department of Defense, told Zuckerman on one occasion that the whole thing was regarded as 'very speculative'.[23] Not surprisingly, Zuckerman himself was outspoken in his criticism of the project, believing it to be overambitious, expensive and with little relevance to the overall British or American strategic plans. He predicted that the weapon would reveal itself sooner or later to be a white elephant and cautioned his superiors about becoming too dependent on it. Zuckerman's warnings obviously did not have the effect intended. Why? One possibility is that the precise criticisms he had of the project were not easily understood by those outside the scientific community.[24] One of the aspects that the scientific adviser disliked most was the guidance system. As Neustadt has pointed out, to his non-scientific colleagues it sounded 'hypercritical', especially when they were in regular receipt of confident reports from the RAF, USAF and the Douglas Corporation.[25] Ironically, despite Zuckerman's close contact with and knowledge of the project in the crucial period preceding the cancellation, he could contribute little to the discussion because his usual sources were silent.[26] He did hear from Will Hawthorne, an English Professor of Engineering at Cambridge currently on a visiting year at MIT, who told him that he had heard that McNamara was serious about cancellation, which now appeared to be a certainty.[27] Although this was passed on to Peter Thorneycroft, the minister did nothing.

McNamara's briefing of Ormsby-Gore and Thorneycroft on 8 and 9 November removed any lingering hopes the British might have had about the Skybolt weapons system. Officially notified that some change could be anticipated, Thorneycroft faced the problem for the first time. After writing a memoradum to the prime minister summarising McNamara's telephone message, he briefed Macmillan face-to-face, in what one official recalled as a very extensive meeting.[28] Although Neustadt believed that, from this point on, Thorneycroft had written nothing more about the matter, there is evidence to suggest otherwise. Thorneycroft did correspond with Macmillan before the Nassau Conference, mainly to discuss alternatives to the Skybolt weapons system.[29] There is nothing to suggest, however, that he tried to contact McNamara, or anyone else on the

American side, to discuss the problem or possible solutions to it. Communication was strictly at the highest levels of the British government, and the British government alone. Macmillan behaved in a similar fashion. Having cabled Ormsby-Gore on 15 December with instructions to secure a number of procedural assurances from President Kennedy pertaining to cancellation, Macmillan then asked the Ambassador if he thought a private phone call to the president would help the situation. Ormsby-Gore, believing that Kennedy was not yet fully briefed on Skybolt, advised Macmillan to wait, fearing that such a gesture might only complicate matters. Macmillan deferred to Ormsby-Gore's assessment, for, after all, he was much closer to Kennedy. He had his reasons.

Both David Ormsby-Gore and David Bruce, the US Ambassador, it has been claimed, played uncharacteristically minor roles in the Skybolt affair. Henry Brandon has suggested that Ormsby-Gore knew little or nothing of his government's intentions until he arrived with President Kennedy at Nassau; while his American counterpart was effectively sidelined, neither consulted nor instructed during the unfolding crisis. This, however, is quite inaccurate. Ormsby-Gore was the first on the British side to be contacted by the Secretary in his bid to cancel the project. The Ambassador immediately informed both his prime minister and the Minister of Defence, and then awaited instructions about how to proceed in Washington. Throughout the period leading up to the Nassau Conference, he was receiving communications from London. For example, on 11 December he received a telegram from Macmillan's Private Secretary, Philip de Zulueta, telling him that Macmillan was considering asking Kennedy for a loan of three Polaris submarines while other arrangements were being made, and wanting to know if the president might plead Congressional difficulties to avoid agreeing to this proposition.[30] Nor was he left without instructions. Macmillan requested his advice on whether or not he thought a private telephone call to Kennedy would benefit the situation, and asked for a number of procedural assurances from Kennedy about consultation.[31] Ormsby-Gore's job was to prepare the ground for a successful resolution of the Skybolt issue. It would appear that he fulfilled this role.

David Bruce, it has been said, received one telegram from McNamara advising him of the situation. The fact that this communication had come not from his superior, Rusk, but from another Department entirely, caused him to wonder if there was not more going on than he was privy to. Instinctively, he recoiled from pushing any further and, like Ormsby-Gore, awaited instruction. According to Neustadt, Bruce had no instructions to approach and probe the minds of the British politicians and therefore found himself without a portfolio. For all this, Bruce managed to send a number of pertinent cables about the highly charged political atmosphere, urging full and immediate consultation with the British.[32] Bruce was subsequently recalled to Washington to help prepare for the Nassau Conference. His attempts to alert his superiors to the impending crisis somehow failed to hit home. Those who received his warnings evidently believed that everything was under control.

On the American side, as in Britain, the breakdown in communication went further than Ambassador David Bruce. At the top Kennedy had little to do with the crisis until he set off for the Nassau Conference. Many of his staff, including McNamara, Rusk, Bundy and Nitze, were well aware that the affair had the potential to cause major political fireworks in Britain but all failed to drive this message home. At one meeting on 7 November, both Rusk and McNamara indicated their concern that the problem might destabilise the Conservative government in Britain.[33] According to Bundy, it was left to the British Ambassador to alert the president as to what was unfolding.[34] It is possible that until that point his advisers believed the affair to be under control, thus making it unnecessary to argue convincingly of a life-and-death situation. Perhaps Kennedy understood the dangerous ground the cancellation decision had pushed them onto but was unmoved, believing the problem to be in the expert hands of his most trusted staff. Whatever his thoughts before the crisis broke, afterwards Kennedy reflected on the affair in frustration demanding to know from one of his aides why 'Bruce . . . Ormsby-Gore, or Macmillan himself, or Rusk, or Someone, had not warned both sides in advance of the storm?'[35]

McNamara, on the other hand, was intimately involved. For all his good intentions (Zuckerman had met him on 9 December in Washington and was convinced he was trying to be helpful),[36] McNamara confused matters and failed to communicate his plans effectively although he too had reasons for keeping quiet. In light of Skybolt's strong support in Congress and the USAF and among the Joint Chiefs of Staff (except Maxwell Taylor who was against continuation of the project), the Secretary could not openly set out his agenda without incurring the combined wrath of these powerful forces.[37] Although he was of a mind to cancel the weapon certainly from August 1962, he could not say so, even to his British counterpart visiting in September for fear that word would get out and hamper his plans.[38] In fact, although Thorneycroft later complained that McNamara should have informed him earlier, the Secretary of Defense was really in a position to do so only on 23 November when the president officially approved the cancellation plan after receiving the recommendation of the Joint Chiefs of Staff.[39] McNamara had volunteered to handle the cancellation and both the President and Rusk had agreed. In deferring to the Secretary of Defense, Rusk effectively bowed out of the picture even though the affair concerned matters traditionally under the jurisdiction of the State Department. Although it has been suggested that, as Secretary of State, Rusk either failed to recognise the full extent of the problem or, for some more obscure reason, felt unwilling to become involved (perhaps out of fear that an Anglo-American crisis would hurt himself and the President), the real reason might be more simple. Capable and confident, McNamara had presented the issue to his colleague as a simple technical and budgetary decision that just happened to involve an allied country.[40] Rusk was concerned that Britain be given ample time to consider alternatives and urged thorough consultation to decide upon a suitable alternative or compensation package should this be required. He had no sense, however, that this was something that would require his time. It is also possible that, aware of the growing sentiment within his department focusing on revising the so-called 'special relationship', he did not want to open up the debate by actively involving the State Department.

McNamara confused matters further by stressing that the cancellation decision was taken primarily for technical and cost-efficiency reasons. At a distinct disadvantage as a result of their unfamiliarity with the new 'jargon' emanating from the defence community in Washington,[41] the British had trouble accepting and believing the new procedures, facts and figures that McNamara was suggesting explained the new American opposition. According to the Secretary, the highly complex weapon was taking too long and proving too costly to develop. By the time all the problems had been sorted out (if indeed they ever were) there would simply be no justifiable need for Skybolt. This jarred with the sanguine reports reaching Britain from their own personnel working on the project and from the USAF and the Douglas Corporation. According to them, the problems the project was experiencing were predictable and surmountable with time.[42] The secrecy with which McNamara pursued his agenda also caused problems. While at the top of the Administration, it was generally accepted by Kennedy, Rusk and McNamara that Polaris would figure in the final solution to the Skybolt problem, officials lower down the ranks in the Defense and State Departments were not privy to this reasoning and drew up proposals containing alternatives based on the assumption that this would not be the case.[43]

Finally, McNamara had forgotten one crucial thing – the projected leak date that he had set for the probable breaking of the Skybolt story. He had originally told Thorneycroft of his intention to get an official decision and initiate consultation *before* 10 December. Somehow this had slipped from the Secretary's mind. McNamara had planned to have the matter settled before the whole discussion became public. His slip ensured that the story had broken before he arrived in London.

DIFFERENT AGENDAS

The McNamara Strategy: Feasibility vs Cost

McNamara's priority was the rationalisation of the Department of Defense, which he presided over with determination and skill. The inability of his predecessors to seize control of the Pentagon with all its diverse groups and departments contributed to a gross underestimation of the Secretary's will and ability. McNamara's business skills easily translated into blueprints for conducting defence business. 'Cost efficiency' and 'value for money' became the watchwords of his stewardship of the Department. While he did not penalise projects because of their complexity, McNamara did target those that were incurring greatly augmented costs and time lags by refusing them the resources required to produce a viable system.[44]

For McNamara the issue was simple. The US government had decided to develop Skybolt as one of several possible weapons at a time when the only missile system America had fully operational was the Atlas. Ambitious and complicated, the Skybolt missile would only have been useful for a tactical defence suppression mission if its development had been cheap and technically straightforward. However, since its inception in the late 1950s, the nature of strategic planning had completely changed with the development of the long-range missile, rendering obsolete systems that could not effectively penetrate enemy air defences in order to reach a target.[45] During the course of this development the Skybolt system proved to be anything but value for money and repeatedly failed to measure up when assessed against McNamara's 'cost-efficiency' yardstick.[46] It would, the Secretary later explained:

> combine the disadvantages of the bomber with those of the missile. It would have . . . the bomber's disadvantage of being 'soft', 'concentrated', relatively vulnerable on the ground, and slow to target . . . [it] would have . . . the lower payload and poorer accuracy of a missile, without the relative invulnerability and short-time to target of a MINUTEMAN or POLARIS.[47]

In short, according to Zuckert, McNamara felt that he simply 'did not need the weapon'.[48] It was not worth the money needed to see it through to completion because time was diminishing the role for which it had been designed. For McNamara, the *substance* of the technical difficulties was largely irrelevant. Whether or not these were solvable with time had little bearing on his thinking. Facing a defence budget of some $51 billion (the largest ever), and having already spent $500 million on Skybolt, the Secretary of Defense badly needed to make savings – and Skybolt was costly, unpredictable and consistently late.[49] Instead of pumping more money into the project, McNamara estimated that 2–3 billion dollars could be saved if he cancelled the project. Eventually, it was cost rather than feasibility that decided Skybolt's fate.[50]

From McNamara's point of view, the decision to cancel was a straightforward military hardware one, which, handled correctly, would have been resolved without much more than a few anxiety attacks in London. However, when he accepted the instructions issued by the State Department and agreed to handle negotiations with the British their way – not offering Polaris – the decision then turned from technical and military to political.[51] He recognised that this weapon was probably the only possible alternative to Skybolt that the British would accept, but was not prepared at this stage to do battle with the Europeanists in the State Department over the timing or substance of any Polaris offer. Instead, he decided to give them a shot at what they wanted. When this failed, he would offer Polaris and the matter would be resolved without having spilt any blood within the administration. Ormsby-Gore picked up on this subtlety even before McNamara went to London. He wrote in a telegram:

my impression is that he [McNamara] has found it impossible to recommend the continuation of this programme to the President on economic or military grounds. *While he fully understands the political implications for us, it is not of course his job to argue within the Administration.* (emphasis added)[52]

McNamara later explained his reasoning:

I never thought State's three alternatives contained a viable solution. I thought I ought to give them a run for their money in case I was wrong. But I never did think the British were likely to buy any of them and I never thought for a moment that if the British didn't buy them, we could leave it at that. I thought we'd probably end up by giving them Polaris. I'd said that on November 7 and Mac had agreed. The President and Dean hadn't disagreed . . . But my own people were dubious and Rusk's people were dead against it. I thought he wanted me to give them a crack at what *they* wanted. I decided I might just as well do that . . .[53]

In many ways, the British reaction remained the least of his worries (the Secretary was more concerned about Congress and the USAF learning of his plans) until he met Thorneycroft in London when he began to realise the extent of the problems to which he had inadvertently contributed. If the British had done their job, alternative arrangements could have been made and the matter finalised without much difficulty. As George Ball later commented, McNamara's insistence on giving a statement about Skybolt's failures when he arrived in Britain illustrated both the strength and weaknesses of his temperament. Once he had made up his mind that something should be done, 'he would damn the torpedoes and full steam ahead', in spite of any incidental breakage caused by inappropriate timing.[54]

One startling piece of new evidence may account for McNamara's apparent lack of concern about the Skybolt issue developing into an Anglo-American crisis and his bewilderment when this happened. The Secretary of Defense was under the impression until quite late in the affair (the 16 December meeting with the President) that the original Skybolt agreement had been in a *multilateral* as opposed to a *bilateral* context. In believing that the British Skybolts would be assigned to NATO and not the mainstay of a prestigious national deterrent, the Secretary was critically mistaken.[55] This, according to one of his aides, 'significantly complicated' negotiations.[56] In short, McNamara had been making crucial decisions about the weapons system and planning a strategy to deal with the cancellation based upon false information. This goes far in explaining several things. First, it offers a possible explanation for Thorneycroft's insistence that he had mentioned Polaris to McNamara during their telephone conversation on 9 November. McNamara later denied that an independent Polaris had been discussed, but, given his assumption that any replacement for Skybolt would be on similar terms as the original agreement, it is just conceivable that the men discussed Polaris – McNamara thinking he was talking about a multilateral force while Thorneycroft was under the impression that the conversation was about a no-strings-attached replacement for Skybolt. The British records show that Thorneycroft stressed the need for any alternative British deterrent – whether it was Polaris or some other – to have the same degree of independence as Skybolt would have.[57] Given that the two men were approaching the problem from such different directions, it is hardly surprising that confusion abounded.

There is another piece of crucial information that seems to have been overlooked by both sides, which also concerns the original 1960 agreement. Until now historians had thought that the Americans had suggested the 'termination clause' in the original deal.[58] Previous accounts have claimed that Gates had insisted on the inclusion of the clause motivated by the serious doubts he had about the project. The discovery, however, that the insistence was British and not American puts a whole new spin on the Skybolt affair. If this is indeed true, and Richard Neustadt certainly believes it is, the British government had little justification for getting upset about the American decision.[59] At most, British politicians could complain about the lack of extensive consultation and perhaps the speed of the decision, but if the cancellation clause had been added at the behest of British officials, they could hardly accuse the Americans of dealing in bad faith. However, if the British made a mistake with this oversight, McNamara must surely take the blame for a much bigger one. Logic would concur that if McNamara had not known about the details of the original Skybolt agreement he probably had not seen the document and did not know that the technical unfeasibility clause came from Britain and not the US. Otherwise, he would have known that he had a perfect way out. The Secretary of Defense could simply have pointed out the technical difficulties and reminded the British that they had insisted on the clause and left it at that. Unfortunately, McNamara's ignorance about the true nature of the original document disabled him and hampered his ability to deal successfully with the issue.

Intra-Governmental Clashes of Interest

Opinions varied considerably within the administration, not so much about the wisdom of abandoning the Skybolt programme, but about what was to happen to the British independent nuclear deterrent and the 'special' Anglo-American relationship as a result. The British deterrent and the 'special relationship' were highly emotive issues which left a considerable proportion of Kennedy's staff in opposition. For the most part, the Pentagon, and particularly Paul Nitze's International Security Affairs Office, preferred to see the status quo maintained. Nitze was in favour of updating the 'special relationship' to prevent a British slide towards neutralism. He was not in favour of multilateralism and saw no reason why other relationships, for example, with France, could not be upgraded to equal status with Britain. In the State Department, the British desk was understandably primarily concerned with the fortunes of Britain. Feelings were particularly strong in the office of Robert Schaetzel (William Tyler's deputy for Regional Affairs). Schaetzel's priority was British entry into the Common Market. Fearing that the withdrawal of Skybolt might fatally undermine the pro-European Tory government currently in power, while on the other hand, too generous a replacement for the weapon risked inhibiting the government's chances of successfully gaining entry into Europe, Schaetzel and his aides wanted Skybolt maintained as long as these negotiations lasted.[60] Although Tyler let this ride, he gave no support to his deputy's views. The one positive aspect of the cancellation for these men was the demise of what they considered to be the divisive independent nuclear deterrent. For them, British entry into the EEC was the necessary prerequisite for a strong, united Europe, linked in transatlantic partnership to the US. The British deterrent would have to go sooner or later. Perhaps this could now be used to their advantage. Suddenly there was a chance to ensure that beyond the British V-bombers, the British force would cease to exist. Outside Schaetzel's office this logic had appeal. In the Policy Planning Office, Henry Owen (one of the originators of the Multilateral Force idea) also believed the British force to be a hindrance to the realisation of the multilateral nuclear solution.

Opposed to the idea of removing the British deterrent at this junction was Jeffrey Kitchen's Office of Politico-Military Affairs, a general-purpose staff link to Defense which had a tie to Rusk through Alexis Johnson, the Deputy Under Secretary. Kitchen and his deputy, Seymour Weiss, did not oppose the policies espoused by Schaetzel's office but felt that the timing was wrong and that more consideration should be given to the advantages of the Anglo-American relationship.[61] Essentially, like Nitze's office, they too favoured preservation of the status quo. All these groups, however, soon found that they had very little say in what was going on. It was revealed that McNamara and not the Secretary of State would negotiate with the British. The only area where they could hope to have some influence was in the study of alternatives requested by McNamara.[62] When Rowen met Owen, Schaetzel, Weiss and Bowie (a private governmental consultant) to discuss the alternatives to Skybolt the very mention of Polaris as the fourth possibility was enough to cause great consternation. According to Neustadt, the group 'exploded'.[63] When the unfortunate Weiss suggested that this was the most probable outcome, his colleagues, unanimously, denounced him. 'You'd have thought', he recalls, 'that I'd called Christ an atheist in a room full of Bishops.'[64] The idea of replacing Skybolt with Polaris was anathema. For Owen it meant risking German nuclear ambitions, while Schaetzel feared it would prevent Britain gaining entry into the EEC. Furious at the possibility of such a development, no time was lost in preparing a memorandum embodying State's official views. After a minor revision, Rusk approved the document which set out a number of acceptable alternatives, including continuing with the Skybolt programme, switching to the Hound Dog missile and a sea-based MRBM force for NATO. It continued:

it seems essential that we make quite clear to the B[ritish] that there is no possibility of our helping them set up a nationally manned and owned MRBM force . . .[65]

To add credibility to the document and the views it embodied, they told Rusk that the Department of Defense had requested that State make its views on Polaris known directly to McNamara and that Bundy had told McNamara that the White House was opposed to any such deal.[66]

Before McNamara left for London to negotiate, elements within State, still with no official role to play, were again to influence matters. Rowen was concerned about the timetable and unsuccessfully urged the Secretary to send an advance party to prepare the way for the meeting with Thorneycroft in London. Kitchen and Weiss, believing that the 'instruction' of 24 November was unrealistic and destined to cause more trouble than conciliation, tried to find a way of limiting the damage by approaching Rusk with an idea for the continuation of Skybolt with a subsidy for Britain to enable them to continue with the weapon's development.[67] According to William Tyler, in other parts of State, this concern then came to be displaced:

> one absolute priority displaced another absolute priority. The NATO meeting was the thing we had to work on in the last week of November and the start of December . . .[68]

By the time officials met for the Defense Policy Conference on 30 November to prepare for the Paris NATO meeting, little time was spent discussing Skybolt. In Paris, after his meeting with Thorneycroft, McNamara discussed the situation with Rusk and agreed that an Anglo-American crisis was to be avoided at all costs. They concluded that a formula containing Polaris would probably be the price to pay for keeping the peace. Nitze concurred, while Rowen acknowledged the decision, but Rostow, Schaetzel and the rest of the Europeanists dissented vigorously, almost frantically.[69] By the time Tyler returned from Paris he was astonished to discover Ball, Kitchen, Weiss, Owen, Johnson, Bowie and Bruce discussing ways to revise this thinking. 'It was', he recalls:

> something like going underwater. Here they were, pursuing the issue with enormous passion, as though they could affect what had already happened . . . I had been at lunch with Rusk and all our people when McNamara flew in from London. Before the meal was over one could tell how this was ultimately to come out . . . Here they were in Washington still passionate, with Rostow and Schaetzel, who had been there, coming back to reinforce them. It was curious . . .[70]

For some time now, men such as Henry Owen had been preparing memoranda about the dangers of continuing to show preferential treatment to the British, claiming that relations with America's other allies were suffering as a result. In September 1962, unaware of the Secretary of Defense's plans to cancel Skybolt, Owen, Walt Rostow's Deputy in the Policy Planning Council, wrote an action memorandum[71] restating the April 1961 National Security Council

Policy Directive outlining a policy of non-preferential treatment for Britain:

> you will recall the April 21, 1961 NSC Policy Directive, which states that 'over the long run it would be desirable if the British decided to phase out of the nuclear deterrent business'. It also states that the US should not prolong the life of the British deterrent . . . after the UK-EEC negotiations, the special US-UK relationship may have to be closely re-examined . . . it is of the utmost importance to avoid any actions to expand the relationship . . .[72]

This accurately reflected the Kennedy administration's views on nonproliferation and bias against small, independent nuclear deterrent forces. For the British, however, it was difficult to know where unofficial feeling ended and official policy began. Moreover, Ministers had difficulty accurately gauging the extent of the commitment the top echelons of the administration had to this. The evidence was conflicting. Under President Kennedy the Anglo-American 'special relationship' had flourished. The administration had protected, even boosted the programme, calming British fears and symbolically reinforcing for them the much-favoured ties.[73] McNamara had even told Ormsby-Gore that the British should not make any hasty decisions about their deterrent. As Gore reported:

> McNamara has specifically said to me that he would not presume to advise us what our attitude to the retention of our own nuclear potential should be but that if we did decide that it was in our interest to abandon an independent nuclear role, he could see no political or military advantage in our promulgating such a decision at the present moment, not unless we received some specific benefit in return . . .[74]

This contrasted sharply with other remarks made by McNamara and senior American figures. In particular, speeches made by Dean Acheson in December 1962 and the Secretary of Defense at the NATO meeting in Athens and Ann Arbor caused many in Britain to wonder about the US administration's intention. Both speeches denounced small, independent nuclear deterrents, Acheson overtly and McNamara implicitly attacking the British force.[75] Although McNamara hastily denied his remarks were aimed at Britain, few believed him.[76] A cartoon in the *Manchester Guardian* summed up the confusion. It shows Macmillan and Iain MacLeod in a foxhole holding an umbrella labelled 'independent deterrent' with shells inscribed 'with love, Acheson' and 'with love, McNamara' falling around them. The caption read: 'What makes you so damn sure they're on our side?'[77] It was clear that an element or elements within the government wanted Britain out of the nuclear club altogether. What wasn't clear, however, was the extent to which this extended to the upper reaches of the administration.[78] If Kennedy did not support this policy, why had he chosen the author of Ann Arbor as his spokesman when the matter seemed to fall more in the jurisdiction of Secretary of State Rusk? Did this have something to do with the new ideas on strategic planning and flexible response emerging from the Pentagon? Macmillan himself professed doubts and wrote in his diary:

> In view of the implications of McNamara's speech in Michigan and again at a NATO meeting in Paris in December, it was difficult to suppress the suspicion that the failure of Skybolt might be welcomed in some American quarters as a means of forcing Britain out of the nuclear club.[79]

The opposition in the State Department to the British independent nuclear deterrent had never been too carefully concealed. As Rusk later conceded:

> British paranoia may also have been fostered by some in our own bureaucracy who wanted to use the cancellation to pressure the British to give up an independent force.[80]

The continuing internal debate among the various departments within the administration prevented a rational, coherent and effective policy from emerging until it was really too late.[81] Poor communication, vested interests and hidden or ill-concealed agendas created a fluid situation, with Kennedy's staff divided over how to deal with the issue and the wider problems associated with it.

The British Agenda

Britain's position vis-à-vis Skybolt could hardly have been more different. Although Macmillan and both Watkinson and Thorneycroft were well aware of the dangers involved in relying too heavily on the American missile, they nevertheless failed to take sufficient action to prevent a catastrophe should the Americans decide to cancel the weapon.[82] While in private they discussed the problems associated with Skybolt, in public they defended both the agreement and the Anglo-American interdependence that guaranteed, they claimed, the missile's successful delivery. Despite remarks to the contrary, the fact remained that, in theory and in practice, Britain's whole independent deterrent was tied up with Skybolt. This worrying dependence on the experimental American weapon should have been highlighted by the repeated efforts of officials in the administration to point out to the British the difficulties facing the project. Why did Macmillan and his ministers fail to take action?

For Macmillan, reports of design problems and technical difficulties were something to be expected in such a complicated undertaking, not feared as a new and disturbing development. From its earliest days, officials across the Atlantic had been predicting the project's imminent demise yet, under Kennedy, it had seen its funding increased. Macmillan mistakenly believed that the Americans appreciated the need for Skybolt as a means of sustaining the independent deterrent – a symbol and guarantor of Britain's *role* as a world power. In order for Skybolt to be an effective deterrent for Britain, it only had to 'appear to work'. In English ears, according to Pierre, 'a guidance system did not sound like a great trouble'. In fact 'British purposes required only that the Russians *think* the weapon could be guided to a city' in order to fulfill the Moscow Criterion.[83] Britain's concern lay not so much in deterring the Soviet Union while it had the protection of the United States, as it was in retaining some measure of influence over American strategic decision-making and over the targeting of the vast arsenal commanded by that superpower.[84] Macmillan remarked in an interview in *The Times*:

> The independent contribution . . . gives us a better position in the world . . . it gives us a better position with respect to the US . . . The fact that we have it makes the US pay a greater regard to our point of view and that is of great importance.[85]

In previous accounts, Peter Thorneycroft's role throughout the affair has been somewhat ambiguous and in need of clarification.

Appointed Minister of Defence in July 1962, he inherited Skybolt from his predecessor rather late in the day, although he had some knowledge of the weapon and the 1960 agreement from his time as Minister of Aviation. Described as highly skilled and politically ambitious, Thorneycroft was anxious to avoid any political embarrassment that would damage his prospects at a time when the question of who would succeed Macmillan was very much common currency.

Unlike his counterpart in the United States, Thorneycroft's control of the Ministry of Defence and the Services was far from assured. In Britain, as in America, the armed forces had traditionally enjoyed relative autonomy, battling with each other for budget funds and power. Thorneycroft was unable to submit them to his will and suffered from powerful RAF and Navy lobbies which pressured him to support a course of action favourable to their interests. The RAF, in particular, had strong links with industry and the military-industrial complex and enjoyed the powerful backing of these groups.[86]

Thorneycroft made two initial mistakes. Following the lead of Watkinson and Macmillan, he defended the Skybolt deal and praised the importance, value and necessity of the Anglo-American 'special relationship'. According to Zuckerman, Thorneycroft failed to accept the latter's warnings of trouble and probable abandonment of the weapon by the United States.[87] Second, he was unmoved during his Washington trip in September by McNamara's strong hints and made no effort to prepare for the possibility of cancellation. Thorneycroft appears only to have been activated by McNamara's telephone call, but by then it was too late.[88] Too much was at stake and time was too short. Suddenly the Minister was faced with two options, neither of which appealed to him. He could either continue to support Skybolt and shoulder the accusation of incompetence both for allowing the British deterrent to become dependent on the United States and for failing to have contingency plans in place. Or he could denounce the American decision, declare that he had been told nothing to indicate that Skybolt was in serious trouble and, in private, work to secure a better deal for Britain.[89] Thorneycroft was under no illusions about the weakness of his position and that of the Tory Party in general over Skybolt. Logic should have compelled him to make sure he had assurances from the US administration about a replacement weapon for Skybolt. For reasons best known to himself, he decided to follow his own plan.[90]

The difficulty for Thorneycroft lay in the fact that he could not be seen to champion Polaris openly until Skybolt – now a 'dead duck' in his eyes – had been well and truly buried by the Americans. Polaris seemed like a much better bet both as a possible trump card vis-à-vis Europe and because it was undeniably a more useful weapons system.[91] However, he had to be very careful and wait for the appropriate time.[92] To act precipitously would, according to Neustadt:

be tantamount to treason, selling Skybolt down the river . . . He could not advocate a change in everyone else's treasured *status quo* until he could show cause and chart another course.[93]

Thorneycroft kept his counsel and said little about the matter other than to Macmillan, a small number of colleagues and his private secretary, Arthur Hockaday, for fear that discussions with the Americans would leak out in Britain. According to Hockaday:

> In terms of personal and bureaucratic politics, silence with his colleagues was the safest course for *him*, and lack of talk to us assured security at home: McNamara–USAF–RAF, or any variant, was a potential channel of communication . . . weakness in his personal position . . . counselled silence everywhere.[94]

Macmillan was in a similarly precarious position. Having brokered the original Skybolt deal, its cancellation would reveal not only the fallacy of the independent British nuclear deterrent, but in doing so, could also fatally undermine Macmillan's position. Retention of the national force, as his biographer stated:

> represented a major plank of his political platform . . . the unrequited removal of Skybolt would be as if Britain were unilaterally disarmed.[95]

Aware of the difficulties facing the project, Macmillan nevertheless disregarded the warnings in the hope that the USAF would protect the missile.[96] Unfortunately for him, according to Gilpatric, the Douglas Corporation had been unjustifiably sanguine in its reports to the USAF and, in all probability, to the British military as well.[97] The project was in bad shape as McNamara had discovered, but the problems had been well concealed. The Prime Minister was not unduly concerned about cancellation, believing Kennedy would let him know if there was any serious danger that the project would be cancelled and that the President was conscious of the fact that he had inherited a 'moral obligation' to provide Britain with an alternative arrangement.[98] Macmillan had gambled the British independent deterrent on an experimental missile.[99] The warnings he had received, far from galvanising him into action, had served rather to immobilise him.[100]

> McNamara's warning raised a horrid prospect: Pandora's box might open . . . the issue for Macmillan in November was how to sit on the lid.[101]

Macmillan, like his Minister of Defence, had his reasons for keeping silent. First, along with the 1960 agreement had come an arrangement whereby America was granted docking facilities in Holy Loch. Although the two agreements were not formally linked, it was considered, by Macmillan especially, that they had been quid pro quo. But this was something that could not be said in public. It was better to use a private conversation with Kennedy when the two met to remind the president of this deal. Second, Macmillan was adamantly opposed to having to choose between his three major policy aims. Unfortunately for him, the alignment of these three key policies – independent nuclear capability, close Anglo-American relations and entry into the Common Market – were to coincide with Skybolt's demise. Third, Macmillan feared that any discussion of the Skybolt arrangements and the possible acceptable alternative might lead to backbench dissent and possibly the Cabinet to withdraw support for the whole notion of an independent deterrent, citing cost as unacceptable. According to the Cabinet Secretary, Tim Bligh:

> For several months . . . there had been growing an uncrystallized, uncanvassed, latent Cabinet sentiment against prolonging the effort to sustain the independent deterrent . . . if a change had been put to the Cabinet in November, especially if it involved more money, all those latent feelings might have crystallised *against* going on . . . the hell with it . . . the PM was not unaware of that . . .[102]

A fourth reason why Macmillan made no effort to initiate discussion of the issue was that even an informal inner group would have to include the Chief of the Defence Staff, Lord Mountbatten, whose loyalties Macmillan doubted. Mountbatten might alert the Services and word might spread before Macmillan was ready. Finally, Macmillan had a factor of another type to take into consideration. Britain was just days from completing the tests necessary to produce a nuclear warhead suitable for the missile delivery system. Any action he might take ran the risk of upsetting this work and the aim at which it was intended.[103]

Initially, according to Bligh, Macmillan felt that it would probably be better to 'try and play Skybolt along for another year to eighteen months in order to avoid political difficulties at home', although he did concede that it was necessary 'to get on to a Polaris deterrent at some stage'.[104] However, a startling new piece of evidence has revealed how the British government's position came together just days before the crucial Nassau meeting. Although Skybolt was still officially an option when the British delegation headed for Nassau (out of loyalty and a sense of obligation to the RAF), a secret meeting with McNamara on 15 December had placed Polaris firmly on the agenda as a substitute weapon for Skybolt.[105]

External Factors and Domestic Problems

No event in foreign affairs can fail to touch or be touched by other events unfolding around it. In the case of the Skybolt affair it was the Cuban Missile Crisis followed by the Sino-Indian dispute. The Cuban crisis not only delayed McNamara's plans, but it distorted perceptions and numbed usually sensitive antennae to a potential crisis they would otherwise have been on top of. When the administration returned to the Skybolt issue after the euphoric but exhausting Cuban episode, the problem was not given the same consideration it might have received had many key members of the president's staff not been so distracted. As one official remarked:

if there had not been a traumatic experience like the Cuban crisis, Skybolt would have seemed like a big problem. But it didn't. Golf was the order of the day, not (more) missiles . . .[106]

After the success of Cuba, officials in the American administration were understandably buoyed up. This pervaded all aspects of policy and decision. Quite suddenly, the government began to exude this confidence. This was picked up by the media like the *Christian Science Monitor* which quickly identified the subtle change in approach pointing out what they described as the new 'candour' of the administration.[107]

Likewise, for Macmillan's government, other concerns seemed more pressing than the admittedly disconcerting rumours reaching Whitehall about the probability of cancellation. Macmillan's leadership had never looked so precarious. His popularity had declined badly over the previous year and the domestic policies he had championed like the 'pay-pause' and entry into the Common Market had not been well received. Alarming by-election defeats had prompted him to lose his characteristic *sang-froid*; axing a third of his Cabinet in a desperate attempt to retain the credibility of his government. In addition, the prime minister had difficulties in Katanga and Rhodesia and the Vassal scandal to contend with, not to mention months of Cabinet agonising over agricultural concessions to the EEC. Macmillan's reputation was further damaged by the furore in the British press over what they called the impotence of British power. This was demonstrated, it was claimed, by Kennedy's failure to consult during the Cuban missile crisis.[108]

Macmillan's many difficulties had resulted in a hardening of his position. Backed into a corner by domestic problems and a cutthroat press, the Skybolt crisis threatened to unbalance him to a degree he might well have survived in an earlier time. With less at stake politically, Macmillan's handling of the affair would arguably have been more low-key, focusing on technical rather than political issues. Although he knew that the offer of Polaris was now more than likely, what he could not predict was the strength of the element within the US government that was anxious to prevent this from happening at all costs and indeed the conditions (if any) that might be attached to an agreement. Many uncertainties remained and, as Macmillan prepared to go to the conference, he noted in his diary, 'I shall have a difficult time with the Americans in Nassau.'[109]

5 Finding a Solution – The Nassau Compromise

When Harold Macmillan stepped into the balmy air of the picturesque Caribbean island, he hardly noticed his surroundings. Neither was his mood lifted by the winter sun. It was obvious that he was under great strain, events of the past twelve months having taken a visible toll on the ageing prime minister.[1] Feeling that his time in office was drawing to a close, Macmillan bitterly contemplated the end of his political career. Everything he had worked for, all his key policies, appeared dangerously close to disintegration. Now he had to face the Americans over the abandonment of the Skybolt missile. Everything hung in the balance. Nassau would be the deciding factor.[2]

Macmillan had every reason to be concerned. Only days before he had had a difficult meeting with President de Gaulle at Rambouillet. De Gaulle had been in fighting form, making little effort to disguise his plans for Britain. Macmillan, tempted to return home early, only stayed on in an effort to explain to the French leader his own intention to find a means of preserving the British independent nuclear deterrent at the forthcoming Nassau Conference.[3] When Macmillan did take his leave he was in little doubt that de Gaulle intended to keep Britain out of the European Economic Community.[4] The encounter had depressed him, sweeping away any vestiges of hope that had lingered before Rambouillet. But with Nassau just days away Macmillan turned his mind to a fight where he could still perhaps influence the outcome. Arriving in the Bahamas before Kennedy, Macmillan's mood was not improved by the news that Kennedy had given a television interview two days earlier in which he had very abruptly denounced Skybolt, saying:

> we are talking about two and a half billion dollars to build a weapon to hang on our B-52's, when we already have billions invested in Polaris, and Minuteman . . . There is just a limit to how much we need, as well as how much we can afford to have a successful deterrent . . . we don't think that we are going to get $2.5 billion worth of national security.[5]

Much to Macmillan's chagrin, Kennedy's staff had not even bothered to inform the British delegation officially of these remarks.[6] For Kennedy the comments were a fair assessment of the project as explained to him by the Secretary of Defense (the president had not yet been alerted to the grave political implications of the crisis), but for the British, it was a thoughtless and damaging gaffe adding to the strain of an already volatile situation. Kennedy appeared to be heaping insult on injury when he really should have been sensitive to the problems his cancellation decision was causing in Britain. Macmillan and his colleagues wondered if there was not some other hidden agenda in place in the US administration.

In contrast, as Kennedy made his way to the conference, he belatedly became aware of the problems he was about to encounter in Nassau. Having invited David Ormsby-Gore to accompany him on Air Force One, the President soon learned that the Skybolt issue was threatening to split Anglo-American relations wide open. Time was short. Although Kennedy had been kept fully briefed on the developments in the Skybolt cancellation, he seems not to have grasped the full significance of the problem until his talk with Ormsby-Gore en route to Nassau. The British Ambassador informed him that America was being accused of betrayal and worse, Macmillan's Conservative government might fall on the matter. The decision to abandon the weapon was seen as dishonourable treatment of America's closest and oldest ally. This perception was causing serious problems not only for Macmillan, but also for Kennedy himself, who was facing a growing body of negative opinion in the United States about the crisis. Kennedy needed to produce tangible evidence that his decision was purely a technical one and that no thinly veiled attempt to manoeuvre Britain out of the independence business was in play. The solution they arrived at was simple and, according to Neustadt, 'nearly perfect'.[7] In order to repudiate the accusations of bad faith being levelled at Kennedy and his government, the men constructed a formula that allowed America to give up the project as planned, while Britain continued on alone. The 'cancellation fee' to be paid by the United States was 50 per cent of the remaining development costs. Britain would pay for the remaining costs estimated to be around 100 million dollars, as well as 1.5 million dollars for every missile it then decided to buy.[8] Although considered by Nunnerley and others to have been a serious attempt to salvage Skybolt – Arthur Schlesinger described it as a 'wise and generous offer'[9] – later comments by Ormsby-Gore have indicated the opposite. Some years after the crisis he wrote:

> neither of us entertained any lively hope that this formula would
> be acceptable to the Prime Minister and his colleagues . . . the
> fifty-fifty scheme was therefore conceived more as a holding op-
> eration designed to spike the guns of those in the British party
> who were suspicious of American motives, rather than as a for-
> mula which would prove acceptable so late in the day . . .[10]

The proposal may have stood some chance of reaching the negotiating table had it been produced at an earlier date. This is borne
out by Schlesinger, who wrote:

> the British faced with spiralling development costs, might have
> decided to give up Skybolt anyway, but it was too late; Kennedy's
> television comments had destroyed any lingering interest Macmillan
> might have had in Skybolt . . .[11]

The 50–50 offer, as it became known, may not have been intended
as a serious solution to the Skybolt problem for Ormsby-Gore was
well aware that Macmillan had turned towards Polaris as the preferred alternative, but perhaps there were good reasons for proposing
the idea when the negotiations began. After the airport ceremon-
ies had been dispensed with, Ormsby-Gore joined Macmillan for a
briefing on the delegation's position. A short conversation confirmed
that Macmillan had now lost all interest in Skybolt, adopting instead
Thorneycroft's posture of Polaris or nothing. That evening Macmillan
took Kennedy for a walk and the two leaders discussed the range
of problems confronting them. Meanwhile, Ormsby-Gore with the
aid of various other members of the British delegation was engaged
in 'sitting on' Thorneycroft, who had grown increasingly intransigent and combative since arriving at the conference.[12] The Minister
of Defence, it seemed, was more concerned with appearing to stand
up to the Americans, preferring a breach to a settlement. One associate later remarked:

> Thorneycroft wanted to leave in a huff, rally the country, go it
> alone, and 'let [the United States] take the fall out'.[13]

Ormsby-Gore, Home and Sandys had some difficulty with their
colleague. Thorneycroft's tactics simply would not work, they told
him. The Americans had every right to do what they were doing.
Moreover, as Ormsby-Gore pointed out:

if we try to claim that the Americans have let us down, they will publicize their 50–50 offer, which they'd have every right to do . . . Once publicized, we wouldn't be able to sustain the claim at home that they are against our deterrent. The offer will show that's false. It's a fair offer . . .'[14]

The offer, therefore, served an important purpose. It represented American goodwill towards Britain and proof that the cancellation of Skybolt was not a calculated move to force the relinquishment of the national deterrent. Moreover, it provided the evidence that cost was very much a dominant factor in the whole business. While the 50–50 proposal offered Britain the chance to preserve the status quo, it highlighted the country's dependence on the United States, for a decision to pull out of the missile's development, even if Britain were allowed to continue, was clearly impossible given the huge costs involved.[15]

Tensions were running high when the two delegations met the next morning. 'The atmosphere was tense', one principal recalled, 'because for the first time we were competing.'[16] According to Brandon, Macmillan quickly took centre stage, opening the conference like a 'Marcus Antonius giving the funeral oration' before launching into a nostalgic recollection of the history of Anglo-American relations.[17] Pointing out to the Americans that 'his memory of government perhaps went back further than that of anyone else in the room', the prime minister, in an emotional and eloquent oratory, detailed the triumphs and heartaches shared by the two nations and commended the special friendship that had helped them endure and overcome many setbacks and injustices. He then went on to recall the recent agreement he had made with his old friend President Eisenhower allowing Polaris submarines docking and service facilities in Holy Loch, reminding the company that this agreement (which incidentally had caused both he and his government substantial political difficulties), though not legally binding, had always been understood as a quid pro quo arrangement, with Skybolt as the British prize. In essence, President Kennedy had a moral obligation, inherited from his predecessor, to see Britain fairly treated.

Having established themes of friendship and betrayal, shared glories and hardships and an indivisible common purpose, Macmillan then turned to the question of Polaris and the European reaction to this development. He told the delegations that there was no reason why any outcome involving the sea-launched ballistic missile should affect Britain's chances of successfully negotiating entry to the Common Market; after all, these were two entirely separate matters. The real stumbling block in Europe, he added, was the issue of agriculture. Nuclear delivery systems had no bearing on the issue. Besides, Macmillan offered, President de Gaulle had had little to say when informed of the prime minister's intention to pursue Polaris as a substitute for Skybolt when the two men had met in Rambouillet a few days previously. As for the other allies, it was foolish, he suggested, to conceive of any adverse reaction coming from them as it was widely accepted (although admittedly not liked) that Britain and the United States had a special defence relationship dating back to the wartime Manhattan Project.

Macmillan then turned to the talk of a multilateral nuclear force about which he expressed doubts. He could see no contradiction, however, he told them, between the concepts of independence and interdependence which were really only 'two sides of a coin'. He saw some possibility that British forces might be put into an independent arrangement, but until there was a supranational political authority that would exercise juridical control there would have to be interdependence with an ultimate national authority. In conclusion, Macmillan stated his belief that the weapons were not fundamentally different, but merely varying ways of delivering ballistic rockets and a switch from the 'lame horse', Skybolt, to what was now the favourite, Polaris, should not cause any significant upheaval within the NATO alliance.

When Kennedy's turn came he presented the 50–50 offer saying that any arrangement involving Polaris would in his opinion seriously compromise America's relationship with her other allies, namely France and Germany. Not only were the two weapons systems very different, but they 'appeared' to be so and this appearance was crucial. Supported by George Ball, Kennedy declared that the United States had a very real worry about what path Germany might take after the departure of Adenauer and that relations with France had soured considerably due to the fact that the United States had consistently refused to help that country with its nuclear programme. In these circumstances, President Kennedy thought it would be better for Britain to accept the Skybolt offer.

Macmillan, however, was not to be placated. He rejected the 50–50 deal explaining that 'while the proposed marriage with Skybolt was not exactly a shot-gun wedding, the virginity of the lady must now be regarded as doubtful'. Skybolt had been dragged through the mud and no Prime Minister would be able to 'sell' the weapon at home.

Kennedy pressed harder, saying that 'if the United States gave Polaris to Britain it would be difficult in logic not to say that if in future any country developed a nuclear bomb the United States would give them a missile system', adding that 'to give Polaris to Britain would be a new step and so regarded in Europe'. He suggested that if Britain still saw Polaris as the only possible alternative, this would have to be discussed but could not be decided straight away.[18] To this end, Kennedy proposed the setting up of a joint study of alternatives for the British in lieu of Skybolt.[19] One major concern of the United States, George Ball suggested, was the worry that Germany might be seduced to follow the nuclear path by the actions of General de Gaulle and even the very existence of the British independent deterrent. Some mechanism, he proposed, must be found to head off any such development. To this end, the US government was suggesting a multilateral solution.

Macmillan and Home between them dismissed the German question with gusto. The Foreign Secretary pointed out that few people in Europe would be happy with the idea of any form of German participation in a nuclear force. He noted that President de Gaulle had rejected the idea of Germany becoming in any way a nuclear power because of the difficulties that it would cause with Russia and with the countries in Eastern Europe. Soviet distrust of Germany would be so intensified as to lead to a serious deterioration in East–West relations and the prevention of any détente. Thorneycroft, who suggested that it might not be entirely wise to press this concept too heavily at the outset lest it cause major upheavals, backed him up. In reply Ball stated that this 'did not help the German problem and would not be sufficient'.

Macmillan again stressed his belief that there was not a great difference in the two weapons systems, saying that 'Polaris for Skybolt was not a new step in principle, since the weapons were basically the same, that is ballistic missiles. One was fired from an aeroplane, the other from ship'. He did not think that the French would make an issue out of Skybolt being swapped for another missile. Kennedy, however, was unconvinced. His government, he said, was most concerned with how de Gaulle would react to any arrangement involving Polaris. The original Skybolt deal had been made in 1960 when France was not yet a nuclear power. Since then, they had acquired this capability and deeply resented the amending of the prohibitive McMahon Act which facilitated Anglo-American nuclear co-operation but no aid to France. Theoretically, France could now be given assistance. In these new circumstances, the offer of Polaris to Britain would be seen as further proof of America's willingness to discriminate against her NATO ally. The conversation then turned to Skybolt, with Macmillan asking McNamara about the weapon. The Secretary of Defense replied that the United States would have completed development of the missile had it not been for the existence of a number of other weapons systems, including Polaris and Minuteman, although estimates were putting the reliability of Skybolt at 20–30 per cent. Regardless of this, Macmillan had no desire to continue with the project. He admitted that he 'had been wrong' to opt for Skybolt instead of Polaris in 1960. Thorneycroft reiterated the point that no matter how the US government tried to present the decision to cancel, the British press would not be dissuaded that the United States had a clear responsibility to provide an alternative and, incidentally, Hound Dog would not suffice.[20]

Conversation then arrived at the heart of the issue, with Macmillan addressing the issue of Polaris. As Neustadt remarked: 'the President now got the treatment McNamara had received from Thorneycroft . . . in still more vivid form with the Prime Minister's full weight behind it'.[21] He was like 'an Edwardian Shakespearean actor overplaying the drama of poor old Harold at the end of the road', according to Walt Rostow.[22] Macmillan conceded that he was quite prepared to agree that some form of multilateral arrangement should be studied and that as much as possible should be done to help NATO allies with information about joint planning, targeting, and so on. But he did not think the United Kingdom should be expected to contribute Britain's entire force to a supranational authority. According to Brandon, 'with something of a Churchillian palette he painted the future of Anglo-American relations in gloomy colours', adding that Britain would certainly not renege on any of the agreements made in the past with the United States. However, this would put Britain in a position where she was running a great many risks without benefiting at all, perhaps causing a deep rift in Anglo-American relations. Macmillan had presented the Americans with two crucial statements: he was prepared to consider the multilateral idea (with conditions, of course), but if a suitable solution could not be found, the United States would have to bear the consequences of a damaging split in Anglo-

American relations. The inference was that, if unresolved, the crisis would inspire a substantial public surge of anti-Americanism for which he could not be held responsible. Now everything was on the table. The two delegations then adjourned for lunch. In the afternoon, they exchanged drafts outlining the earlier discussions and possible agreements.

Kennedy was impressed by Macmillan's arguments and suggested another possible alternative: Britain could either accept the offer of Hound Dog or a force consisting of Polaris missiles which would have to be assigned to NATO. He understood that, for purposes of policy, Macmillan had to be able to say that Britain had an element of control over the force and therefore suggested that a clause could be inserted allowing for its withdrawal 'in a case of real emergency, of mortal peril'. In which case, the deterrent would revert to UK control. As Neustadt remarked, the president was facing:

> an impassioned older man embodying a valued weaker ally, who invoked in his own person a magnificent war record, an historic friendship, and a claim upon our honour – in Eisenhower's name – to say nothing of one politician's feeling for another. McNamara and Thorneycroft had spoken different languages; these two spoke the same.[23]

Macmillan sensed Kennedy's willingness to help and questioned the president closely on what he meant by 'assigning' forces to NATO. The crux of the problem lay in the whole nature of independence. Kennedy wryly admitted that for their different reasons, Britain wanted the word 'assigned' interpreted as 'loosely as possible', while the United States wanted quite the opposite. The reason for this, he explained, was so that his government could not be accused of aiding in the development of or protecting small national deterrent forces. Macmillan, however, wanted Polaris on the same terms as the Skybolt agreement – a no-strings-attached deal, and pressed harder. He told his audience:

> we were really between two worlds, the world of independence which was now ceasing to exist and the world of interdependence which we had not yet quite reached, though we were moving towards it. The nearer we got to it the more surrender of sovereignty there would have to be in practice, but until our design for interdependence was completed, we must be able in the last resort to control our own forces.

Macmillan admitted that there might perhaps be 'little purpose in doing so except an emotional one', but the United States must be clear that Britain also wanted an independent deterrent as an instrument of policy. The following day it had become clear that Kennedy was not prepared to risk a serious rift in Anglo-American relations over a missile system. He had known some time before that this was where the negotiations would probably end and had discussed as much with his advisers before coming to Nassau.[24] He could no longer put off the inevitable. All that remained was for the two leaders to thrash out an acceptable agreement that saw neither of them fatally compromised. What followed was a series of meetings focusing on the language of the agreement and the nature of the concessions both sides were agreeing to.

Macmillan opened for the British admitting that 'perhaps he had been wrong' in proposing that Polaris would be no more than a substitute for Skybolt because Polaris had 'implications both in character and in time which meant that it marked the beginning of a new phase'. He conceded that part of the reason for wanting nuclear weapons was 'to keep up with the Joneses'. 'This was a universal and perfectly respectable feeling in the world', he told the delegations, but it must be understood that they also 'satisfied the instinct of great nations that they should not become clients – not to use the word satellites'. In short, the possession of these weapons would avoid a 'weakening of British foreign policy and would enhance the value of the advice that the United Kingdom could give'. To make it easier for the president, he thought an offer of some or all of the British V-bombers into a NATO pool with US forces and possibly French would satisfy any difficulty he might have at a later date when asked about the role of a British Polaris force. He could then say that these weapons had a similar role to that of the V-bombers.

After lunch Macmillan played his last hand. The drafts prepared by the Americans were not acceptable. They failed to make clear the independence of the British Polaris force. He had to be able to tell the British public that, in the last resort, the force 'was as much part of Her Majesty's Government's forces as were the Brigade of Guards' and emphasised that 'if the Queen's Ministers gave orders Her troops would obey'. If agreement could not be reached on this matter, Macmillan told Kennedy, the British government would have to make a reappraisal of its defence policies throughout the world.

After numerous drafts had been prepared and rejected, a formula was eventually agreed upon. To satisfy both British demands for independence and American demands for a multilateral force component, Kennedy and Macmillan agreed that the United States would sell Britain Polaris missiles (minus warheads which Britain would manufacture), which would be assigned to a NATO multilateral force. To preserve the independence of the British national deterrent, Macmillan secured an escape clause. With the agreement reached in principle, numerous aides and bureaucrats set about producing an official communiqué. A 'Statement on Nuclear Defense Systems' was jointly drafted as part of the general communiqué.[25] While the communiqué was being put into final form, Macmillan requested that he be allowed time to consult his Cabinet as he could only act with their approval. Strictly speaking, Macmillan had no real need to delay proceedings in order to get clearance from London; with the weight of Home, Sandys and Thorneycroft behind him, he could have 'told' London rather than 'consulted' his colleagues back home.[26] Macmillan, however, had a very good reason for insisting on this procedure. What he wanted was insurance against any accusation of being arbitrary. Having been consulted, the Cabinet would assume collective responsibility for defending the agreement in Britain. Somewhat reluctantly, Kennedy agreed to wait a day for London's response.

With agreement reached, the president's mind turned once again to France. Almost as an afterthought, it was agreed that the same offer be made to France in order to entice General de Gaulle to commit himself to some degree to the NATO framework which he had been shunning. After hasty discussion it was decided to send this by way of a personal letter, to be followed up by discussions with Ambassador Bohlen.[27]

Macmillan returned home exhausted but jubilant. It had been three – almost four – days of hard negotiation. The talks had been so intense and speedy that he wrote, somewhat pessimistically in his dairy:

> we have had a tremendous week . . . the Americans pushed us very hard and may have 'outsmarted' us altogether. It is very hard to judge whether they speak the truth or not . . .[28]

Not only had he managed to walk away from Nassau with Polaris, having acquired it at a knockdown price of less than 2 per cent of Britain's national defence budget, but he had effectively saved almost

800 million dollars worth of research and development costs already carried out by the US government. If Britain had been forced to build independently a similar Polaris-type missile, the cost would have had to come out of the national defence budget.[29] Moreover, Macmillan had secured a weapon (and the right to use it independently if necessary) which promised Britain a national deterrent well into the 1970s and perhaps further.[30] This in itself was a remarkable achievement, not least because it had largely depended on President Kennedy's willingness to dismiss the opposition loudly articulated by a substantial element within his administration. Macmillan acknowledged the role of the president in a letter to the Queen shortly after his return:

> I must pay tribute to President Kennedy's sense of fairness and willingness to be persuaded by argument and over-rule those of his advisors who were not sympathetic to our views.[31]

When Parliament resumed, the prime minister faced the House to defend the Nassau agreement saying:

> I believe – and I hope that a greater part of the House will agree – that the arrangements reached are both sound and imaginative ... But it will be for the House and the country to judge, and I am not ashamed of the stand which we have taken on this agreement and in relation to these grave matters ...[32]

Macmillan's triumph was short-lived. The British press saw him returning home *without* Skybolt. In its place was the promise of a weapon that would not be available for at least another couple of years (the Prime Minister had insisted on the Polaris A-3 missile – the most advanced version that was not yet in production).[33] As if this wasn't bad enough, Britain was going to have to build a fleet of submarines in which to carry the missiles as well as warheads to arm them. The cost, they argued, would be massive. The final contentious point was that, upon completion, this Polaris force would be assigned to NATO. The deal, the press claimed, was a 'sell-out', the escape clause 'paper-thin'.[34] It seemed that 'almost everyone in Britain had some objection to the agreement'.[35] A telegram from the American Embassy in London captured the mood:

> nearly all comment agrees that Nassau marked [a] fateful turning point in Anglo-American relations, less by way of initiating [an] absolutely new line than by confirming one already in progress.

[The] fact that France [was] offered same terms as UK within framework of projected European deterrent concept underlined ending [of] unique Anglo-American relationship in nuclear field, and probably in others. Retention of British independence over nuclear weapons is regarded as largely fictional . . . what Macmillan secured, comment implied, is tarnished Christmas bauble without more than tinselled meaning and effect . . .[36]

As Rostow later commented, it was a 'tragic victory'.[37] In the House of Commons Hugh Gaitskell's Labour Party capitalised on the press criticism. George Brown, the Shadow Defence Minister, opened Labour's criticisms saying that the record should show that the House:

can have no confidence in a Government whose defence policy had collapsed and which, at Nassau, entered into an agreement which, by seeking to continue the illusion of an independent British nuclear deterrent, imposes further economic burdens upon the nation and makes more difficult the solution of Great Britain's defence problems . . .[38]

What was the point, they demanded, in Britain spending millions of pounds on a national deterrent that was not even independent? Macmillan had sold out his party and his country, reducing Britain to a satellite state, dependent upon the goodwill of the United States.[39] The communiqué, they pointed out, was almost intolerably vague and lent itself to a plethora of conflicting interpretations so as to effectively render it useless.

Unfortunately for Macmillan his troubles did not end here. Much to his embarrassment, just two days after the conference ended, the USAF enthusiastically announced that Skybolt had at last tested successfully.[40] Macmillan, though initially startled and appalled by the apparent lack of good judgement,[41] quickly got over his annoyance and made light of it in a letter to the president. He accepted that it had been a desperate, last-ditch effort on the part of Skybolt's supporters to save the missile. Kennedy, on the other hand, was furious and took a considerable time to calm down. He treated the British Ambassador who just happened to be present to an 'awe-inspiring exhibition, notable for the fact', the latter reported to his Prime Minister, 'that [Kennedy] again and again emphasised with the most vivid choice of words the trouble it might cause in London'.[42] As Henry Brandon said, 'it was like the final twitching of the tail of a dead lizard'.[43] There is little doubt that the Nassau

Agreement represented the apogee of Anglo-American defence relations in the postwar era. Kennedy's decision to sell Polaris missiles to Britain was singularly responsible for maintaining the British independent nuclear deterrent well into the 1970s. Moreover, the offer of this same deal to the French signalled a willingness to change US–French nuclear policy and the acceptance that both Britain and France would continue indefinitely to be nuclear powers. These decisions were nothing short of momentous. In order to get a fuller understanding of the importance of the Conference, one must examine the negotiations in some detail.

ANALYSIS OF THE NASSAU CONFERENCE

There are several aspects of the Nassau Conference that must be closely examined. These include the American and British roles in the resolution of the Skybolt crisis at Nassau; as well as the communiqué and its contents and significance for British, American and Anglo-American policy.

Why did Kennedy concede to Macmillan's demands and agree to sell Polaris to his ally when the very idea contradicted many of his administration's key policies, including non-proliferation of nuclear weapons and condemnation of small, independent nuclear forces? What pressures were on the president to withhold this weapon? Did he have the support of all his advisers? What did the Americans think they were getting from Britain that might compensate for this agreement to sell Polaris? What was the reaction of the Europeanists and the other elements within the administration who rejected the continuation of preferential treatment for the British? Why did Kennedy decide to make a similar offer to President de Gaulle when his administration until that point had refused to give assistance to the French nuclear programme? How seriously was this offer intended? What did the president hope to achieve by embarking upon this radical new policy direction?

Kennedy had known before he set out for Nassau that some formula involving Polaris would probably be required in order to resolve the problem caused by the cancellation of Skybolt. As early as 10 December, at a top-level meeting at which the President had presided, this possibility had been discussed and, on 16 December, plans had been drawn up outlining the alternatives to be offered to the British, which also included the weapons system. But Kennedy was under immense pressure not to 'give away' this highly sophisticated piece of American technology. As seen in the previous chapter, elements within the State Department had united in an attempt to influence presidential thinking against a decision that would perpetuate the discriminatory 'special relationship' cherished by the United Kingdom. Kennedy was initially unwilling to incur the combined wrath of these groups and their supporters in Congress, fearing that this would rock the political boat to an unnecessary degree. Instead, he began negotiations with the British by offering an assortment of alternatives that would counter any suggestions or criticism that the United States was attempting to force Britain to relinquish its nuclear status. He argued his case, according to Brandon, with little enthusiasm, for he knew that Macmillan was unlikely to be pacified with the hotch potch of ideas and alternatives being offered.[44] His talk with David Ormsby-Gore en route to the conference had put the affair into focus for the first time.[45] Kennedy knew Macmillan was in trouble and that his government bore some responsibility (though certainly not all) for this crisis.

Kennedy had two weighty problems to contend with. First, as already mentioned, he was under considerable pressure from an element within the administration who wanted him to use this opportunity to extract the United States from the restrictive and damaging constraints of the 'special relationship'. A number of them were also concerned that a policy concept – the multilateral nuclear force – should not be fatally undermined by any arrangement that Nassau might produce.

Second, Kennedy was deeply concerned with the impact a Polaris deal might have on America's other NATO allies, particularly France and Germany. His government firmly believed that there was a very real danger that Germany might grow tired and resentful of the non-nuclear status she had committed to and decide to seek redress. The example of France, it was felt, did nothing to ease this worry. President de Gaulle's reluctance to involve himself in NATO and his unerring commitment to the *Force de Frappe*, if anything, only made things worse. Now Macmillan was suggesting that the United States sell Britain Polaris missiles to preserve and extend the life of the British deterrent. Some in the Kennedy administration were concerned that the United Kingdom might turn to France and some form of Anglo-French nuclear collaboration if an acceptable agreement could not be reached. On 13 December, *The Times* commented:

if Britain is without a role in deterrent nuclear strength, she may be driven closer to the French who could no doubt profit greatly from British know-how . . .[46]

The merits of these arguments were obvious and Kennedy could see what attracted many of his staff to view the situation in these terms. On the other hand, the president was faced with a number of pressures from the opposite direction.[47] To begin with he instinctively recognised that Macmillan was in great political difficulty over the matter and genuinely wanted to do something to help Macmillan out. Kennedy greatly valued the good relations he had managed to establish with Macmillan and was acutely aware of the fact that Macmillan was the only counterpart the president had such an easy and close working relationship with. If the Skybolt crisis were to provoke a split of the magnitude that Macmillan was predicting, Kennedy knew that he could lose a valuable ally.[48] Also motivating him was the fact that he had inherited a commitment from his predecessor, President Eisenhower, and that the whole business had seemingly got out of hand when news of his administration's plans were leaked in the United States.[49] Kennedy also understood what many in his administration had apparently failed to grasp – that the close Anglo-American relationship was a tangible reality as opposed to the non-existent united Europe that was distant and elusive. For the president, the here and now was of more importance than the appealing yet distant future.[50] Kennedy was obviously impressed by the British leader's emotional and eloquent pleas for fair treatment and justice. Brandon noted in his report that 'a burgeoning and blossoming of the two leaders personal affection for each other' seemed to take place when the two men got together.[51] Remarkably, a change came over the proceedings in which goodwill replaced the tense and suspicious atmosphere in which the talks had opened. Neustadt also confirmed this when he recorded in his report that 'it was a case of "king to king", and it frustrated the court'.[52]

Another concern for Kennedy was how the Skybolt cancellation was being portrayed in the United States. Much to his surprise, a large proportion of the American press was highly critical of his administration's handling of the affair. Editorials in several leading papers claimed that the president was treating America's closest and oldest ally with disdain. The *Washington Post*, on 15 December, published one of the most stinging criticisms of the government announcing that:

weaknesses of Skybolt as a weapon are less alarming and less disappointing than the weaknesses in the conduct of American foreign policy . . .

. . . the Government of the United States has handled its relations with Great Britain with little consideration for British feelings, and not much evidence of real concern about the British position . . .

. . . the United States Government, disclosing its inherent misconception of the nature and gravity of the crisis, dispatched its able Secretary of Defense to England . . . But this is not solely a weapons problem and it is alarming to see that this Administration is handling it as though it were . . .

. . . if we don't respond as a friend ought to respond . . . their emotions will be justified and fears about the adequacy of the State Department confirmed.[53]

As Neustadt commented: 'Rusk was the ostensible target, but the White House knew at whom the *Post* was shooting.'[54] A personal call from the publisher of the *Washington Post* drove the message home. Britain had a large body of support in the United States. Kennedy wondered how the bipartisan establishment would react to a British accusation of betrayal of the original Camp David agreement. He did not want to be blamed for the collapse of Macmillan's Conservative government or for a situation where the British leader might be forced to adopt an anti-American platform in order to stay in power.[55] Furthermore, the president was worried about losing the American 'elite' support for European policy which had been assiduously cultivated by Democratic presidents since the Second World War. American media such as the *Washington Post, Time-Life, Newsweek,* the *New York Times, CBS* and others had it in their power to influence the opinions of millions of Americans.[56] A lot of damage could be done to Kennedy's presidency if the weight of public opinion went against him.

The president and his senior staff could live with the idea of making Polaris available to the British (even with the 'escape clause') because of 'concessions' he felt Macmillan had offered in return. First, Macmillan had agreed to 'work hard' for the creation of a multilateral force, towards which the British had hitherto shown barely concealed hostility. This appeared to be a departure that was certainly welcome in Washington. The multilateral force idea had been germinating for some time but had lacked strong official backing and commitment as well as support from key European

allies. Britain's promise to collaborate with the United States in
further exploration of a mixed-manned multilateral force appeared
to signal a new policy and was perhaps the key to solving the vex-
ing German problem. The second 'concession' Macmillan offered
was a commitment to put the British V-bomber force 'into NATO'
which, together with a similar American contribution, would form
the basis of a NATO multinational force. Third, the prime minister
had accepted the need to increase the strength of Britain's non-
nuclear forces. In recent years Britain had fallen noticeably behind
in its conventional force goals agreed by NATO. Now, it appeared
that Macmillan had re-committed his government to increasing the
effectiveness of these forces. Kennedy felt that while the outcome
of the talks would not please a great many of his staff, the reaffirmation of the Anglo-American alliance and the commitments given
by Macmillan augured well. The crisis had been resolved and an
old idea given new life. All in all, it was not a bad outcome.

The decision to make a similar offer to the French was perhaps
even more controversial than the British Polaris agreement.[57] The
debate about whether or not to aid the French nuclear programme
had been raging within the administration but eventually had been
won by those who were opposed to the idea.[58] Kennedy himself
had said in the course of the Nassau negotiations that although
the United States was helping France with very marginal nuclear
problems, this was 'minuscule' and at the very outer circle of the
nuclear world, while his government had no plans to increase or
extend this assistance.[59] At some point it appears that the president changed his mind. But was the offer genuine? With hindsight,
many of the key players at Nassau recognised that the offer to
France did not appear as attractive as they might have first thought.
It was decided to inform Chancellor Adenauer about what had been
done for Britain and what was being proposed for France. A hastily composed letter was dispatched outlining the offer of Polaris
missiles on the 'same terms' as the British agreement to France.
Upon further consideration, the drafters realised that this was in-
sulting given the fact that France's nuclear programme was not
sufficiently advanced to make use of these terms. Polaris missiles
were of no use to de Gaulle unless something was done to help
France to a point where the weapon could be utilised. Panicking,
'same' was changed to 'similar' in the letter to be sent to de Gaulle.
Unfortunately it was too late to change Adenauer's letter and as
Neustadt commented, 'no doubt the Elysée read both'.[60] After Nassau

there was much discussion about what the United States would be prepared to do in order to enable France to make use of the American offer.[61] Perhaps Kennedy, encouraged by Macmillan's promise to consider multilateralism and to assign the British V-bombers to a NATO force, felt that the time was now right to reach out to de Gaulle. The balance of independence and interdependence might just be enough to tempt him to give up his hostility and return to the NATO fold.[62] There is also the suggestion that the president recognised that the Nassau agreement was a radical departure which risked fatally compromising his administration's European and NATO policies. The offer to France could be regarded as a 'damage limitation' exercise – if de Gaulle could be contained, the fall-out might not be so severe as to cause any major problems. This view, however, is less likely, mainly because Kennedy and his staff appeared to be quite optimistic not only about the possibility of France accepting or at least opting to begin negotiations based on the offer, but that Nassau was the catalyst that would stimulate and inspire a new era in US–European relations.

From Macmillan's point of view the deal secured at Nassau was more than he could have hoped for. His Foreign Minister, Lord Home, agreed, calling the agreement 'a first-class bargain'.[63] The British independent deterrent had been preserved well past the decade that Skybolt would have covered. Moreover, Britain would be saving billions of pounds on research and development costs of a home-grown missile. In order to gauge the importance of the crisis from the British point of view it is necessary to pose a number of questions. How important was it for the prime minister to get a deal at Nassau? Would his government really have fallen or been forced to embrace an anti-American platform had the crisis not been satisfactorily resolved? Was the prime minister prepared to permit a split in Anglo-American relations had Kennedy refused to satisfy British demands? How important for Macmillan was the 'escape clause' and why did he press for a settlement at Nassau and not agree to the joint study group idea? What pressures were on the British leader?

With the independent nuclear deterrent and the restoration of close Anglo-American defence relations, two of the very cornerstone policies of Macmillan's government, the American decision to cancel the weapon was a major blow. The prime minister quickly realised that Skybolt's progress and chances of success had been highly subjective and at times misleading. He had placed too much trust in the might of the USAF and the military-industrial complex. He had been wrong. Britain had neither detailed contingency plans nor an alternative weapon.[64] Macmillan knew that the original agreement contained an escape clause and the Americans were well within their rights to abandon the missile. It was the manner in which this had been announced and the embarrassing fact that despite all the warnings Britain had been caught foolishly unprepared that was problematic. Thorneycroft had been unable or unwilling to make any headway with McNamara when the two men had met in early December. Now it was up the Macmillan to negotiate some solution with Kennedy.

Macmillan was personally compromised by Skybolt's demise. As he told the Americans at Nassau, he had been the one who had chosen the weapon at Camp David some years before. It had obviously been a mistake – his mistake. It was up to him to redress the damage. At Nassau Kennedy tried to placate the prime minister by offering him a number of alternatives to Skybolt – the 50–50 offer which would allow Britain to continue with the weapon, Hound Dog, and a proposal to set up a joint study group to consider alternatives over a longer period. None of these, however, was of any use to Macmillan. Skybolt had been too discredited; Hound Dog impractical and the study group would prevent the prime minister from being able to return to Britain with a tangible replacement.[65] The only possible solution was Polaris. Macmillan knew that Kennedy was under immense pressure not to give him the weapon but could accept nothing less. Macmillan had a number of pressures to contend with. First, he was not entirely confident that the Cabinet was fully behind him on the matter.[66] Second, his personal prestige and the credibility of his Conservative government were very much at stake. As Bligh recalls:

> The PM pressed Kennedy out of fear that if he didn't get a concrete offer at this juncture he would never get it later. If he went for a joint study . . . there would be no Polaris at the end of the road . . .[67]

Macmillan carefully laid his cards on the table one by one in an eclectic mixture of promises and thinly veiled threats, all delivered in an emotional and hypnotic oratory. As Gilpatric recalls, the room was 'spellbound' as they listened to him plead his cause.[68] This was not the man to whom they had become accustomed.[69]

Macmillan had gambled and won.[70] In a difficult position and little to bargain with, the only ammunition the prime minister could use was the threat of what he might be forced to do if adequate compensation was not forthcoming. He implied, during the course of the conversations, that a deep split in the Anglo-American alliance was a likely consequence of an unresolved crisis. If let down by the United States, Macmillan might find himself having to adopt an anti-American stance in order to retain power in Britain. He also hinted at the possibility of Anglo-French nuclear collaboration if Kennedy was not prepared to fulfil his obligation to provide Britain with a viable alternative weapon. This was an unwelcome scenario for the Americans which would have disastrous consequences for the Anglo-American relationship. Any Anglo-French collaboration would certainly have enormous implications for NATO and an unimaginable effect on Germany – a worry that the Kennedy administration was increasingly struggling to address. In order to play this hand it was necessary for Macmillan to refrain from telling the Americans about his depressing meeting at Rambouillet with de Gaulle. He knew that the General almost certainly meant to keep Britain out of Europe and possibly felt that if Kennedy and his pro-European staff were aware of this, it would be unlikely that they would consider Anglo-French collaboration a possibility, nor would they agree to a deal that would almost certainly provide de Gaulle with an excuse to keep Britain out of Europe. Macmillan was fairly sure that his European policy had failed, at least for the time being. All that was left was the independent deterrent and the 'special relationship'. It seems unlikely, however, that he would have followed through with any of these threats. He had made the restoration of the 'special relationship' the cornerstone of his foreign policies since coming to power in 1957. Moreover, he was aware that short of any unlikely Anglo-French collaborative venture, the United States was the only ally Britain could turn to for technological and scientific assistance. As for the Conservative government falling over the issue, again, this seems to have been a remote possibility. No one on the British side ever believed that this was probable.[71] Tim Bligh concurs, recalling his impressions at the time:

> If the president had responded 'I'm sorry but I can't...', the PM wouldn't have taken to drink, or resigned or anything... If Kennedy had said those words the PM would be sitting in office yet, just as he is now...[72]

The escape clause that Macmillan negotiated was of central importance. He would certainly have found it very difficult to explain to the press and the public that he had been forced to give up the independent British national deterrent and commit the existing British forces to a multilateral effort. Fortunately, Macmillan managed to preserve the perception of independence so that he could claim a major victory in the shape of a highly advanced, second-generation missile that would enable Britain to maintain national control over defence. As he told the House of Commons on his return:

> this is perhaps the most vital argument of all, there may be conditions, there must be areas, in which the interests of some countries may seem to them more vital than they seem to others. It is right and salutary that a British Government, whatever may be the particular conditions of a particular dispute, should be in a position to make their own decision without fear of nuclear blackmail . . .[73]

In return, Macmillan's concessions, whilst appearing at first glance to be substantial, were in reality too vague and open-ended to be of any real worth. 'Assigning' the British V-bombers meant little or nothing in practical terms. The agreement to consider a multilateral nuclear force and to work towards this goal was vague and contained no specific commitment to participate in such a force or indeed in discussions about it. The same applied to the NATO conventional force goals commitment. Britain had been trying to meet these levels for some time but had found it difficult to find the money. The Kennedy team had thought that the deal was a fair one with similar concessions made by both sides. It was not long before they realised that Macmillan had in fact gained a lot more than he had actually given.[74]

'Swaddled in masterly ambiguity', the Nassau Agreement was a document to which numerous often contradictory, interpretations, could be and were applied.[75] In the weeks and months that followed, much debate and controversy ensued. Both sides found themselves struggling to advance the policies and commitments they believed the document had secured. Several questions beg to be answered. Why was the wording so ambiguous and obscure? Was this deliberate or the result of pressures on time, manpower and expertise? How did each side interpret the agreement and did these interpretations differ substantially? How seriously did the United States take British commitments to multilateralism and conventional force increases? What did the agreement mean for the MLF proposal and American plans to allow NATO greater say in nuclear affairs? The controversial elements of the Nassau Agreement are to be found in paragraphs 6, 7 and 8 of the document. Paragraph 6 referred to the pooling of national nuclear forces under a single NATO command. This would form the basis of a multi*national* force and would comprise of mainly British and American elements. If General de Gaulle could be persuaded to become more NATO-friendly, it was envisaged that France might also contribute something to this force. Paragraph 7 committed both Britain and the United States to work towards the creation of a multi*lateral* nuclear force that would incorporate a mixed-manned element. This mingling of national personnel was necessary in order to make indistinguishable the individual contributions from each country and to prevent any one nation from attempting to dominate or even seize control of weaponry, submarine or ship. Paragraph 8, however, did not make clear which of these two forces, multilateral or multinational, the British Polaris force would be assigned to. In addition, nowhere in the document was a timeframe set out as a guide to when both forces might be expected to come into being. The agreement did not explicitly commit Britain to a multilateral course, stating only that they had agreed that the 'purpose of their two Governments with respect to the provision of the Polaris missiles must be the development of a multilateral NATO nuclear force in the closest consultation with other NATO allies', adding that 'they will use their best endeavours to this end'.[76] This wording was vague enough to allow Britain any number of ways out for, if the NATO allies failed to reach agreement or decided not to make use of or go ahead with the American proposal, the force would not come into being. In this case, there would be nothing for Britain to either assign or commit forces to.

The ambiguity of the Agreement was widely recognised when it was made public at Nassau. It looked very much like a 'rushed job', blamed by participants on the lack of available and competent staff. This was less a criticism of the abilities of the two delegations than an observation about the 'type' of personnel both sides had brought to the meeting. On the American side, Secretary of State Rusk had not even thought it necessary to attend the conference, going instead to a diplomatic dinner. Few were qualified to work efficiently on the problems being discussed or on the policy areas that risked being affected by the decisions being taken. The

British delegation was similarly handicapped.[77] As Theodore Sorenson remarked, it was a 'hasty improvisation' which was full of high level imprecision.'[78] Moreover, it had:

> an ambiguity that was perhaps the inevitable result of inadequate preparatory staff work, tight deadline pressures and the inherent difficulty of reconciling British strategic independence with an integrated MLF concept.[79]

Others point to the fact the very nature of the agreement necessitated a form of words that allowed both sides to claim a victory. Macmillan could stress the independence of the British deterrent and the fact that Kennedy had 'given in' and made Polaris, a much more advanced weapon, available for British use. The Conservative government could also claim that the close Anglo-American relationship had not only been preserved, but had been strengthened as a result of the agreement. The United States had demonstrated that the maintenance of the 'special relationship' was of the greatest importance. Similarly, Kennedy could point to Nassau as a great turning point, the beginning of a new phase in US foreign policy. By playing down the escape clause and emphasising the renewed British commitment to NATO force levels and the multilateral nuclear force, the president could use the agreement to demonstrate a fresh new effort was being made, led by the United States and the United Kingdom to create a strong and politically cohesive NATO. For the most part the Americans returning to Washington after Nassau were relieved that a difficult and potentially disruptive confrontation had been resolved. In the Defense Department, McNamara and Nitze were particularly pleased, regarding the agreement as an excellent point from which negotiations with the French could begin. For them, it contained just the right amount of independence and interdependence to entice the General to 'rejoin' the alliance. Even French rejection could improve the present situation which had become contaminated by American refusal to assist de Gaulle's nuclear ambitions, by countering the accusation of American negativism.[80]

The agreement had significant meaning for another group who had initially been outraged at the notion of preserving the independent British national deterrent – the Europeanists inside the Kennedy administration. For Ball and his colleagues, the Agreement was nothing short of a disaster.[81] From their point of view, as long as these negotiations dragged on, Britain would have to be supported, but once this had been achieved, all effort could then be made to get back to the multilateral solution. For those who advocated a multilateral approach to NATO's problems the clauses referring to both multinationalism and multilateralism provided the official platform from which this proposal could be launched, stressing the mixed manning multilateral element.[82] For the first time, what had always existed in proposal form had the backing and potential to become a Kennedy administration policy, and one, its proponents claimed, which could solve the worrying German and French problems. As Neustadt was to write in his report to President Kennedy:

> Each man looked to the future from his own predisposition; each saw in Nassau's outcome opportunities to further the particular perspective with which he himself viewed 'basic NATO policy' and European prospects.[83]

Nassau afforded an opportunity for numerous groups and individuals within the two governments to further the interests of the policies closest to their own heart. On the British side, Bligh, among others, certainly felt that several of Macmillan's Cabinet colleagues would have preferred to 'renegotiate' the independent deterrent, possibly to be replaced with a less costly and more realistic deterrent force. Thorneycroft, while supporting a Polaris deal, displayed all the characteristics of a man who might have preferred a break with the United States in favour of a more Europe-oriented defence policy. He was a well-known Francophile and continued throughout 1963 to press for greater co-operation with the French on nuclear matters. For Macmillan, the Polaris arrangement offered him both the opportunity to reaffirm his policy of Anglo-American collaboration and the independent British national deterrent. On the American side, Nassau provided an entirely different set of opportunities. Unable to dissuade Kennedy from preserving the independent British deterrent by giving his British counterpart Polaris, the Europeanists and Theologians within his government had to move fast to recover some of the ground their chief had given away. The Skybolt decision had been, in their opinion, the perfect opportunity finally to disassociate the United States from the debilitating 'special relationship'.[84] Kennedy's decision to overrule their objections had left little room for manoeuvre. What they could still do, however, was to emphasise the need for the Polaris agreement to be tied into a multilateral framework. In this they were successful. As the conference drew to a close, the men with the multilateral outlook began to digest the implications of the meeting.

6 A New Foreign Policy Initiative – Are There Any Takers?

The Nassau Agreement recognizes that the security of the West is indivisible, and so must be our defense. But it also recognizes that this is an alliance of proud and sovereign nations, and works best when we do not forget it. It recognizes further that the nuclear defense of the West is not a matter for the present power alone ... We remain too near the Nassau decisions, and too far from their final realization, to know their final place in history. But I believe that, for the first time, the door is open for the nuclear defense of the alliance to become a source of confidence, instead of a cause of contention ... We are not lulled by the momentary calm of the sea or the somewhat clearer skies above. We know the turbulence that lies below, and the storms beyond the horizon this year ...[1]

Thus spoke President Kennedy of his hopes that the decisions reached at Nassau would pave the way for a new era in alliance relations. His words have a prophetic resonance in the light of what transpired that year. In fact, the Multilateral Nuclear Force proposal survived the death of the President, only to fade into obscurity as a new leadership exerted itself in the United States. Its path was fitful, turbulent and always highly controversial. Even the mention of the project never ceased to elicit a mixed reaction ranging from 'messianic zeal'[2] to antipathy and, in some cases, downright opposition. One inescapable truth, however, is that the concept occupied a premier place in foreign policy debates in the corridors of Whitehall and the White House, the Elysée, Bundestag and the parliaments of Europe for many years. The year 1963 saw it reach its pinnacle.

The Nassau Agreement had resurrected with some vigour an issue that had been simmering on the administration's back burner since the days of the Eisenhower administration. The complex question of how to respond to what the United States perceived as allied demands for an augmented role in NATO nuclear planning and decision-making had long troubled policy planners in Washington,

105

who had an additional worry that while the complicated issue of Britain's bid to enter the EEC was unresolved, the situation in Europe threatened to exacerbate the problem. Much time had been devoted to the matter, but as yet no concrete proposal had been successfully implemented. While suggestions had been floated, none appeared to embrace adequately the problem which was ultimately to remain unresolved until the Skybolt crisis and the Nassau Conference conspired to force the British and American governments to deal with the thorny issue. The announcement that the MLF route – albeit in a decision taken bilaterally – had been identified as the most suitable way to address the problems confronting the NATO alliance, combined with de Gaulle's blunt rejection of Kennedy's 'Grand Design' policy, turned the matter into a priority project almost overnight.[3] Suddenly, what had been discussed in various forms for several years was represented as a new, officially sponsored, presidentially-backed policy. To the perplexed NATO allies, the new Anglo-American initiative looked like an unlikely bet. All the governments of Europe waited to see what Washington's next move would be. Few cared to speculate on what the months ahead would bring.

The decisions reached at Nassau not only provided high-priority backing for the MLF concept, but also gave it a high voltage jump-start. While officials in Washington busied themselves with post-Nassau planning matters, work quickly got underway on the multilateral aspects, with 'feelers' going out to the various European capitals to assess allied reaction to the previous months' work. As Under-Secretary Ball explained to Chancellor Adenauer, the United States favoured quick action. He told the German leader:

> We have been talking about a multilateral force for some time but the principal difference in our position after Nassau is that we no longer are waiting for a European initiative but are now forced by decision to use Polaris to take the initiative ourselves in proposing a plan to key European countries. We are no longer prepared to proceed in leisurely fashion but wish to proceed as soon as possible . . .[4]

With President de Gaulle's peremptory rejection of Nassau and Britain's bid to join the EEC came the realisation that America's relations with France had deteriorated. The French leader's bombshell 14 January press conference had once again emphasised the extent to which de Gaulle was determined to remove himself and

France from the 'interfering' hands of the United States or any of its 'cohorts'. It was clear that much work had to be done to mend the rift and control the damage wrought by de Gaulle's negativism. In addition, the Franco-German Treaty signed on 23 January heightened fears about direction de Gaulle was moving in. Amidst the confusion and disorientation that followed these two events, the administration found itself floundering. This allowed the pro-MLF staff to push the proposal forward as a solution to the setbacks suffered. Invigorated by the highly charged atmosphere in Washington, the multilateralists began a vigorous campaign dedicated to achieving the implementation of this proposal.[5] It was now tagged as a major diplomatic initiative.[6]

With the creation of a special office within the State Department headed by Livingston Merchant, the proposal had a base.[7] For the next 20 months the MLF advocates worked tirelessly towards their goal.[8] Never enjoying a particularly smooth path, the fortunes of the proposal fluctuated from relatively promising to seemingly bleak at times. Likewise, reaction in the European capitals for much of the time followed a similar course. The story is a complicated one, full of twists and turns characterised by a diversity of feeling ranging from passion to antipathy through to opposition. In order to get a full understanding of this policy and the effects that it had on Anglo-American and NATO relations, the development of the proposal must be examined in some detail.

THE PROPOSAL

A position paper produced in late January 1963 outlined a proposal for a NATO Polaris Force made up of either submarines or surface vessels. The document set out at length the arguments for and against each mode of missile delivery.[9] A submarine fleet would be made up of eight nuclear-powered boats each equipped with 16 Polaris A-3 type missiles with a range of 2,500 miles. This would cost an estimated $1,770 million in initial investment with an additional $160 million annually in operating costs. If, on the other hand, the surface mode were preferred, the force would consist of 25 ships carrying eight Polaris A-3 missiles each. This projected cost was marginally lower, with an initial bill of $1,650 million and an annual operating cost of $90 million. It was expected that the costs of the force would be split between participating nations in order to decrease the share of the total NATO costs borne by the United States.

Manning the proposed multilateral force was a crucial issue if the force were to have any credibility at all. Three proposals were initially put forward: national manning, bilateral manning and mixed manning. The two forms of control would be political and military. A political control formula might have two parts: a pre-arranged allocation of authority to fire the force upon confirmation of unmistakable nuclear attack and an agreement that in all other contingencies the force would be launched by consultation between the allied participants, perhaps by some pre-arranged voting system. This was unmistakably one of the most difficult problems facing the realisation of the multilateral force idea. Given the fact that the creation of the force would take place over a period of several years, it would be naive to expect allied attitudes not to change. Several factors might influence a shift in perception, including increased European political and economic integration and changes in the Atlantic alliance. It would be hoped that improved NATO conventional capabilities and increased allied involvement in other aspects of Western defence would encourage European understanding of the needs and desirability of a cohesive, integrated and centralised defence structure. Military control, it was anticipated, would require a force commander to whom all units and elements would be directly responsible.

As it stood, US law allowed co-operation and assistance in certain conditions but stressed that atomic weapons must stay in American possession. In short, the law prohibited the transfer of completed atomic weapons to any other state or defence organisation. For an integrated Polaris force to receive completed atomic weapons or nuclear reactors from the United States, there would have to be changes made to current legislation in the form of the Atomic Energy Act. If it was decided that the United States would retain sole possession of the atomic weapons, a formula would have to be constructed which would not require any legislative changes.

This was the basic set of blueprints on which negotiations with the NATO allies were to be based. Although Kennedy stressed during subsequent discussions of the MLF proposal that the idea was to be presented as one of a range of possibilities to be offered to the Europeans for their consideration, even by this early stage the basic format of the discussions had been decided.

MOTIVATIONS: THE GERMAN PROBLEM AND OTHER CONCERNS

Why did the Kennedy administration feel the need for this particular proposal? What motivated those advocates of the proposal? How seriously did they regard the 'German Problem'? Why did the MLF supporters feel that this was the only workable solution to the problems the United States faced in Europe and NATO? The Multilateral Nuclear Force proposal had varying amounts of support within the Kennedy administration. Its proponents were known as the 'Theologians' or 'Cabal', and included Robert Bowie, Henry Owen, Robert Schaetzel and Walt Rostow among others. Some of these men were also known as 'Europeanists' and George Ball, one of the most fervent of this grouping, was also a keen MLF exponent. These men had two main reasons for advocating this as the best hope of resolving some of the government's most testing foreign policy commitments. First, they firmly believed in the existence and possible resurgence of a dangerous latent German nationalism which would manifest itself in a demand for access to and control over nuclear weapons. Going by past experience, they argued that if Germany were not securely tied into a stable European politico-military structure and successfully cured of its sense of being a second-class citizen within the NATO alliance the moderate leadership in that country would not be able to withstand or overcome these pressures to attain the prestigious status of a nuclear power.[10] The current provocative yet seductive behaviour of President de Gaulle was adding to the complexity of the problem. According to Arthur Schlesinger, the MLF believed that if the plan failed:

> moderate leadership in Bonn would be undermined, West Germany would start pressing for nationally manned and owned missiles and if denied them by us, a right-wing government might turn to the French.[11]

Germany, it was thought, held the key to stability and prosperity on the European continent. Much of the United States' foreign policy in the last half-century had been based on finding mechanisms for containing Germany. There existed a widespread expectation among officials that it was only a matter of time before Germany once again began to flex its considerable muscles and began to move in a dangerous pro-nuclear direction and possibly towards to acquisition of an independent nuclear weapons capability.[12] It was considered that the example of France and Britain only exacerbated the problem and further encouraged the development of nationalist tendencies. Why did this fear exist? The assumptions underlying these expectations were quite diverse. They ranged from a belief that a desire for nuclear status was a natural result of the process of rehabilitation and possibly rearmament – a reassertion of the traditional German military expertise – to the belief that the tremendous economic and industrial success of the country would provide more than enough skills and financial means to utilise what must also be regarded as one of the most advanced technological developments of the twentieth century.[13] Whether compelled by tradition, frustration at having been 'kept down' and treated as a second-class citizen, envy at the prestige and influence afforded by its nuclear allies, Britain and France or simply as a natural consequence of having the money, skills and perhaps desire to make use of nuclear energy, Germany was regarded as a ticking time-bomb which could not be ignored.[14] Walt Rostow referred to the problem in a detailed memorandum to President Kennedy:

> It may seem odd to create such an elaborate structure merely to solve the problem of Germany's nuclear role. The truth is that most of our creative innovations in European policy since 1945 have been more or less directly the result of efforts to solve aspects of the German problem ... In short, we are on a familiar and reasonably distinguished track in offering a multilateral formula to Europe in nuclear matters primarily to solve the question of German participation. Europe has had to discipline itself in order to discipline the Germans ...[15]

The 'German problem' was compounded by the recognition that the Adenauer era was drawing to a close. The ageing Chancellor was expected to retire soon and speculation was rife about his successor and his ability to maintain the stable political environment Adenauer had managed to preside over.[16] Some American officials feared that the new leadership would be unable to resist what they imagined to be the growing clamour for restitution and satisfaction as a premier power in Europe. With Adenauer gone, Germany might find it impossible to prevent a slide towards nationalism and perhaps nuclearism also.[17]

The second motivating factor for the MLF proponents was the need to find a formula that would enable them to rebuild relations with France. Franco-American relations had deteriorated considerably over the previous few years, culminating on General de Gaulle's rejection of Kennedy's 'Grand Design', the Nassau Agreement and British entry into the Common Market. Arguing that the so-called 'special relationship' the United States had with Britain was anachronistic, debilitating and generally counterproductive, they saw multilateralism as an effective means of 'levelling' the playing field in order to put all America's allies on an equal footing and to counter once and for all the accusations of discrimination and favouritism. This, they maintained, would serve America's foreign policy interests better than what was currently in place, enabling the United States to proceed with a non-discriminatory policy that would build up relations with all the NATO countries.

Another reason the MLF advocates pressed their proposal was to promote political cohesion in the Atlantic Alliance. With so many genuinely co-operative political and economic ventures in a state of suspension, if not disarray, the *New York Times* reported that 'the basic purpose here has been to create a sense of forward motion on the military front to keep alive the notions of interdependence and Atlantic Partnership'.[18] To this end, even as an educational experience to familiarise the Europeans with all aspects of nuclear problems, the proposal would certainly have great benefit.[19]

An additional motivation not widely known was information in the form of an intelligence report that the United States had received from British sources. Not long after de Gaulle had rejected Britain's Common Market bid, the Nassau Agreement and its MLF component, Kennedy was shown a report claiming that de Gaulle was contemplating some sort of master negotiation with the Soviet Union – that he had seen the Soviet Ambassador and had confided to Couve de Murville, and one or two others, that the time had come for him and Khrushchev to settle all these matters. Sorenson, who tells the story, recalls that the president understandably was 'extremely concerned' and worried about what this would mean for the security not only of the United States, but West Germany, which was bound to be involved in any such settlement. He was also concerned about the NATO alliance and how it would be affected by de Gaulle's actions. 'All this', according to Sorenson, 'gave added impetus to the studies of how to approach Western Europe which were going on at the time in connection largely . . . with the MLF'.[20]

Of Kennedy's top advisers and staff, only George Ball was obviously an MLF supporter in early 1963 although even he viewed the project as a means to a greater end, the unification of Europe.[21] Both McNamara (whom Henry Brandon claims was 'lukewarm')[22] and Nitze were dubious. McNamara in particular was more concerned with internal politics and re-organisation of the Department than the force idea, which he did support.[23] In an early meeting about the force in February 1963, the Secretary of State expressed his preference for a surface fleet and his concern about current Republican efforts to 'dictate military policy' to the Administration. He told the meeting that he had originally opposed the surface force concept, but he had now come to the conclusion that the United States should offer the Europeans a surface force rather than take on a major fight with the Republicans who would be quick to exploit a proposal to share Polaris submarines with European members of NATO. He doubted whether it would be possible to sell Congress a NATO Polaris multilateral force given the domestic political problems he had encountered during recent Congressional hearings.[24] Secretary of State Rusk appeared happy enough to allow his staff to continue to push the proposal without offering too much by way of resistance or criticism. In fact, he proved quite supportive, telling Kennedy that 'at this juncture the alternative to the multilateral path seemed to be the development of national deterrents and proliferation', adding that if the United States did not take the initiative, 'we could expect greater Franco-German collaboration and a considerably more complicated problem'.[25] Such was his interest, that the President closed one meeting by telling Rusk that he had two weeks to sell 'his' idea.[26] Recalled for a time from London to work on the post-Nassau strategy, Bruce also advised, after careful consideration, that the MLF route was 'a useful instrument for moving towards our basic objectives in Europe'.[27] An ardent pro-European, Bruce felt strongly that something needed to be done in order to stem the tide of nationalist nuclear aspirations. The difficulty, he told a meeting, was that 'the Europeans realized that they would never be able to build up sufficient nuclear forces to ask for control of the firing of NATO weapons because we will always have overwhelming military power'. 'Our problem', he went on, 'is to figure out some way to make it possible for the Europeans to live with this fact.' 'We must find a way', he stressed, 'of giving them a means, even a façade, of answering de Gaulle's argument.' 'What we are seeking is a political solution, not a military answer . . . what we are trying to do is to overcome the present political uneasiness about the nuclear force problem in the hope that the uneasiness will vanish within five years.'[28] Bruce believed that if the Europeans came to the conclusion that nuclear war was indivisible and that it would make no sense for them to think of a force that could be used independently of the United States, they would decide that there was no benefit in the establishment of a multilateral force and would be content with closer organisational and consultation arrangements. In this case, he advised, perhaps it would be more prudent to consider emphasising the first-phase or paragraph 6 force.[29]

Kennedy was by no means in total agreement with the analysis of this section of his staff.[30] He opened an early meeting at the beginning of the 1963 MLF 'push' by expressing caution and stressing the fact that there was a danger in his opinion that the United States might be tying itself too closely to a project that might fail. The President recognised the validity of these arguments and totally accepted the fact that some mechanism was needed if the unity of the Atlantic alliance was to be preserved and enhanced. America's European allies were restless and indignant over their exclusion from decisions involving issues of continental defence, stirrings that could only increase the possibility of West Germany demanding similar restitution.[31] But the manner in which this concept of multilateralism was to be translated into a viable military force, acceptable to all the countries involved, was not only controversial but highly complicated. Kennedy wondered whether the force would have any real attraction unless the United States was prepared to give up its veto, and at this point he saw no justification for this.[32] On two other occasions during the course of the discussions Kennedy again stressed his concern that the United States was risking identification with a proposition that might be rejected and that the country should not find itself in the position of 'attempting to force the sale of the MLF'. He raised an additional concern saying that 'he hated to see the French and the Soviets stirred up by a proposition that could flounder on the issue of the US veto'.[33] The President decided to give the idea more consideration suggesting that both the paragraph 6 force and the MLF proposal be considered as equally important parts of the whole multilateral concept. Still reticent about his administration appearing to have made up its mind about the MLF, Kennedy somewhat reluctantly gave Livingston Merchant permission to attempt to negotiate in Europe an agreement based on the previous October's Smith–Lee briefings.[34] Merchant's instructions contained a mandate for investigating interest and possibly negotiating a Preliminary Agreement. He was told:

... You should conduct this mission as to avoid serious damage to US prestige if our allies do not wish to proceed with an MLF ...[35]

Kennedy also reiterated his concern that an 'effective and presentable alternative' be prepared lest the MLF proposal fail to make sufficient progress.[36] This was to contain a greater emphasis on the so-called paragraph 6 forces and would be the responsibility of Jeffrey Kitchen. The President also gave approval to Nitze's proposal to bring the NATO allies more fully into the planning for the nuclear defence of NATO which he wanted explored as a possible alternative approach.[37]

Before Merchant left for Europe Kennedy warned against over-selling the MLF concept, emphasising that he did not want the United States to be accused of putting pressure on the allies or promising the proposal as a 'cure-all for all our problems'.[38] The important thing, he instructed, was 'not to stick to the MLF too long if it seemed to be a losing proposition but to ensure that the formula offered would have some chance of success'.[39] From Kennedy's perspective, the Merchant trip was very much an exploratory mission, an attempt to 'reach out' to Europe in the hope that enough latent enthusiasm and interest existed to allow discussion about the future shape of Atlantic interdependence to begin. Concerned that the project might 'abort with subsequent discredit to the United States', Kennedy considered that a preliminary 'reconnaissance' of the governments of Europe was necessary before it could be determined whether the plan had the makings of a good and viable policy.[40] Kennedy was also concerned about the reaction to the MLF proposal in the Congress. Early in 1963 he became aware that the proposal as it stood would require changes in, or possibly new, legislation before the force could be implemented.[41] In a closed session, the Joint Congressional Committee on Atomic Energy (the Congressional watchdog body protecting the United States' nuclear interests) interviewed Merchant in order to examine the implications of such a venture before determining that this would contravene existing legislation.[42] The committee strongly opposed relaxing any laws that would allow foreign hands on American nuclear weaponry or targeting or control systems, confirming that this would require an amendment to the Atomic Energy Act of 1954. According to the *New York Times*, committee members indicated that they might consider such an amendment if satisfactory arrangements could be worked out over who was to control the use of the weapons, but at the same time expressed 'serious doubts' about whether or not the critical control question could be settled.[43] The meeting left the administration in no doubt that Congressional opinion was likely to complicate the implementation of the Multilateral Nuclear Force. Indeed, in later months, Kennedy was reluctant even to consult Congress until he considered that he had enough firm commitment from the Europeans to carry the proposal through to completion. He was well aware that the German problem could not be tackled in isolation and at the expense of America's relations with the other NATO countries. De Gaulle's rejection of Nassau had left a considerable vacuum in US–French relations which also needed to be considered. The president understood that the decisions taken bilaterally with the British had profound implications for NATO and that the success of the arrangements and especially the Multilateral force proposal depended on his administration's ability to convince the Europeans that this was the best way to assure Atlantic partnership, stability and prosperity.[44] The next few months would be crucial.

In a January meeting, Kennedy expressed his concern that the timing was going to be tight. 'As soon as the French have a nuclear capability', he told the group, 'we have much less to offer Europe and the Europeans may conclude that continuing their ties with us will create a risk that we will drag them into a war in which they do not wish to be involved.' 'If we are not vital to Germany', he warned, 'then our NATO strategy makes no sense.'[45] Kennedy saw no harm in continuing to discuss the idea with America's allies in an effort to fashion a solution that would satisfy the needs and aspirations of all the countries involved, including, if at all possible, France. To mend relations with General de Gaulle's France was an important motivating factor for Kennedy, who believed the country to have a crucial role in achieving Atlantic unity.

The president's reluctance to embrace the MLF without reservation at this point grew out of his concerns that the project, while attractive enough in American eyes, not only failed to contain enough of the right ingredients to satisfy the Europeans but quite possibly contained more than enough to cause serious concern to the Soviet Union. While anticipating some reaction to the proposal from the USSR, the initial sounds coming from Moscow appeared to be more vituperative and hard-line than many of Kennedy's advisers had been expecting.[46]

THE MERCHANT MISSION: THE BEGINNING OF
ATTEMPTS TO CONVINCE CONTINENTAL EUROPE:
GERMANY, FRANCE, ITALY AND THE OTHERS

How did each of the countries respond to the proposal? Who was
enthusiastic and why? Who was opposed or lukewarm, and what
motivated them? Did American tactics change as the mission progressed? What information was being sent back to Washington?
Did Merchant and his staff feel confident that their message was
getting across in Europe? Did enthusiasm increase, fluctuate or
decrease as time went on? Was this an accurate assessment of what
was happening in Europe?

It is perhaps ironic to find that Merchant himself was unconvinced at the outset about the project's chances of success. In a
meeting with the president before he left for Europe, Merchant
expressed his opinion, saying that 'if the MLF worked, we would
have extricated the Germans from the exclusive French embrace',
but added that he was 'not optimistic' about the project.[47] He began his mission sceptical about the chances of success. His weeks
in Europe appeared to change his mind. Of all the allies, West
Germany alone showed signs of genuine enthusiasm for what Merchant was proposing.[48] The discussions in Bonn lasted longer and
took place in greater depth than anywhere else in Europe, with
perhaps the exception of Britain. In the eyes of the MLF advocates, Bonn was the key to the success of the plan. German support
was a virtual precondition for preliminary negotiations to begin
and it was essential to have a strong signal from Adenauer that his
country fully backed the proposal and continued to support the
ethos of Atlantic partnership and interdependence. The discussions,
according to Merchant, were 'quite satisfactory', allowing him to
report back to Washington that the Germans gave what he termed
'clear evidence of willingness to match any United States share in
the cost of the MLF', indicating that it was a strong candidate for
eventual participation.[49] Support in Bonn, however, was far from
unconditional. The German government was not unanimous in its
approval of the scheme and there was some disagreement about
the nature of the force being proposed by the Americans. A strong
preference existed for a submarine instead of a surface fleet.[50] In
addition, there was much debate in the Bundestag about the proposed control mechanism. As the talks progressed, more divisions
appeared to be opening up. Von Hassel, the German Defence

Minister, was reported as expressing himself 'much more cautiously' on the MLF in the Bundestag Foreign Affairs Committee session and at a press conference because, the report claimed, of recent discussions with Adenauer in which the President reiterated his belief in the political and strategic need for land-based MRBMs.[51] The German press appeared similarly unconvinced, with an influential weekly paper suggesting that the entire project should be dropped in favour of a formula that would produce guidelines on nuclear weapons use. Restored NATO co-operation, the paper claimed, would render the multilateral nuclear force obsolete, for without a restoration and redefinition of these issues, any such force could not hope to function anyway.[52] However, by the time the team left Bonn, Merchant felt sure that the difference of opinion could be worked out and that Germany was definitely on board.

The Italians, Merchant found, in spite of some confusion over what appeared to them to be a shift in American preference from submarines to surface ships, seemed prepared to support the MLF with substantial resources. Although it was unclear how much popular support existed for the project, the Belgian government also appeared enthusiastic. Although Spaak (the Belgian Foreign Minister) was personally in favour of the proposal, the Senate and Defence Ministry were strongly opposed and more predisposed to supporting the multinational force idea favoured by the British.[53] All indications pointed to the fact that this small country would prefer to remain on the sidelines of any nuclear matter offering perhaps only 'loud vocal support' rather than any firm commitment. As an official report stated:

> sparse Belgian press coverage and comment on Merchant visit to Brussels, and fuller coverage in other capitals, is accurate reflection of deep-seated current popular preference to be on sidelines in nuclear matters. While this does not mean Belgians would not eventually participate in MLF if other members joined and cost problem met, much inertia to be overcome . . .[54]

In his opinion, if the project managed to get up and running with the US, Germany and Britain as the founding members, Belgium would 'scramble aboard the bandwagon'. Spaak did suggest that if participation in the MLF meant that Belgium and the other smaller European countries would be involved in production of part of the MLF equipment it would result in Europeans having greater access to modern technology in nuclear and related fields and would thus add inducement of substantial importance.[55] In short, the non-military benefits of nuclear power would hold considerable attraction for those nations that could not or would not engage in a nuclear programme of their own.

Of the remaining NATO countries, Holland, Greece and Turkey, while interested, would be unlikely to be able to offer any financial or military contribution to the force except perhaps for port facilities in the case of Holland. If the force were to go ahead, Merchant estimated, the other participating countries would more than likely find themselves having to meet the financial fees to ensure Greek and Turkish participation.[56]

France was barely touched. While Merchant did speak to various French officials, including Couve de Murville, this was only in an unofficial capacity to brief the government on what the American administration was hoping to achieve with the MLF proposal. The French made it very clear that they were totally opposed to the idea and would not consider participation under any circumstances.[57] Their unequivocal rejection of the concept of multilateralism left little room for doubt in Washington that de Gaulle would reconsider and agree to participate in such a venture. Nevertheless, it was hoped that at some point in the future, the existence of such a mechanism would facilitate closer French integration with the Atlantic Alliance.

The sceptical man who set off from Washington a month earlier seems to have become more sanguine as he made his way through Europe. In a letter to the Secretary of State he warned of the consequences of failure to implement the proposal:

> if the United States does not move with this European pro-MLF drive, Gaullist forces will be encouraged and Atlantic community hopes set back. . . .[58]

Merchant did, however, come up against difficulties, some created by his own government. One of the problems the Ambassador encountered almost straight away was in the form of instructions on cost sent from Washington. He replied somewhat laconically:

> I believe persuasive presentation [of] our concept MLF and hence its prospects for success seriously damaged by instructions contained in TOPOL 1248 re costing. Cost differential in favor [of] surface [is] dangerously thin. Moreover, facing possible participants with possible necessity [of] bearing some R&D expenditures

prior to January 1, 1963 seems to me not only damaging but indefensible. In my judgement, any downward negotiation will find no one to express gratitude for our generosity, all candidates having died of initial fright.[59]

The issue of surface ships versus submarines was another bone of contention mainly for Germany and Italy. The delegation was initially concerned about getting consensus on this matter. Finletter wrote to Rusk, 'it seems to me that there is enough risk that one or more of three key European countries will refuse to accept surface vessels, or will be seriously disturbed at having to accept them, that this problem should be reviewed after return of Merchant team, and definitive decision made once and for all . . .'.[60]

By mid-March, Kennedy and Rusk were becoming more concerned with the lack of progress made in getting British commitment to join negotiations. The President recognised that if Britain refused to join in the MLF discussions, the project would necessarily take on a new US–German shape which might not be beneficial to any of the parties concerned. In a telegram to the American Embassy in London, Rusk outlined Washington's concern:

I fear that, if the Macmillan Government cannot be brought to see these larger issues of the UK's relation to the Continent, the natural evolution of events may conspire to damage British basic interests and position in the world . . . a continued sense of drift and lack of purpose could encourage Little Englanders and niggling and sterile anti-Gaullism . . .[61]

In London Ambassador Merchant found his reception decidedly less enthusiastic.[62] Negotiations with the British in February had produced consensus on the multinational paragraph 6 aspect, but on little else. The talks in Washington had made it clear to the Americans that Britain had every intention of following through on this, but would prove reluctant and difficult about committing themselves any more deeply to the multilateral dimension.[63]

The United States had reservations about pushing ahead too rapidly with the creation of this force until the multilateral element had been explored further. It was felt that a simple transfer of current NATO tactical nuclear equipment to a multinational force would contribute no additional strength and risked greatly complicating the present military command and organisational arrangements of NATO.[64]

Merchant described the first meeting the team had in Britain as 'tepid'.[65] Nevertheless, by the time he left the United Kingdom, the Ambassador was sure that he had succeeded in convincing Macmillan's government of the merits of the proposal. In his judgement, Britain could not afford to remain outside of the MLF initiative for fear that the cherished 'special relationship' would be replaced by a new German-American closeness. Merchant wrote to Washington:

> the UK and/or Italy are the key to the enterprise . . . I believe strongly that we should not delay our decisions, reserve our attitude or otherwise act on the assumption that the worst and least likely combination will develop. My belief is reinforced by the leverage we possess with Britain to prevent them wrecking our policy in so vital a matter as the MLF . . .[66]

He took heart in the fact that Ministers had spoken to him about trying to find the money in their budget to finance a 10 per cent stake and perhaps even a contribution of nuclear warheads.[67] However, despite Merchant's belief that he had found support, albeit cautious, for the MLF, as he prepared to return to the United States, he could boast of little more than a restrained British endorsement for the proposal. The communiqué issued after the talks was limited to a statement referring to Britain's 'continuing support' for the proposal and the 'hope' that a way might be found to enable participation in the nuclear force.[68] Writing to the Secretary of State, he offered his opinion that the reaction to his mission had gone as well as could be expected:

> I would like to register my belief that [the] existence [of] some confusion and absence [of] optimism as to final results is in important respects to our advantage. Firstly, [the] venture is by no means assured of success and insupportable optimism at this point would be misleading and possibly in the end harmful. Secondly, undue precision and emphasis on firm elements in US MLF concept impairs [the] image [that] we seek to maintain, the purpose [of] this mission at this time is to consult and listen to [the] views of interested allies rather than appearing that we are 'peddling' or attempting to dictate to others [a] US complete and rigid in all details . . .[69]

One of the reasons why Kennedy was reluctant to give his full and unconditional support to the proposal was because of the lack of positive statements about the MLF coming from London. Arthur Schlesinger had told him of his recent experiences in Britain:

The sudden US excitement about the MLF has given people an impression that US policy in Europe is hopelessly vacillating and unstable, and, therefore, un-thought-out and unreliable ... In short, I could not find anyone in England who showed any enthusiasm about the multilateral force ...[70]

Kennedy was now deeply concerned that Britain's lack of support, given the agreements reached at Nassau, would seriously endanger the proposal's chances of success. For him, a multilateral force without British participation would probably create more problems than it hoped to solve. But why did his closest ally not feel able to join in this project?

7 Do or Die – The Making and Breaking of the Multilateral Nuclear Force

INITIAL BRITISH REACTION – THE MLF THROUGH BRITISH EYES

How did the British government respond to the Merchant Mission? Did their position differ from what they had agreed to support at Nassau? Was the Cabinet unanimous in its reaction or was there a difference in opinion? How did the military and other interested parties feel about the proposal? What concerns, fears and factors motivated the British response to the proposal? Was the government afraid of jeopardising the recent Polaris Agreement or the 'special relationship' that appeared to have been reaffirmed by this deal?

At Nassau the price Macmillan had to pay in order to maintain the semblance of independence was the espousal of multilateralism and, in particular, the concept of a NATO multilateral nuclear force proposal. In its final form, the communiqué issued at the close of the conference spoke of two forces: one multilateral and one multinational. It was unclear at the time if these were to be phases of development of the same force or two wholly separate entities. From the outset, the two allies habitually stressed fundamentally and essentially opposite aspects of the final agreement. Macmillan needed to emphasise the independent nature of the deterrent he had just secured while, for internal political reasons, it was absolutely crucial for Kennedy to stress the multilateral aspect of the deal. Macmillan's Conservative government had shown little enthusiasm for the idea of a multilateral force even before Kennedy insisted that the British would have to endorse the proposal in order to get Polaris for themselves. Not surprisingly, after Nassau little changed. If the Americans believed that assurances given in the course of the Polaris negotiations amounted to a firm commitment to participate in the MLF proposal, they soon found out that this perception was far from accurate.

From the British point of view, Nassau gave them what they wanted with only a vague promise to participate in some form of multinational force and to consider expanding this into a multilateral force at some point in the future.[1] As Sir Pierson Dixon wrote to Lord Home shortly after the conference:

> it is the charm of the Nassau agreement that provides for things to be done now and aims to be achieved later. It fits in with the realities of the time scale before us . . .

Of the multilateral element he concluded:

> how can these questions be resolved when we do not know whether Britain will be part of Europe or whether a European political union can be created. To take such a line as this seems to me to have great advantages. It provides us with a convincing and sincere argument to put to the Americans for not going multilateral now, or even discussing the concept in any detail. It is consistent with what we said before Nassau . . .[2]

Macmillan, supported by the Foreign Office and the Ministry of Defence, was reluctant to give into American pressure to commit Britain to participation in the multilateral force for a whole range of political, military and financial reasons that they ranked in no particular order.[3]

MILITARY OBJECTIONS

One fundamental problem the British government had in accepting the MLF proposal was the fact that initial studies had arrived at the conclusion that no actual military need existed for such a force. This was highlighted by the visit of the American Admiral Ricketts, who was sent in early June to brief and attempt to convince the British that the proposal was for a viable and necessary force. Ricketts was under instructions to explain the merits of a mixed manned multilateral force comprised of surface vessels. Unfortunately, he failed to produce a convincing *raison d'être* of a military kind for the addition of this force to the deterrent strength of the West. The briefing did not go well. Compounding his failure to impress his British hosts with the benefits of participating in such a venture, Ricketts admitted that an evaluation done for the US Navy had concluded that in military terms 'the system [of surface vessels] was significantly more vulnerable than submarines'.[4] Not surprisingly, those listening to Ricketts heard nothing to reassure them about the military and strategic benefits the nuclear force would bring to the defence of NATO. Macmillan's instructions to his colleagues (at the behest of President Kennedy) that they should endeavour to try and take the American seriously did little good. The British government was simply not convinced.[5] Thorneycroft was unequivocal in his denunciation, calling the proposal 'the biggest piece of nonsense that anyone had ever dreamt up'.[6] Not surprisingly, the British Chiefs of Staff were also particularly critical of the proposal, regarding it as 'entirely superfluous' in military terms and highly vulnerable to destruction.[7] As for the Royal Navy, apart from the fact that the American preference for a fleet of surface as opposed to submarine vessels was known to be more vulnerable, the whole concept of mixed manning was abhorrent to them. Many politicians (including Macmillan) also shared these sentiments.[8]

FINANCIAL DIFFICULTIES

It was not simply that militarily the MLF proposal was regarded as being superfluous. Financially, too, the force described by the Americans sounded like a fairly expensive venture especially for a country that had just recently taken a costly decision to upgrade her nuclear deterrent. The NATO MLF plan far from being a 'one-off' payment of funds or weaponry, could involve, British government analysis suggested, a commitment of at least ten years. Moreover, if Britain did decide to participate in this force, the additional expenditure would almost certainly restrict or prevent Britain from being able to follow through with her own Polaris force. Technically, a report claimed, Britain's warhead programme would be 'stretched' even to provide for its own forces and financially it would be a formidable extra load on the defence budget. The pressure of having to manufacture additional warheads could prove not only crippling in terms of cost, but impractical and perhaps even impossible to produce.[9] By March 1963 estimated cost studies predicted that any British contribution would amount to something in the region of ten million pounds per year over a ten-year period.[10] On top of this, the United States was also insisting that as yet unattained NATO conventional force levels be met requiring an additional three to four hundred million pounds from NATO over a three year period.[11] Unwilling to incur more financial burdens, especially after the Chancellor warned that the country could simply not afford to spend any more money on defence, the Cabinet decided in March to try and avoid committing Britain to the proposal, stating:

> it would be important, particularly since the Nassau Agreement has not yet been signed, to avoid discouraging the United States in their attempts to win support for the concept of an inter-nationally-manned force, while at the same time avoiding any obligation to contribute to it...[12]

In addition, the British government was reluctant to consider such a large financial contribution because of an argument that had been going on for some time with the government of West Germany. The cost of maintaining the British Army of the Rhine (BAOR) was causing Britain serious balance of payments problems putting a not insignificant strain on the Exchequer. For their part, the German government had always refused to contribute directly to this cost.[13]

POLITICAL DIMENSION

If, militarily, the MLF proposal was an unnecessary addition to the Western nuclear deterrent, and financially its creation promised to impose heavy burdens on the participating countries, its value had to lie in the political field. The MLF advocates were attempting to sell the force by stressing the need for something to combat the disaffection and disunity permeating NATO. Playing down the military aspect as a 'useful addition', they concentrated instead on identifying the political need for such a force. The big political prize for the United States was the tying of West Germany securely and irrevocably to a strong Atlantic partnership. A large proportion of the Kennedy administration, including the president himself, believed that the German problem posed the most important challenge and possible threat to Atlantic unity. In a letter to Macmillan, Kennedy wrote:

the Germans are the heart of the problem, and I simply cannot escape the conclusion that one of the courses available to us in dealing with them, the MLF is the only safe one. If it fails, the Germans are bound to move in much more dangerous directions...[14]

The fear was that below the surface of moderate, co-operative, complacent Germany there was a groundswell of discontentment, tension and resentment centring on its non-nuclear status which, if not dealt with swiftly and completely, would explode in a dangerous lurch towards nuclearism, shattering in the process the relative stability of post-war order. This concern was reinforced by comments from certain German officials who seemed to be thinly disguising a pro-nuclear agenda. For example, von Hassel, the Minister of Defence, reportedly suggested in an interview that as soon as it became apparent that the multilateral force was about to become a military instrument, 'it must be possible to make the American partner waive the veto and bring about a majority decision for the political and military utilisation of the force'.[15]

In considerable contrast, however, Macmillan and his colleagues were unconvinced of Germany's aspirations to this end. There was some feeling in Germany, they acknowledged, that amounted to a mild resentment of the country's perceived inferior position in the world order but this was a natural sentiment which was highly unlikely to develop into anything dangerous.[16] The British government pointed to a number of reasons why this was likely to be the case. First, in 1954 the German government had voluntarily assumed an undertaking not to manufacture nuclear weapons and there was little or no evidence, Ministers remarked, that 'internal pressure in Germany for an effective share in some nuclear capability had yet reached a point at which the need to contain it could be used as a reason, which public opinion in this country would find convincing, for our consenting to the creation of a mixed manned force'.[17] This, according to the government, was simply not a realistic or probable course of action for Germany. In order for the Federal Republic to go down that path, the nation would first have to breach the international treaty that prohibited the manufacture of nuclear weapons on German territory. Such a move would almost certainly cause isolation from the rest of Europe and, more importantly, the United States, bringing with it not only the loss of friendship but the withdrawal of NATO's protective cloak, leaving West Germany vulnerable to the threat of domination by the forces of the Soviet Union. In addition to the certain exposure to aggression from the East, the political, economic and diplomatic isolation would leave Germany a very late starter in the nuclear game having no prior knowledge of nuclear bombs or delivery systems and without any suitable testing ground to enable them to catch up. Ostracised, the country's politicians would have to proceed without the help of allies which would save Germany crucial time and money. Fundamental to the survival of the country would be the speed at which the nuclearisation process took place.[18] Enormous costs would almost certainly prevent a rapid development and it hardly seemed likely to the British that the Soviet Union would stand idly by while her old adversary built up the capability to launch another even more deadly attack. Essentially, by deciding to acquire nuclear weapons, the German leadership would be signing the country's death warrant. Such a move would almost certainly strip Germany of its defences and its allies, and impose heavy financial burdens on its citizens. Meanwhile, the first indication of nuclearisation would alert the Soviet Union, who would swiftly move to prevent this development.[19] Quite simply, it was unlikely that Germany would be 'allowed' to chart this particular course.

Second, in order for Germany to avoid the punishing costs and fatal delay in attaining a nuclear status, it would have to seek an alliance with a current nuclear power.[20] The American argument was that Germany's nuclear ambitions might compel the country's leaders to turn to France and General de Gaulle's *Force de Frappe*. This would both enable Germany to circumvent the clause in the treaty forbidding the manufacture or ownership of nuclear weapons and remove the need for commencing with a brand new and unassisted nuclear programme. A joint venture with France would also remove the threat of complete allied desertion, although it would certainly cause major upheavals in NATO and especially in Germany's relations with the United States. This scenario was also deemed unlikely by the government in London. The notion that de Gaulle would share the fruits of France's labour was far-fetched to say the least. Anyone who was familiar with de Gaulle and his philosophies was fully aware of the French leader's intentions. The primary purpose of the *Force de Frappe* was to claim and preserve France's status as a first-rank world power. It represented the primacy of the nation-state and the theory that each nation was responsible for its own defence. De Gaulle might seek close relations with his neighbours, but suddenly to embark on a joint nuclear strategy would contradict everything he stood for.[21] The Cabinet concluded that 'if the Germans cannot make, or get, weapons of their own, need we pay too much attention to the fact that they would like to take an active part in the nuclear business?'[22]

Third, the British government had no reason to believe (as the Americans apparently did) that Germany would embark on a national nuclear route if denied participation in some form of multilateral force. German Ministers had consistently reiterated their commitment not to seek to develop a nuclear capability both in public and in private conversations with their British counterparts.[23] Thorneycroft received numerous assurances from the German Minister of Defence, who told him that 'in no circumstances will the Germans seek to acquire nuclear weapons of their own'. 'Neither do they intend', he added, 'to work with the French in the development of the *Force de Frappe*...'[24] On this, as a memorandum points out, they were reasonably certain:

> To the best of our judgement, there is no sign – rather the contrary – that the Germans hanker after control of their own nuclear warheads...[25]

If anything, British Ministers thought, Germany merely wanted the most concrete and irrevocable guarantee possible that the United States would not withdraw from Europe and leave them at the mercies of the Soviet Union. According to Lord Home, 'the Germans actually wanted to see the Americans physically in one ship with them...'[26] British scepticism was not assuaged by revelations during an Anglo-American defence conference in England in September 1963. In the course of discussions the American delegation were asked whether or not they had evidence to substantiate their claim that Germany was likely to embark upon a nuclear course if something was not done to prevent this. The answer the British received was evasive and totally unconvincing. Even when it was suggested that the sharing of such information might make it easier for the British government to agree to co-operate in the MLF venture, the American team could not offer anything of note.[27] Even if US thinking on Germany was correct (and Ministers severely doubted this), was limited participation in a multilateral nuclear force not more likely encourage interest in nuclear power rather than satisfy these dangerous aspirations? As Harold Wilson put it: 'if you have a boy and wish to sublimate his sex appetite it is unwise to take him to a striptease show...'[28]

Essentially, in British eyes, the MLF represented a costly venture that was designed to deal with a threat which in their opinion did not exist. Moreover, officials were concerned about the impact the proposal might have on the current test ban negotiations. Macmillan told a Cabinet meeting that the implications of a mixed manned force 'gave cause for serious anxiety, particularly in terms of its probable effect on the chances of securing an agreement to ban nuclear tests and to prevent the proliferation of nuclear weapons, which must', he stressed, 'remain our overriding objective'.[29] The prime minister had committed himself very publicly to working for this treaty (to such an extent that some officials in the Kennedy administration believed the British to be too favourable to a détente with the Soviet Union and perhaps a little 'soft'). Any move that might prejudice the outcome of these talks would reflect badly on Macmillan and his government, presaging accusations of having sold out on arms reduction and test ban policies in order to retain a vestige of the cherished 'special relationship'.

Finally, there was an element of suspicion within British government circles that the MLF proposal was not all that it seemed. Many believed that the Americans had ulterior motives in pushing the dubious plan and were trying to outmanoeuvre Britain and perhaps negate the recent Nassau concessions.[30] Although the original terms of the agreement were ultimately adhered to (the Polaris Sales Agreement was signed in April 1963), profound misgivings lingered in London about the sincerity of the Americans, as one official wrote:

> one cannot avoid the suspicion that by pushing the mixed manned force to the exclusion of all other provisions in the Nassau Agreement the State Department may be hoping to do precisely this, namely, transform our plans away from a British force to a British combination to a mixed manned force . . .[31]

THE SEARCH FOR A SOLUTION

Despite the fact that the MLF proposal appeared to the Macmillan government to have little merit, other considerations compelled them to study carefully their response to the American proposal. To begin with, Macmillan and his colleagues were anxious not to announce any decision that might antagonise the Kennedy administration, at least until after the Nassau Agreement had been finalised.[32] Because the two concepts (multilateralism and multinationalism) had been linked in the negotiations, there was a danger that a British refusal to consider the multilateral proposal as agreed at the Conference would cause the Americans to call the whole thing off. Although such a radical move was considered highly unlikely, it was nevertheless a possibility that was not beyond the bounds of reality considering the disastrous Skybolt episode not six months earlier. Since the December meeting, Macmillan and his colleagues had attempted to minimise the linkage between the two concepts, emphasising instead the independence of the British Polaris Force and Britain's desire to commit to a multinational NATO force. Strategy, therefore, concentrated on keeping an MLF option open for as long as possible without committing Britain to participating in either negotiations or actual planning. Macmillan also wanted to defer making a decision, at least until after the parliamentary recess in August or if possible until after the British general election, which was expected to take place in the autumn or following spring.[33]

The Anglo-American relationship was one of Macmillan's most fundamental policy successes. The prime minister was acutely aware of the fact that he had a very delicate tightrope on which to balance on and had to negotiate a steady path between keeping the Americans happy and preserving the successful Nassau deal of independent Polaris for Britain. Moreover, if Britain did decide to remain outside the multilateral force, Macmillan's government ran the risk of isolation from NATO decision-making, planning and targeting. If such a force were created, it would certainly become the central focus point of US NATO planning from which British nuclear forces would probably be excluded.[34] In these circumstances it would be unlikely that the United States would continue to attach the same importance to the maintenance of the 'special relationship'. The government feared a loss of prestige and ability to influence European and world affairs if they relinquished control over any future German participation in nuclear matters. British non-cooperation risked encouraging, some Ministers feared, a new US–German special relationship which would jeopardise and possibly replace the traditional Anglo-American intimacy much vaunted by Macmillan. The prime minister had too large a political stake in remaining strongly associated with the United States to consider seriously a move that would certainly alienate the present administration to the point where Britain lost this prize.[35] Another consideration pointed out by Lord Home in a Cabinet memorandum was the fact that British abstention from positive involvement in the proposed nuclear force would remove one of the key reasons used by Britain to justify its own nuclear deterrent. He informed his colleagues that:

> one of the arguments by which we have justified the retention of our own independent nuclear arm is that it will ensure that we will take our place by right in all discussions in bodies concerned with nuclear matters. If we are absent from the Board of the Multilateral force this argument will no longer hold.[36]

Macmillan did not want to commit himself to participation even in exploratory negotiations for fear that this concession would be taken as an indication of eventual compliance. The Cabinet did not find the decision an easy one. In the months after Nassau considerable pressure was put on the British to embrace the MLF positively – pressure from the Merchant and Ricketts Missions to Kennedy himself, who urged Macmillan to amend Britain's position in favour of the force:

> every day that passes makes it plainer that a move from the United Kingdom toward participating in the MLF will be a major step forward in our joint effort to bind the alliance safely and strongly together in the face of General de Gaulle's opposite course . . .[37]

Talks earlier in the month had not been very productive. Walt Rostow had attempted to convince Lord Caccia of the need to contain German nuclear ambitions, saying that 'the prize was within grasp'. 'That prize was to satisfy the German desire for some satisfactory participation in a nuclear force for . . . sooner or later . . . there would be a movement in Germany either to obtain an independent nuclear capacity of their own or to join with the French *Force de Frappe* . . .'[38] Caccia responded bluntly. He told the American that Britain had not yet seen 'clear and direct evidence of the German attitude' and that the military doubts and financial strains associated with the proposal made it highly unlikely that Britain would find itself in a participating role.[39] Information now reaching the government suggested that the United States wanted Britain to contribute warheads to the proposed force. A telegram from Ormsby-Gore outlined the current thinking across the Atlantic. He reported that the Americans were prepared to 'go a long way' to enable Britain to participate in the MLF venture.[40]

At a Cabinet meeting at Chequers in mid-May, the Foreign Office set out their view:

> Refusal by us to contribute to the force would be likely to have a deplorable effect on our relations with the United States and German Governments. Moreover, if the force were set up without us, we should probably lose all influence on its command and control arrangements, which may be of great international importance . . . If, on the other hand, the idea of the force collapses because of our refusal to join, we shall incur special blame from the United States; and the French, who have always argued that the Nassau proposals offered Europe nothing, will have won a major victory.[41]

Rather than turn the MLF proposal down flat, British tactics consisted of responding to the American prodding by replying that although prepared to listen to the arguments, Britain was unwilling to give any more of a commitment than to await the outcome of the studies being conducted.[42] In May, Macmillan telegraphed the Foreign Secretary in Ottawa instructing him how to approach the MLF discussions. He told Home: 'the important thing is to play this along and prevent any definite agreements being reached, still less announced, during the President's European visit'.[43] Macmillan had just sent this communiqué when another arrived from his Ambassador in Washington reporting a conversation with the president. It was evident that Kennedy was not thrilled about the current state of affairs. He told Ormsby-Gore that he was 'deeply committed to the Germans and did not see how it would be possible to go into reverse'. The president was very concerned that if the United States backed away from this policy, de Gaulle would be tempted to enter into a 'joint enterprise' with the Germans.[44] Ormsby-Gore was concerned about the damage that a British rejection of the proposal might have on Anglo-American relations. He warned the prime minister:

> Kennedy would be deeply disappointed and disturbed if that was our final decision. He would almost certainly feel compelled to go ahead without us . . . I fear that our relations with the United States would in future be significantly and adversely affected . . .[45]

By the end of the month Macmillan was presented with memoranda from his Secretary of Defence and Foreign Secretary detailing recommendations for dealing with the increasingly insistent American demands. The Foreign Office's position had shifted noticeably from an earlier downright opposition to the proposal. Now Home counselled co-operation:

> in judging our response to the multilateral force proposal we have to give full weight to its effect upon our relations with the US on the one hand and with Europe on the other, particularly the Germans and the Italians... Whatever the position may have been at Nassau, things have now moved further and faster... consequently the importance of the multilateral force lies mainly in the political field. The motives for establishing it are at the lowest respectable and at the highest imaginative, namely preventing the spread of nuclear weapons on a national basis and creating an arm which is international in the fullest sense...[46]

He concluded by admitting that a refusal to participate might thrust Germany into a new and intimate relationship with the United States at Britain's expense. Moreover, Britain would certainly lose any means of controlling the new nuclear force or influencing its use.[47] In short, the country risked losing the special Anglo-American relationship as a leadership role in Europe and NATO.[48]

In contrast, Thorneycroft's memorandum painted a very different picture. The Ministry of Defence had been opposed to the force since it was first proposed and had sought to discourage any serious consideration of the idea. Thorneycroft did not try to disguise this sentiment saying:

> the force would be of no significant military value to NATO. The additional power that it would provide would add nothing to the deterrent and would be superfluous to the military nuclear power that already exists... The net result of creating the force would therefore almost certainly be to weaken rather than strengthen Western defence...[49]

The subsequent Cabinet discussion questioned whether or not it would be better to be candid and tell the Americans that Britain was simply not interested in the MLF and did not want to participate:

> the American anxiety to persuade us to join implies that they still have serious reservations about going ahead on their own; and, if they do go ahead, it is not certain that a clear refusal on our part to participate (on French lines) would do us any more harm than half-hearted participation...[50]

Macmillan's government was still undecided and few believed that the decision was going to get any easier as the months wore on. Newspaper reports in the United States claimed that, despite saying that they would give the US case a thorough hearing, observers of British political affairs had been left with the conviction that the British hoped something would happen to lead to the scrapping of the idea.[51] Meanwhile, back in Washington, Kennedy and his staff had been discussing the proposal and the progress Merchant's negotiating team had made so far.

BACK IN WASHINGTON: REASSESSMENT OF THE PLAN

What had the Merchant Mission achieved? How strong and committed was support for the project in Europe? What did Kennedy and his top staff think of the proposal's chances of success? Did this differ from the assessment offered by Merchant and his staff? How strong was support for the force within the administration? Had this support grown since the Nassau Conference? Why did Kennedy allow the proposal to continue? If Kennedy himself was not convinced about the sagacity of the proposal, why then did he let it continue?

By the time Merchant arrived back in Washington he was convinced that every effort must be made to give the MLF proposal a fair chance of success. His visits to the European capitals had impressed on him the need for some sort of formula to bind Europe and the United States closer and more irrevocably together. The multilateral solution, while complex and fraught with difficulties, was the only strong contender presently available to the administration. He told Rusk:

> I return encouraged over the prospects for an MLF, of a character which is sufficiently responsive to certain of our European allies' desires and at the same time acceptable to the United States. A substantial element of the leadership of important members of the Alliance wants an MLF ... If the United States does not move with this European pro-MLF drive, Gaullist forces will be encouraged and Atlantic Community hopes set back ...[52]

He had managed to get qualified support from virtually all the countries visited, with the exception of Britain, where the government was reluctant to commit at any level. Not surprisingly, it was

West Germany that had displayed the most interest and agreed in principle to the setting up of a multilateral nuclear force. With Germany on board, the Italians, Merchant felt sure, would not back away from a tentative commitment after the Italian elections had produced another government. Cheered by the absence of strong negative reaction to the proposal, Merchant and his colleagues emphasised the need to have British participation.

While the delegation failed to gain a consensus on a number of fundamental elements of the MLF proposition, notably the type of force (i.e. surface or submarine), the control mechanism and specific cost sharing, they did manage to reach agreement on several points. The European allies accepted the fact that the force would be managed and controlled by its owners, assigned to NATO and integrated into the NATO military command structure. It was also agreed that no single member should contribute more than 40 per cent of the total cost and that an administrative body should be necessary to handle budgetary and other administrative matters. The concept of mixed manning was generally accepted, especially in relation to surface ships and general agreement held that the force should not hinder progress towards meeting conventional force goals.[53]

In a meeting with Kennedy, Merchant stressed the need for commitment and action.[54] He told the gathering that they now had the advantage of 'momentum'; 'delay', he cautioned, would 'lose this advantage'. Asking for new instructions authorising negotiations for a Preliminary Agreement, and presidential action with Adenauer, Fanfani and Macmillan to close out the possibility of submarines as an option, Merchant argued that at some future period the possibility of submarine-launched missiles should be considered as an addition to the force. On the vital points of costs and controls, the Ambassador suggested, further negotiations were necessary. He stressed, however, the need to have an exploratory agreement ready in time for the president's European visit in June. This was necessary if a final agreement was to be reached in time for presentation before Congress in the autumn (thus avoiding the presidential elections the following year). 'If we do not take the opportunity now', he told the meeting, 'it will fail'. Merchant's apparent success in Europe persuaded Kennedy to agree to press on with the mission.[55] The president decided to postpone Congressional consultation and to send letters to the German and Italian leaders to emphasise presidential backing and to gauge the support in those countries for the proposal.[56] To Adenauer, he wrote:

I have read with interest comments of all sorts on the multilateral force, and . . . it seems to me that it is the proper course now for us to move firmly forward on the basis of a proposal which is clearly good, and not to get bogged down in a profitless search for ideal answers which do not exist . . . I am convinced that if we can act promptly together we have a chance now to set in train an enterprise that can fix the direction of nuclear defense along safe and sound lines for future generations . . .[57]

In a letter to Italian Prime Minister Fanfani, Kennedy expressed his desire that the force proposal have the full backing of the Italian government:

Such a force . . . would meet the healthy desire of the great nations of Europe for a larger role in nuclear defense without contributing to the dangerous situation in which many nations throughout the world would own separate national nuclear forces. It would mark a long further step toward effective Atlantic cooperation, and give body and substance to the Atlantic Partnership . . .[58]

However, despite Merchant's enthusiasm, by this point it was difficult to know exactly what stage the MLF negotiations were at. The key issues of mode and control still plagued discussions. Secretaries McNamara and Rusk as well as Ambassador Merchant travelled to Europe for meetings with the various interested and not so interested parties. Admiral Ricketts was despatched to Bonn to try to convince the doubting Germans that accepting surface ships now would not preclude a change in the force's composition at some later date.[59] It also emerged that doubt surrounded the full extent of German acquiescence about the control issue. One staff member pointed out that recent discussions on the subject had consisted of Ambassador Dowling asserting the United States' position while the Germans offered no objection. This was a shade less affirmative, he suggested, than a position in which the Germans had spoken out positively on the issue.[60] This assessment was upheld with the arrival of a letter from Adenauer that essentially agreed to the American outline for the force, but added two important conditions: reconsideration of the use of the control formula and a re-examination of the surface ships/submarine debate after some years of operation.[61]

During the spring months, whilst the British Cabinet was debating the best way to handle the MLF pressure,[62] the Kennedy administration again debated the benefits and drawbacks of the proposal. In Europe, a period of 'lame duck' governments had brought things very much to a standstill. Not everyone in Washington, however, was convinced of the merits of the multilateral force. In April, Kitchen wrote a strong memorandum to Gerry Smith (a State Department consultant) on what he perceived as some of the dangers associated with the project:

> In my view if we are to stem the seep of missile technology from the MLF into national hands we must assure ourselves that our policy is based on a positive approach and that it truly meets national needs. I am by no means satisfied that the MLF, even if accepted by the Europeans as currently constituted, provides a satisfactory answer over the long term ... Indeed ... I am inclined to think that time is working against us, and that unless we can make something like the MLF truly responsive to *national* needs, technological breakthroughs will combine with national aspirations to thwart our non-proliferation policy. It is entirely possible this could occur even if the MLF is successful.[63]

Kitchen was also concerned about the feasibility of the proposal and suggested in a memorandum a number of alternatives that might also be taken into consideration including 'SAC internationalization' – substantial military and nuclear integration between the nations of Europe and the United States.[64]

Meanwhile, in Britain, Macmillan's government had still not given a definitive response.[65] In May, David Ormsby-Gore reiterated his government's position, telling Ball and Tyler that 'the trouble was that the UK Government had taken on recently a new commitment to buy Polaris missiles and build submarines and warheads for them'. 'The Prime Minister's idea', he told them:

> was that a UK national force would thereby be built up which would be added to, and thus form part of the multilateral force. HMG would naturally give the multilateral force 'a fair wind' and support it in general, but he doubted whether the UK would be prepared to assume a commitment to join in a mixed manned force and to accept a specific percentage of the costs of such a force.[66]

Bill Tyler was not surprised by the Ambassador's response and recorded his own thoughts on the British position:

> While David's position was obviously pretty negative, and doubtless reflects present UK thinking, I think that the political implications,

pro and con, of going in now or not going in, will sink in as the British consider the matter further.[67]

Kennedy quite possibly spoke to Ormsby-Gore about the situation, for by now he was frequently discussing British intransigence with the Ambassador. He also wrote to Macmillan stressing once again the need for reaching consensus on the MLF issue.[68] This was followed several days later by a letter urging Macmillan to make up his mind in support of the project.[69] By the end of May, the president was again being pressed to broach the subject of British intransigence with Macmillan.[70] The State Department presented another effort to persuade the prime minister to adjust his position. The memorandum that came through Rusk counselled:

> if it should appear in Europe that the MLF were losing momentum, the advantage would fall to de Gaulle, and much less satisfactory proposals for dealing with the nuclear problem would begin to be pressed.[71]

The letter suggested that the United States would consider going ahead without the United Kingdom and offered some possible changes to make it easier for the British to join:

> On the basis of a UK commitment to participate in this process, the formal convening of a multilateral drafting group could be postponed until August or September. In the meantime, the preliminary drafting process can be carried on quietly in the NATO headquarters in Paris, and, to some extent, in capitals . . .[72]

Macmillan's Cabinet had not managed to make a concrete decision and in his response to the president, the prime minister continued to stall.[73] The MLF advocates in the State Department responded immediately with a memorandum via Rusk to the president:

> this kind of delay would make it impossible for us to get a Treaty up to Congress by early January, as we have planned, in order to meet the problem posed by the fact that 1964 will be an election year . . . The best way to counter this tactic is probably to make clear to the United Kingdom that the train will not wait – that we have in mind going forward with the informal and unpublicized substantive discussions with interested countries . . . I believe that we should now focus on Rome, as well as London, in getting ahead with the MLF . . .[74]

But by June, the project was looking decidedly less robust than it had done a few months earlier, and Kennedy was beginning to entertain some serious doubts about the project and the manner in which it was being handled by some in his administration. He had recently learnt that Macmillan was under the impression that Britain's Nassau commitment was to contribute Polaris submarines to the NATO Nuclear Force and not necessarily to participate in the mixed manned element of this force.[75]

At some point in late May or early June the president requested that Kitchen prepare a 'fall-back' exercise of alternatives to the MLF proposal. Kitchen had been involved in the preparation of similar exercises in the past and had authored an earlier 'package' designed to provide a range of alternative proposals. The MLF was by no means assured. As Weiss (in the Bureau of Political and Military Affairs) wrote:

> it would appear that reinstituting the exercise is in order as a matter of prudence, if not as a reflection of the judgement that the MLF is, as was frequently reported about the recent demise of the Pope, close to expiration . . . It does appear from second-hand reports, that it is by no means a sure thing and, indeed, unless the British can be brought about to join the enterprise . . . it might have to be abandoned.[76]

Weiss in his memorandum pointed out a crucial problem facing an Administration that wanted to reassess this proposal and possibly the reason why the project had been left virtually unhindered in the last months – the fragmentation of views within the State Department and indeed throughout the government.[77]

Opinion may have been divided, but a conversation in Washington with Lord Home soon revealed to the president that considerable pressures emanating from his own bureaucracy were responsible for trying to pressure Macmillan's government into agreeing to involvement in the MLF project.[78] Schlesinger believed the president to have been 'surprised' at the hostility to the MLF in Europe and had thought that the Europeanists were correct in their assessment of the situation.[79] Some of his top advisers were also beginning to wonder out loud how the matter was being handled. Shortly before his departure for Europe, Kennedy received a long memorandum from his National Security Adviser, McGeorge Bundy. The latter pulled no punches in his criticism of the current state of affairs.[80] He wrote:

In Great Britain, where almost no one with any political standing is personally favorable to the MLF, the decision would be regarded as an extraordinary case of subservience to US pressure. We should not believe those who tell us that the Foreign Office is favorable; in unguarded remarks to others, Home and other Englishmen have indicated their doubts, and the few who are for it are for it because we are, and they wish to be loyal allies . . .

. . . There is no strong affirmative German sentiment for the MLF as something the Germans themselves want . . .

. . . If we press the MLF through in the next twelve months, we shall have only grudging support among the very people in whose interest the force has been designed . . .

. . . if this is an accurate picture of the troubles that lie ahead with the MLF, you may well ask how we got as far as we have. The answer, I think, is a double one: One turns on people and the other on policy. It happened that the people with the direct responsibility here (Ball, Merchant, Rostow, Schaetzel and Owen) were and are passionate believers in the MLF as a means of blocking national deterrents, General de Gaulle, and all other obstacles to European unity. They have pressed the case more sharply and against a tighter timetable, at every stage, than either you or the Secretary would have chosen. I myself have not watched them as closely as I should have, and more than once I have let them persuade me to support them where I might well have been more skeptical . . .

. . . The MLF is in trouble now, and we have a real problem in framing our next steps with it . . .

. . . It is essential that we not back away too sharply from the MLF. A hasty reversal would not only be wrong on the merits but very damaging to our prestige . . .[81]

Bearing in mind Bundy's warning about backing away from the proposal too sharply, Kennedy went to Europe in June stressing a need to promote Atlantic unity and co-operation, deliberately playing down the previous month's frantic efforts to sell the MLF in Europe. Discussing the situation with Adenauer in Bonn, Kennedy admitted that 'the picture had become somewhat obscure'. The two leaders agreed to keep the concept alive for a year or maybe more, judging that what was needed was 'a period of time to consider building up of alternatives as well as strengthening of existing mechanisms'.[82] On his return, the president again warned against trying to recreate any impression that the United States was trying to 'sell' the force proposal to reluctant European purchasers.[83] Allowing the talks to continue, he made it clear to his staff that he wanted to see the parameters of discussion expanded to allow for a full and comprehensive analysis of all the possible alternatives suspecting that the apparent lack of enthusiasm for the proposal was due to the 'failure to work through the alternatives'.[84]

Although the MLF negotiations continued, Kennedy's personal commitment to this particular policy had probably reached an all-time low. The failure of its advocates to identify and harness a strong positive demand in Europe for such an initiative compounded his suspicion that the idea had been unviable from the beginning.[85] Now, Kennedy's lukewarm endorsement of attempts to see the proposal bear fruit was extremely tentative and almost certainly contingent on other foreign policy developments and issues. Crucially, it was in the summer of 1963 that the test ban negotiations had again become a priority for the administration and a personal goal for the president. In a revealing conversation with his chief negotiator, Averell Harriman, Kennedy made his feelings about the MLF quite clear. During a discussion of the Ambassador's forthcoming mission to Moscow, the President suggested to him: 'our first response to this issue should be to repeat our argument that it was consistent with the purposes of non-dissemination.' But added 'if, however, there seemed to be some purpose in going beyond this in terms of the China problem or otherwise, Harriman should be guided by his judgement of how useful it was to indicate to the Soviets that in certain circumstances we might not need to go forward with this proposition . . .'.[86] Whether the president's willingness to shed the MLF became part of the official package is doubtful, but his lack of hesitation reveals just how much Kennedy had moved away from placing any real faith in its ability to deliver the promised goods.[87]

RENEWED EFFORT

By July Kennedy was losing patience.[88] Britain was still refusing to commit to participation and no real progress had been made. The Cabinet was still divided and generally felt that any decision should be postponed until after the Test Ban Agreement Talks had concluded.[89]

Word from the UK delegation to NATO had confirmed that while at one time Britain might have stood alone in its lack of enthusiasm for the MLF proposal, support in NATO for the scheme 'had now diminished considerably'.[90] The president suggested that a mixed manning trial on board an experimental ship might help the process along.[91] Pressure was again put on Britain to sign up to the proposal after the nuclear test ban treaty was signed in August.[92] This had created renewed enthusiasm in West Germany for the force that would provide physical reassurance that America would not withdraw from Europe.[93] In September it was beginning to emerge that some staff had been circulating much more positive reports than they were authorised to. Howard Furnas told Weiss that the project was moving along quite well and that he was very optimistic about the future. Furnas insisted that a recent meeting had reaffirmed that the White House was completely behind the proposal and that Kennedy believed it to be 'the only feasible solution to a very difficult problem'.[94] This confused Weiss, who had been under the impression that since the president's European trip, the proposal had been 'put on ice' so as not to cause problems for the administration if it should expire due to lack of interest.[95] David Klein suggested that the White House was motivated by two considerations:

> the President obviously wishes to avoid a blatant reversal or rejection of US policy. Accordingly, the single experimental mixed manned US vessel is intended as a transition toward a policy 'turn around' and . . . the White House desires to keep the MLF alive in the event that it can subsequently be utilized as a bargaining chip in Western–Soviet negotiations.[96]

When Bundy found out he was furious with the interpretation that Furnas and Schaetzel had been articulating and demanded that the latter withdraw and rewrite a memorandum relating to the meeting in question.[97] By the end of September, the Ministry of Defence and the Foreign Office had been unable to agree on an approach. Whereas the MOD had become more intransigent and opposed to the proposal, pressure from the United States had persuaded the Foreign Office to favour participation, if only to keep the 'special relationship' secure.[98] October finally saw Macmillan give way and announced that Britain would participate in talks about the MLF proposal without any commitment to actually participate.[99] The statement read:

if they are to take part in the discussions it must be on the clear understanding that it does not commit them to participate in such a force . . . subject to this reservation, the United Kingdom Government are prepared to join in an objective examination of the project in all its aspects and variations . . .[100]

Just prior to Britain joining the formal discussions on 7 October, Kennedy and Home met to talk about the MLF and the experimental ship that had been proposed. During the course of their conversation Kennedy revealed his current thoughts on the matter. He told Home:

> there was no hurry. The Germans were in no rush as long as they could see progress being made. The ship could sail around for as much as a year and a quarter or a year and a half and the Germans would be satisfied. By then we should know what the situation was. It was better to get the ship sailing than try to get an agreement on a blueprint for the MLF . . .[101]

What he was in fact saying was that the mixed manning exercise was a way of putting the MLF on ice until it became clearer how much real support the plan enjoyed.[102] So long as Germany was reassured that the United States had no intention of pulling out of Europe and NATO, they would be prevented from looking elsewhere for protection and security.

By the time the talks got under way, any momentum that had been built up was lost. Almost immediately disagreements about voting procedures and a control mechanism stalled the proceedings. Just over a month later, President Kennedy was assassinated in Dallas, Texas. The multilateral force idea was an unfinished legacy inherited by the new president, Lyndon B. Johnson.

Conclusion

In the period 1961–3, the 'special relationship' was beginning to be reassessed by elements within the new Kennedy administration who were increasingly coming to regard the close alliance as detrimental to America's other foreign policy interests. President Eisenhower's measures to restore close nuclear relations between the two countries was viewed as a mistake which was responsible for having created an artificial situation within NATO. The New Frontier in the United States largely consisted of a new generation of officials who did not have the same wartime collaborative ties or who had been too far down the ranks to develop any strong associations with Britain. Of those that had developed close ties during and after the Second World War, men such as Dean Rusk, George Ball, Robert Schaetzel and others, most had developed a more Europhile than Anglophile outlook. A number of Kennedy's senior staff, including Ambassador David Bruce, were much more 'European' in their outlook and had strong views about the unification of the continent rather than the prolongation of the 'special' Anglo-American relationship. These men were more interested in the ideas of multilateralism than bilateralism and believed that the United States should treat all its allies equally. In short, this was a period that saw Britain having to come to terms with the conflicting policies of independence and interdependence against a background of increasing debate in the United States about the existence of and necessity for a special relationship with Britain.

Against this backdrop Kennedy and Macmillan developed a quite remarkable relationship. Although a recent book on Macmillan by Lamb[1] claims that there was no meeting of minds, the wealth of evidence refutes this.

The two leaders, although widely different in so many ways, formed a bond that facilitated generally amiable exchange of views. This was obviously helped by the presence of David Ormsby-Gore who had known Kennedy for many years and was counted among the president's closest friends. The combination of Macmillan and Ormsby-Gore facilitated the development of unprecedented relations that saw an exchange of ideas and problems that would have been unthinkable between any other allies.

Before the period under review, an important change had taken place in Anglo-American relations. President Eisenhower had presided over the re-establishment of the close nuclear and defence relationship the allies had established during the Second World War. The changes in American atomic legislation had allowed Macmillan to extract a promise from Eisenhower to provide Britain with a weapon that would postpone the obsolescence of the V-bomber force (the mainstay of the British force) and thus the life of the independent British nuclear deterrent. The agreement reached at Camp David had enormous implications for the debate about the British independent deterrent – independence vs. interdependence – because it made Britain more dependent than ever on the United States. Ironically, however, this move towards integration and interdependency was taking place at a time when the United States was beginning to reassess the strategic doctrine of the 1950s and deciding that what was needed was a more flexible approach to defence that incorporated a formidable non-nuclear as well as a nuclear capability. This doctrine had little meaning for Britain which could not afford both a strong conventional as well as a varied tactical and strategic nuclear force. Having opted for a dependence on the nuclear, Britain relied on the acquisition of one single weapon that would ensure this capability. With two fundamentally different defence strategies and the dependence of one country upon the other, it is hardly surprising that cracks in the alliance began to appear. All the signs pointed to the fact that a crisis was imminent.

The story begins at Camp David with the question of whether or not Skybolt was the only choice the British government had when they approached Eisenhower for a weapon with which to replace the costly Blue Streak. It would now seem likely that Polaris *was* discussed as an option and that British politicians perceived that, at an unofficial level, even after they had decided on Skybolt, Polaris was never completely ruled out as an option.[2] Although efforts later in the year failed to secure any kind of promise relating to the provision of the weapon, even at a later date, Macmillan and his colleagues nevertheless remained confident that Polaris would in time become the next guarantor of the independent British nuclear deterrent. The crucial point is that the British government *believed* that Polaris had been secured or, at the very least, *could* be negotiated out of the US government at some future date. This is highly critical for future developments. The fact that the British believed that America had a moral obligation to provide Britain with an alternative weapon coloured perceptions of the crisis caused by the cancellation of Skybolt in December 1962. When this decision was announced by Secretary of Defense Robert McNamara, Macmillan, Thorneycroft and their colleagues felt justified in demanding the weapon that had been offered in 1960 when the deal had first been struck.

The agreement had other dimensions, again with implications for the later problems. There was a link between the Skybolt deal and Macmillan's agreement to provide America with docking facilities at Holy Loch. While the two 'deals' were never explicitly linked, the British government insisted at various times, especially when the Skybolt crisis broke in 1962, that they had been a quid pro quo. The only evidence to support this is a memo from Washington to the Foreign Office referring to the agreements. What is indeed worthy of note is the fact that this document does not contain simply a reference to these two deals, but refers to another element – a proposed NATO MRBM force. This would suggest that if the Skybolt and Holy Loch deals were indeed linked in an unofficial reciprocal agreement, then this also included the tacit acknowledgement to work towards the realisation of this nuclear force for NATO. This makes Britain's refusal to consider multilateral arrangements in 1962 and 1963, whilst berating the US government for first betraying and then misinterpreting the Nassau Agreement, sound lame to say the least.

Skybolt started out life badly. The rationale for this particular weapons system was already in doubt because questions were being asked about the future of manned bombers as a credible deterrent. The missile's designers had almost immediately to reinvent its use, redefining its role as a defence suppression weapon that would clear the way for other missiles to destroy targets on the ground. Ironically, this dubious role for Skybolt, which had questionable appeal for the American military, was a highly attractive weapon for Britain. It would give the ageing British V-bombers a stand-off capability that would be more than enough to deter aggressors, thus preserving Britain's ability to act unilaterally. Once again, differing needs and defence strategies were already threatening to cause problems in Anglo-American relations.

Negative reports reaching British officials about Skybolt were not scarce. Thomas Gates, the Secretary of Defense and his Deputy, James Douglas, never concealed their doubts about the project and whether or not it would overcome the enormous technical problems associated with the new technology it hoped to employ. Confusion over the intentions of the new administration followed a decision by Gates to cut the project's funding. Several scientific panels had recommended against the missile, confirming Gates' misgivings. The new Kennedy administration heralded fundamental changes in the way in which defence was assessed and structured. It was not long before the rationalisation practices of Robert McNamara began to identify the struggling project as an undesirable burden on resources. Having initially increased the missile's funding because he was sure that Gates' decision was not logical or practical, and would not prove either way how well the missile was performing, McNamara soon acknowledged that it would cost too much to overcome Skybolt's problems. The new Secretary of Defense, however, was not in a strong enough position to risk a fight with Congress or the powerful USAF over the project and, therefore, decided to keep it going until it was more expedient for him to make a decision and the situation was clearer. For this among other reasons, McNamara decided to keep his decision to cancel the weapons system as quiet as possible – something that would have serious consequences later on. The insistence on secrecy had implications for the creation of crisis conditions by allowing a veil of secrecy and fears of conspiracy to take over, with those who were opposed to Britain being given Polaris as a substitute to work without any formal supervision or authorisation. Those elements within the State Department who were unhappy with the idea of the British deterrent being propped up by Polaris swiftly moved into action with attempts to dissuade and prevent their superiors from offering this deal. Not enough discussion and interaction between the various agencies, groups and individuals within the administration enabled confusion to dictate policy and prevented the emergence until too late, of a coherent, well-thought-out approach to the problems facing the government.

McNamara's taking the matter onto himself increased the likelihood of problems emerging. The Secretary of State realised when he had received Thorneycroft's telegram that the British would have to be informed about his decision and set up a meeting with Rusk and Kennedy to tell them of his plans to cancel the missile. Although he agreed to inform and consult the British, other factors prevented him from successfully following his original line of thought. The Secretary of Defense was of the impression that once the British were informed about the probability of cancellation, they would prepare for this eventuality. Unfortunately, they did not. He also neglected to keep his own schedule and did not arrive in London before the cancellation news broke. McNamara still believed that everything was moving according to plan but was unaware that Macmillan had asked for and received a promise from Kennedy about consultation prior to cancellation. Kennedy, thinking that McNamara already had this under control, had not thought to reiterate the prime minister's vital requests to his trusted Secretary of Defense. McNamara, therefore, stepped off the plane in London and straight into a crisis, fanning the flames by recounting Skybolt's failures.

Another factor that bore some responsibility for the developing crisis was the deep links between the RAF and USAF and the other services. They kept in close contact and supported each other's policies and interests. The links they maintained were often more powerful than those shared by other inter-governmental agencies, especially over weapons procurement, research and development. In the case of Skybolt, the USAF had been in contact with the RAF before any official government inquiries had been initiated about the possibility of acquiring the weapon for the RAF.[3]

The question of whether or not the crisis was largely the result of a breakdown in communication depends on which side is being referred to. In Britain, there was enough information reaching the government to alert officials to the possibility that the weapon might not make it to its production phase. As early as November/December 1960, Macmillan and Watkinson discussed this possibility and even prepared a document containing alternatives to the weapon. Their correspondence indicates that they had serious doubts about Skybolt. Watkinson was in the best position to know. A great deal of the negative information reaching the Minister of Defence came from Sir Solly Zuckerman who had been from the earliest days a critic of Skybolt. Perhaps because the Chief Scientific Adviser had never backed the project, Watkinson stopped listening to disparaging reports, believing them to be unrepresentative of the true nature and potential of the programme. Moreover, the Minister of Defence was in receipt of information and reports from British personnel liaison with the project in the United States, the RAF and the Americans. All the channels of communication and procedures for reporting, according to the Minister of Defence, were 'most satisfactory'. In particular, the information from Skybolt's Progress Officer, Group Captain Fryer, must have played a substantial role in blinding both Watkinson and his successor to the realities of the Skybolt programme. In his correspondence, Fryer developed an intriguing style – outlining the difficulties associated with the project whilst delivering a personal, concluding assessment that never failed to offer optimism and encouragement – even during the darkest hours of the missile's life that turned out to be among its last. Although the Minister of Defence was aware of the ills of the programme, he was also given to understand that these would never develop into a fatal condition. Given the vast amount of information available to both Ministers of Defence, it should not have come as much of a surprise to the British government in late 1962 to find that the discouraging reports and subsequent rumours of cancellation turned out to be true. The truth about Skybolt had never been concealed, but the spin (originating with those who had a personal interest and desire to see the weapon succeed) had muddied the waters allowing Ministers to believe that all would be well. The British government, was, however, caught out and did not have any up-to-date cancellation alternatives prepared. Moreover, it was known at the highest levels that apart from the defence issues at stake (the preservation of the independent British nuclear deterrent), a potentially huge public relations disaster would almost certainly exacerbate the problem. Cancellation of Skybolt without an immediate replacement weapons system would plunge the government into crisis, forcing them to admit that Britain was entirely dependent on and apparently at the mercy of another country. At this point, the shutting down of channels of communication and therefore potential for debate was essential in order to allow Macmillan and Thorneycroft to prepare for an encounter with Kennedy. Macmillan and Thorneycroft did discuss the problem among themselves and with their top advisers.[4] Each had his own reasons for restricting talk and discussion on the matter. Macmillan was concerned that the Cabinet would be divided on the issue, especially as this was an important element of his party's electoral platform and of his own personal prestige. The prime minister wanted to deal directly with Kennedy, face to face, believing that this would afford him a better opportunity to convince the president to favour a package that would allow Macmillan to claim a victory. Thorneycroft had quickly set his sights on Polaris and, like Macmillan, he had his political career in mind and was anxious to avoid any accusations of incompetence or worse. The Minister of Defence had quickly reached the conclusion that Skybolt was not a viable option and that the only way Macmillan was likely to secure Polaris was for the prime minister to threaten a breach in Anglo-American relations. Ormsby-Gore was aware of Macmillan's mind turning to Polaris and knew that Thorneycroft had already weighed in behind the weapon. His job was to make sure the president understood the full implications of the potential for serious crisis and to make sure that all possible alternatives had been examined so that there could be no charge of negligence or incompetence.

On the American side, confusion abounded. There was a distinct lack of coherence in policy during the affair. McNamara and his staff were working on one agenda while Rusk and the State Department were following another. Not everyone understood, or indeed was clear, about what policy was being executed. At the highest levels, Kennedy, Rusk, McNamara and Bundy recognised that a problem existed and had agreed *before* Nassau a package that included Polaris. Problems began to emerge when lower-level officials and operators failed to grasp this deviation from official policy which stated that Britain should not receive any help to preserve or prolong the national nuclear deterrent beyond its natural life which was now coming to an end. Therefore, McNamara and the Department of Defense were working on the assumption that the cancellation of Skybolt, while potentially a major problem for the Kennedy administration with regard to Congress and other powerful bodies, did not view the matter as having serious implications for Anglo-American relations if Britain was afforded adequate time for discussions and consultation. In contrast, Rusk's State Department was desperately trying to avoid a situation where Polaris was offered as an alternative to the doomed Skybolt while Kennedy and Rusk did not interfere, believing the situation to be in the capable hands of McNamara. Kennedy, for his part, had somehow managed to miss the point of the various warnings he had received about the possibility of an Anglo-American crisis over Skybolt. He was told by Rusk, McNamara and Ormsby-Gore, but still failed to realise how serious the problem was until he was en route to the conference.

McNamara's confusion about the terms of the original agreement explains both his casual approach to the situation and his disastrous meeting with Thorneycroft in London. His poor briefing had perhaps the most serious implications for his handling of the Skybolt crisis. McNamara's approach depended on his concept of what the difficulty was and what was expected to be done for the

British in terms of the provision of a replacement. He was thinking in terms of a multilateral context and was replacing in his mind,
one weapons system with another. There was no thought of the
additional difficulties that a solution not tied to these parameters
would create. Had he known, there is little doubt that the Secretary would have approached the cancellation in a completely different
way. It is important to note that McNamara took the responsibility
for handling the cancellation upon himself after informing the president and Rusk of his intentions. They were also, therefore, under
the impression that the deal was multilateral and thus had no understanding of how the British were likely to react. In the meetings
before 16 December (when McNamara learned of his mistake), they
decided that Polaris should be considered as an alternative for Skybolt
providing that this could be agreed in some kind of multilateral
framework. Neither Kennedy, Rusk, nor any of the other players,
when these decisions were being taken, envisaged having to deal
with Britain asking for a bilateral Polaris deal with no strings attached until just days before the conference when the mistake had
been recognised and the crisis had already reached worrying proportions. This oversight did not give Kennedy or his advisers much
time to plan or prepare for the confrontation at Nassau. Given
these circumstances, it is hardly surprising that the meeting produced a hastily prepared and almost intolerably vague agreement.
     If McNamara did not know the basic premise of the 1960 Skybolt
deal it is fair to assume that the Secretary of Defense was not
familiar with the details of this agreement. Had he been better
informed, McNamara would have known that not only had Skybolt
been offered to the British in a bilateral context, but that the deal
contained a termination clause that provided a technical 'opt-out
clause' so that if the missile proved infeasible, either side could
pull out providing that they consult with the other. In short,
McNamara could have simply informed the British that Skybolt
was technically too complicated, cited the original agreement and
then entered into talks to discuss the provision of an alternative
weapon. He had the perfect way out, if he had only known and
been able to produce the evidence.
     It did not help that United States had been sending out mixed
signals to Britain about its nuclear deterrent and how the US felt
about it. On one hand, under Kennedy, the 'special relationship'
appeared to be flourishing – his administration had increased funding
for the Skybolt project and McNamara had told Ormsby-Gore that

Britain should not be hasty in giving up this force. On the other hand, McNamara and other highly regarded American figures like Dean Acheson had made very public speeches criticising, it seemed, Britain's deterrent and role in the world. Even though the American administration went to great pains to establish that McNamara's criticisms had not been directed at Britain, government Ministers strongly suspected that elements, especially within the US Department of State, actively desired the removal of Britain from the prestigious nuclear club. It was just not clear how much of this activity was officially sponsored or top-level policy. Matters were not helped by the fact that McNamara appeared to have been chosen as Kennedy's representative in charge of the Skybolt business. This was the man who only months before had been at the centre of a controversy surrounding America's attitude towards the British independent deterrent. Why had Kennedy chosen him? Observers in Britain could only speculate that this was part of a Kennedy administration agenda.

The Cuban Missile Crisis did not have the entirely negative impact on Anglo-American relations that has traditionally been attributed to it. The crisis in the Caribbean did play a part in the Skybolt crisis by numbing the Kennedy administration and distracting officials from the row that was brewing. But, there is little evidence to support the charge, levied first in the national press, that the affair caused great tension in the alliance and between Kennedy and Macmillan. It has now been shown that, if anything, the Cuban episode was considered by Macmillan to have been one of the most satisfying events he experienced because of the close and easy exchange of views he had with Kennedy. Cuba distracted, delayed and deadened but it did not create annoyances that, compounded with the cancellation of Skybolt, created a crisis. Macmillan, however, did not benefit from the success of his exchanges with Kennedy. The press and public were unaware of the details of what had gone on. The prime minister was reeling from a variety of domestic problems and crises. His popularity looked shaky, domestic policies like the 'pay pause' and entry into the Common Market had not gone down too well among voters and the Tory Party had suffered a number of alarming electoral defeats in the last year. In addition, several scandals including the Vassal case and the Profumo Affair had been very damaging to the Conservative Party's image.

The Nassau Conference produced a solution to the Skybolt crisis and in doing so, created a new set of problems and difficulties for the Anglo-American alliance. The 50–50 offer traditionally viewed as a belated and hastily improvised solution to the problem created by the cancellation has needed some clarification. Arthur Schlesinger, for example, believed it to have been a genuine attempt to produce an acceptable compromise. While this may have been a small consideration (there was a slim chance that Macmillan would find favour with the idea) Ormsby-Gore later confirmed that the proposal was more of a damage-limitation exercise, designed as proof that all possible alternatives had been considered. This point of view has been further reinforced by the revelation that Thorneycroft and McNamara had had a secret meeting on 15 December during which they discussed Polaris as the only possible alternative for the British government. One of the rationales behind this document was to ward off later accusations that the decision to cancel had been an attempt to prevent Britain from remaining a nuclear power. In this, its success is questionable.

The question about Kennedy's motives in overruling the majority of his advisers has been shown to be a complicated one. The president had a great number of wide-ranging pressures on him that contributed to his eventual decision. To begin with, Kennedy had grave reservations about the wisdom of giving Britain Polaris. He feared adverse French and German reactions and was concerned that this might prevent Britain from gaining access to the Common Market. He had no real desire to cause internal administration divisions about European or NATO policy to become more pronounced and personally did not believe the British deterrent to be of any real value to the defence of the West. On the other hand, the president felt some responsibility for the crisis (undoubtedly American confusion about the terms of the original Skybolt agreement had contributed to the crisis) and felt compelled to help out a fellow politician in need. More than this, Kennedy was concerned that refusal to furnish Britain with Polaris would force Macmillan either to adopt an anti-American stance or to turn to France for nuclear collaboration. The American national press had made it clear that an unfavourable outcome for Britain had the potential to damage the administration and hinted about how the bipartisan establishment would react to a British accusation of betrayal of the original Camp David agreement or a situation where the British Prime Minister might be forced to adopt an anti-American platform in order to remain in power. Also important was the sense that Kennedy had of Anglo-American relations as a tangible reality. While the promise of a united Europe was attractive, it was still a distant and rather elusive reality. It is clear that many of his advisers who advocated giving up the 'special relationship' had not grasped this yet. Macmillan, like Kennedy, had pressures limiting what he could agree to at Nassau. He needed an agreement that he could defend to his colleagues and to the public at home. Skybolt had been publicly discredited and Polaris had remained the only viable option. Macmillan was negotiating from a position of weakness and had little leverage – he could hint about possible Anglo-French nuclear collaboration, his government being forced to become anti-American and the possibility of a major rift in Anglo-American relations that could damage United States policies in Europe and towards NATO also. It is highly unlikely that the Conservative government would have fallen on the matter, but the crisis seemed so alarmingly volatile that it *appeared* that anything might have happened. The Kennedy administration had too much tied up in good relations with Britain to risk this being destroyed by a row over the cancellation of an unreliable and costly weapons system. Macmillan had been caught out badly and forced into a position where he had to choose between his key policies. The prime minister had hoped these might all have come to fruition around the same time, thus cementing both the party and his own personal position. He had doubts about whether he could rely on the full and unequivocal backing of his government.

The agreement itself was the result of bad preparation and planning arising out of the confusion and misunderstandings about the original deal and possible solutions to be offered at Nassau. The Americans were very badly prepared and certainly not clear about the phraseology and concepts being discussed and incorporated into the official agreement and government policy. In addition, there was a lack of relevant technical staff and military advisers on both sides who would normally be expected to be present at such a meeting. The result was ambiguity that could be translated into a victory for both sides. For Macmillan, the agreement secured the preservation of the independent nuclear deterrent at such low cost to Britain. For Kennedy it meant the avoidance of a major crisis with America's closest ally and the opportunity to initiate a new approach to de Gaulle and a possible solution to the NATO problems that had been worrying the administration. Especially for the multilateralists on Kennedy's staff, this was an optimal chance to see the MLF proposal backed as official government policy.

One of the key elements in the Nassau treaty was the agreement to work for a multilateral solution to NATO's nuclear problems. The MLF exponents in the Kennedy administration believed in the existence of a latent German nationalism that would propel the country to seek the acquisition of nuclear weapons as a symbol of prestige and as a means of influencing affairs. They also perceived the need to find a formula that would enable them to rebuild relations with France. The multilateralists saw the MLF proposal as a way of getting rid of the 'special' Anglo-American relationship so that America's relations with all her other allies might be conducted on the same level basis, thus removing the accusations of discrimination and favouritism frequently levied by France. They hoped that the proposal would also promote and maintain political cohesion in the Atlantic Alliance – a new co-operative venture might be just what was needed to stimulate fresh commitment to NATO and keep alive the concepts of Atlantic Partnership. By giving all the allied partners some insight into the many aspects of nuclear weapons planning, targeting and decision-making that had been denied them before, non-nuclear countries might be discouraged from wanting to become nuclear powers.

Another factor that seems to have motivated Kennedy and his advisers was a report that claimed that General de Gaulle was contemplating some sort of direct bilateral negotiations with the Soviet Union without the involvement of the United States, Britain or the rest of NATO. This caused a considerable degree of concern in Washington where it was worried that this would have disastrous consequences for Berlin, West Germany and the NATO alliance.

Kennedy's staff was divided and Kennedy himself wavered in his commitment to the proposal. He was initially very cautious and made it clear that he wanted the proposal explored with the European partners and not pushed down their throats. Over the months he become more convinced that something needed to be done to prevent West Germany from becoming a nuclear power in the future and believed that the MLF was a good enough idea if it was accepted by all the Europeans. Increasingly, however, British intransigence puzzled and worried the president. He had really no desire to proceed without the acquiescence of Macmillan and Britain. Indeed, as the test ban talks began to look more promising and the European allies appeared not as keen as had been reported, Kennedy began to show less support until he appeared willing to sacrifice the MLF in order to get the test ban treaty.

The president's personal views were made evident in two very revealing conversations, one with Ambassador Averell Harriman and the other with the British Foreign Secretary, Lord Home. In the first he gave Harriman, the American representative at the test ban talks, permission to discuss the MLF as a possible bargaining chip if the Ambassador thought this would entice the Russians to make a good deal. In the second conversation, Kennedy revealed to Home his thoughts about the mixed-manned experimental ship he had proposed saying that it was a way of buying time and stalling the proceedings without causing much fuss.

It is now clear that even West Germany – the principal country at which the proposal was intended – was less enthusiastic about the proposal than it was about appearing to please the United States. The Germans feared that the United States was pushing the MLF proposal because of a desire to see more European commitment and participation in the defence of Europe. If the NATO countries did not respond to this they feared that America might withdraw and leave Europe to its own devices. For this reason, and because the German government wanted physical reassurance that America intended to remain, they responded to the MLF proposal very positively. Even in spite of this deep-seated fear of America abandonment, however, West Germany did not embrace the proposal without reservation. They preferred (as did Italy) submarines as opposed to the surface ships proposal.

Britain was always reluctant to show any support for the MLF proposal. The ambiguity of the Nassau Communiqué allowed the government to claim that Macmillan had agreed simply to discuss the venture and that nowhere in the agreement had Britain agreed to participate in such a force. As the months passed, Britain came under increasing pressure from the United States to look favourably upon the proposal. The British government was unconvinced for a number of reasons. First, Macmillan and his colleagues believed that there was no convincing military justification for the creation of the proposed Multilateral Nuclear Force. British studies and meetings with American officials like Admiral Ricketts failed to convince them of anything other than the fact that this was a costly initiative that would add nothing to the defence of the West. Moreover, the mixed-manning component demanded by the Americans in order to prevent Germany or any other country from seizing control of the vessel was judged by experts to be impossibly impractical. For financial reasons too, British politicians did not like the proposal. The resources required would almost certainly detract

from the rapid creation of Britain's own Polaris fleet since a contribution to the MLF would not be limited to a one-off payment
but would stretch possibly to a ten year commitment. In short, it
was highly unlikely that the country could manage to do both. The
United States had admitted that the military and financial considerations were not attractive, but that the real value of the force lay
in its political charms. The MLF promised to combat the disaffection and disunity currently pervading the NATO organisation by
pulling the alliance together in a cohesive and co-operative venture. The proposal promised to tackle the 'German problem' by
giving West Germany a safe outlet for the latent nationalistic elements that threatened to thrust the country down the nuclear path.
The problem Macmillan and his colleagues had with this reasoning
was that they simply did not believe such a nuclear appetite existed in Germany. At the very most, they acknowledged, recent
American efforts to convince the Germans of the desirability of
signing up to this proposal may have inadvertently stimulated some
new interest in nuclear weapons. However, prior to this, and in
general, the British government felt that there was no convincing
evidence to support the theory that Germany was dangerously close
to becoming a serious problem. Too many factors made this possibility highly unlikely, not least of all because for Germany to embark
upon a nuclear course the country would have to give up the protection of the United States and face the unhappy wrath of the
Soviet Union alone and unprotected.

Despite all these factors, Macmillan and his colleagues did not
find it easy to tell the Americans that Britain had no wish to participate in the scheme and would not do so. Other considerations
compelled the prime minister to walk a careful line that did not
commit him either way. Macmillan tried to put off giving Kennedy
a definitive answer for fear that a negative reply would endanger
both Britain's chances of securing the Polaris missiles promised at
Nassau and perhaps damage the 'special relationship'. There was
also a fear that this might be replaced by a new German–American
special relationship. The prime minister hoped that if he were able
to avoid making a British commitment one way of the other, the
proposal would eventually be dropped due to lack of interest and
firm promises of commitment from the other NATO allies. In that
way, Britain would not suffer the rebukes or displeasure of the
United States in a way that might cause serious damage to the
relationship. Negotiations had not begun long in October 1963 when

they ran into trouble. Disagreements about voting procedures and a control mechanism prevented any real progress from being made before the death of President Kennedy. Afterwards, the MLF survived under Johnson who initially gave it his full support only to withdraw it later when he realised that the proposal was nowhere as near fruition as he had been led to believe.[5] Eventually, it disappeared from sight, never having succeeded in gaining the support of the countries in whose interest it had first been proposed.[6]

The Kennedy presidency was a period in which the Cold War became sharply focused and defence issues highlighted in an unprecedented time of near-confrontations threatening nuclear holocaust. Crises over Berlin and Cuba assailed the NATO alliance and prompted determined individuals to reassess and attempt to shore up the Atlantic Partnership. The remarkable friendship that developed between President Kennedy and Harold Macmillan undoubtedly strengthened the Anglo-American alliance, reaffirming it as the lynchpin of the NATO pact. Macmillan's ambition to see the 'special relationship' restored was successful. So much so that, in December 1962, Kennedy overruled the advice of a greater portion of his government and executed the most public U-turn in American foreign policy possibly seen this century. Although Macmillan's critics later decried the deal over Polaris as a betrayal, the Nassau Agreement confirmed Britain's pretensions to being a nuclear power well into the 1970s. One of the side-effects of the conference was the elevation of the Multilateral Nuclear Force proposal causing bitter debate and acrimony to pervade the alliance for the remainder of the Kennedy presidency. Under Kennedy and Macmillan, the 'special relationship' was revived. Even though a vast majority of the Kennedy administration (including the president himself) believed the British determination to preserve the independent nuclear deterrent at all costs was an act of folly, this did not prevent the administration from supporting this decision at a crucial time for Britain.

After Kennedy's death, the new opportunity afforded to the Anglo-American alliance slipped away. This was more than simply the loss of a bright, charismatic president who had befriended an ageing, skilful politician; after the Kennedy presidency the emotional commitment to and desire for a 'special relationship' was lost amidst the changing personalities and circumstances. It has never truly disappeared but lingers on no doubt to be recaptured again, if and when the need arises.

Notes and References

INTRODUCTION

1. R. E. Neustadt, *Report to the President: Skybolt and Nassau, American Decision-Making and Anglo-American Relations*, November 15, 1963, Box 322–323, Staff Memoranda, Meetings and Memoranda, 'Skybolt and Nassau' 11/63, NSF, John F. Kennedy Library (JFKL), Boston, USA.
2. For an excellent account of the period leading up to the Kennedy presidency, see Jan Melissen, *The Struggle for Nuclear Partnership: Britain, the United States and the Making of an Ambiguous Alliance 1952–1959* (Styx Publications: Netherlands, Groningen, 1993); and Timothy J. Botti, *The Long Wait: The Forging of the Anglo-American Nuclear Alliance, 1945–1958* (Greenwood Press: Westport, CT, 1987).
3. Andrew J. Pierre, *Nuclear Politics: The British Experience with an Independent Strategic Force, 1939–1970* (Oxford University Press: London, 1970), p. 234.
4. Ian Clark, *Nuclear Diplomacy and the Special Relationship* (Clarendon Press: Oxford, 1994), pp. 4–5.
5. Clark, *Nuclear Diplomacy*, p. 6.
6. Clark, *Nuclear Diplomacy*, p. 425.
7. Clark, *Nuclear Diplomacy*, pp. 425–6.
8. John Baylis, *Ambiguity and Deterrence: British Nuclear Strategy* (Oxford University Press: New York, 1995), p. 318.
9. Baylis, *Ambiguity and Deterrence*, pp. 322–4.
10. Baylis, *Ambiguity and Deterrence*, pp. 324–5.
11. Although great deal of new evidence has recently become available, many documents (including the relevant files in DEFE 4, 5 and 6) still remain closed.
12. Richard Reeves, *The Kennedy Presidency* (Papermac: London, 1994), p. 474.
13. Neustadt, *Report to the President*, p. 129.

CHAPTER 1   SPECIAL RELATIONS?

1. Paper: 'The Policies Affecting the Anglo-American Alliance' (redraft) from the US Embassy in London to BNA, State Department, 6 January 1961, Box 1236, RG 59, general records of the State Department, Central Decimal Files, 1960–1963, Folder 611.41/1–1361, National Archives.
2. Evidence of the 'special relationship' can be identified after its supposed decline in the 1960s. See John Dickie, *'Special' No More: Anglo-American Relations: Rhetoric and Reality* (Weidenfeld & Nicolson: London, 1994).
3. Conversation between Sir Nicholas Henderson and the author.

4. Henry Kissinger, *The White House Years* (Weidenfeld & Nicolson: London, 1979), p. 90.
5. *Hutchinson Dictionary of Scientists* (Helicon Publishers: Oxford, 1996), p. 210.
6. The fact that the fission process had been discovered in Germany by Otto Hahn in December 1938 prompted British intelligence fears that Germany might take the lead in this field. See Pierre, *Nuclear Politics*, p. 14.
7. American scientists had been concentrating on atomic fission as a source of energy.
8. The British government feared that nuclear secrets might find their way to Germany via the United States which was not at war at this time.
9. The British radar programme exacted increasingly heavy demands on finances while German advances made security an issue in Britain that had to be taken seriously.
10. Margaret Gowing, *Nuclear Weapons and the Special Relationship*, in W. M. Roger Louis and Hedley Bull (eds.), *The Special Relationship: Anglo-American Relations since 1945* (Oxford University Press: Oxford, 1989), pp. 118–19.
11. Pierre, *Nuclear Politics*, p. 15.
12. Botti, *The Long Wait*, pp. 22–3.
13. Secret wartime Quebec and Hyde Park agreements guaranteeing co-operation and consultation which might have had some bearing on the legislation had apparantly been 'lost' in the United States. Margaret Gowing, *Britain and Atomic Energy 1939–45* (Ma cmillan: London, 1964), p. 447.
14. McGeorge Bundy, *Danger and Survival: Choices about the Bomb in the First Fifty Years* (Schwartz & Wilkinson: Melbourne, 1990), p. 463.
15. Rosecrance and Dawson, 'Theory and Reality in the Anglo-American Alliance' (*World Politics*, October 1966), pp. 24–5. In return, Britain gave up the right, secured under the Quebec Agreement, to be consulted by the United States before the latter decided to use her nuclear arsenal.
16. Harold Watkinson, *Turning Points: A Record of Our Times* (Michael Russell: Salisbury, 1986), pp. 144–5.
17. According to Sir Nicholas Henderson, this defence relationship was 'crucial' to Britain. Conversation with the author.
18. S. J. Ball, 'Military Nuclear Relations Between the United States and Great Britain under the Terms of the McMahon Act, 1946–1958' (*The Historical Journal*, 38, 2 (1995), p. 441.
19. J. Baylis, *Anglo-American Defence Relations 1939–1980: The Special Relationship* (Macmillan: London, 1984), p. 35.
20. Peter Malone, *The British Nuclear Deterrent* (Croom Helm: London, 1984), p. 8.
21. John Baylis, *Ambiguity and Deterrence*, p. 236.
22. John Simpson, *The Independent Nuclear State: The US, Britain and the Military Atom* (Macmillan: London, 1983), pp. 113–14.
23. *Agreement for Cooperation Regarding Atomic Information for Mutual*

Defence Purposes, cmd. 9555; *Agreement for Cooperation on the Peaceful Uses of Atomic Energy,* cmd. 9560.

24. According to Ball, the United States Atomic Energy Commission (AEC) attempted to block this transfer of atomic information and weapons. This was ignored by the US military who had an informal agreement with their British colleagues rather than a formal inter-governmental agreement. See Ball, *Military Nuclear Relations*, p. 450.
25. Malone, *The British Nuclear Deterrent*, p. 74.
26. Macmillan was Eden's Chancellor of the Exchequer at the time of the crisis. He had been a strong advocate of intervention before changing his mind at rather the last minute.
27. W. Scott Lucas, *Divided We Stand: Britain, the US, and the Suez Crisis* (John Curtis, Hodder & Stoughton: London, 1991), p. 1.
28. Admiral Sir James Eberle, *The Military Relationship*, in W. M. R. Louis and Hedley Bull, *The Special Relationship: Anglo-American Relations since 1945*, p. 51.
29. Telegram from US Embassy in London to State Department, 17 July 1961, Box 170, JFKL.
30. Simpson, *The Independent Nuclear State*, p. 121.
31. Pierre, *Nuclear Politics*, p. 139.
32. Ball, *Military Nuclear Relations*, p. 452.
33. The previous year a total of five separate sets of Anglo-American discussions connected with nuclear energy were taking place. See Simpson, *The Independent Nuclear State*, p. 121.
34. Ernest R. May and Gregory F. Treverton, 'Defence Relationships: American Perspectives', in W. M. Roger Louis and Hedley Bull, p. 169.
35. Admiral Sir James Eberle, *The Military Relationship*, p. 151.
36. Coral Bell, 'The Special Relationship', in M. Leifer (ed.), *Constraints and Adjustments in British Foreign Policy* (Allen & Unwin: London, 1972), p. 119.
37. 'Britain Through American Eyes', Planning Section, Western Organisations and Planning Department, 13 Feb. 1962, PREM11/5192, PRO.
38. Paper on 'The Policies Affecting the Anglo-American Alliance' (re-draft), 6 January 1961, Box 1236, RG59, general records of the Department of State, Central Decimal File, 1960–1963, Folder 611.41/1–1361, National Archives.
39. *The Times*, 2 August 1963.
40. Clark, *Nuclear Diplomacy*, p. 46.
41. Alistair Horne, *Macmillan, 1957–1986, Volume 11* (Macmillan: London, 1989), p. 279. Macmillan also wrote in his diary: 'Ike was my friend and Britain's friend . . .'. Harold Macmillan Diaries (HMD), d. 42, 11 June 1961.
42. Horne, ibid., p. 280.
43. In one of his less melancholic moods, he recorded in his diary: 'it looks as if Kennedy is going to win this Presidential election. He seems definitely to be gaining ground . . . On the whole, I feel that Kennedy and Johnson will be more friendly than Nixon, Cabot Lodge etc. – that is, the Republicans without Eisenhower . . .'. HMD, d. 39, 20 October 1960.

44. HMD, d. 42, 25 June 1961.
45. Henry Brandon, Oral History, p. 2, JFKL.
46. Horne, *Macmillan*, p. 282.
47. Arthur M. Schlesinger Jr., *A Thousand Days* (André Deustch: London, 1965), p. 85.
48. Horne, *Macmillan*, p. 282.
49. David Nunnerley, *President Kennedy and Britain* (The Bodley Head: London, 1972), p. 33.
50. Schlesinger, *A Thousand Days*, p. 76.
51. Horne, *Macmillan*, p. 289.
52. Walt Rostow, Oral History, p. 142, JFKL.
53. Nunnerley, *President Kennedy and Britain*, p. 31.
54. The PT-boat incident caused Kennedy irreparable damage to his already weak back.
55. James Reston was convinced that Kennedy's appeal lay in his style: 'if you study Kennedy's wit, Kennedy's style, it is not an American style at all, it's a House of Commons Back-bench style . . .'. Reston, Oral History, p. 1, JFKL.
56. Horne, *Macmillan*, p. 289. An indication of the sense of fun the men shared was clear during their last meeting at Birch Grove when they decided to play a practical joke on their advisers by pretending to suggest seriously that a Russian be made Commander-in-Chief of NATO and that the Warsaw Pact and NATO should join in a defensive alliance against China. Harold Macmillan, *At The End of the Day* (Macmillan: London, 1973), pp. 474–5.
57. Horne, *Macmillan*, p. 287.
58. Horne, *Macmillan*.
59. HMD, d. 41, 26 March 1961.
60. Horne, *Macmillan*, p. 293.
61. Bundy, Oral History, p. 2, JFKL.
62. Nunnerley, *President Kennedy and Britain*, p. 28.
63. Kohler to Secretary of State, 31 March 1961, Box 1236, RG59, General Records of the Department of State, Central Decimal File, National Archives.
64. Kennedy took Macmillan's advice and decided to disengage and work for a neutral Laos instead of intervening militarily.
65. Nunnerley, *President Kennedy and Britain*, p. 30.
66. Nunnerley, *President Kennedy and Britain*.
67. HMD, d. 42, 11 June 1961.
68. Ormsby-Gore, speech to The Pilgrims of the United States, 14 November 1961, POF, Box 127, Countries, UK general, 6/61–12/61, JFKL.
69. Nunnerley, *President Kennedy and Britain*, p. 39. Macmillan himself confirms this in one of his diary entries where he says: 'the position of our Ambassador – David Gore is unique. He is *very* close to the President and generally gets on well with the State Department . . .' HMD, d. 45, 6 May 1962.
70. McGeorge Bundy, Oral History, p. 1, JFKL.
71. HMD, d. 45, 6 May 1962.
72. For Macmillan this was something of a front. He projected the

'unflappability' image as part of his political image of a wise and capable statesman. In reality, Macmillan was a highly nervous individual, prone to nausea before a speaking engagement, a constant worrier and prone to bouts of introspection and depression.

73. Nunnerley, *President Kennedy and Britain*, p. 36.
74. Schlesinger, *A Thousand Days*, p. 431.
75. Horne, *Macmillan*, p. 304.
76. McGeorge Bundy, Oral History, p. 3, JFKL.
77. Horne, *Macmillan*, p. 305.
78. Correspondence between Carl Kaysen and the author.
79. For Key texts on the Missile Crisis, see Robert F. Kennedy, *13 Days: The Cuban Missile Crisis, October 1962* (Macmillan: London, 1968); James G. Blight and David A. Welsh (eds), *On The Brink: Americans and Soviets Re-examine the Cuban Missile Crisis* (Farrar, Strauss & Giraux: New York, 1990); James G. Nathan, *The Cuban Missile Crisis Revisited* (St. Martin's Press: New York, 1992); Peter Boyle, 'The British Government's View of the Cuban Missile Crisis' (*Contemporary Record*, 10: 3 Autumn 1996); Gary D. Rawnsley, 'How Special Is Special? The Anglo-American Alliance During the Cuban Missile Crisis' (*Contemporary Record*, Vol. 9, No. 3, Winter 1995); Len Scott and Steve Smith, 'Lessons of October: Historians, Political Scientists, Policy-Makers and the Cuban Missile Crisis' (*International Affairs*, Vol. 40, No. 4, 1994); Len Scott, 'Back from the Brink: The Cuban Missile Crisis Revisited' (*Modern History Review* Vol. 9, No. 3, 1995); Len Scott, 'Close to the Brink? Britain and the Cuban Missile Crisis' (*Contemporary Record* 5 Winter 1991).
80. According to Dickie, Macmillan learned of the crisis on 17 October – a full five days before he was officially informed on 21 October. See Dickie, *'Special' No More*, pp. 106–9.
81. Conclusions C.C. 63 (62) Cuba, Minute 2, CAB 128/39 PT2, PRO.
82. Lord Home, *When The Wind Blows* (Collins: London & Glasgow, 1976), p. 179.
83. Macmillan to Kennedy, 29 April 1962, POF, Box 127, Countries, UA Rep-UK general, Folder 7, JFKL.
84. Although Kennedy had a high regard for Macmillan, this did not prevent him from feeling that the British nuclear deterrent was 'a political necessity but a piece of military foolishness'. McGeorge Bundy, Oral History, p. 3, JFKL.
85. Macmillan's Visit 27–29 April 1962 Scope Paper, RG59, Box 03, General Records of the State Department, Deputy Assistant Secretary for Politico-Military Affairs, Subject Files 1961–63, Messmer (memcons) to Mr Ball's Presentation to NAC, Folder of Macmillan's Visit 1962. National Archives.
86. Policy Directive: NATO and the Atlantic Nations, Washington, 20 April 1961, Document No. 100, Vol. XIII, FRUS.
87. Dean Rusk, Oral History, p. 198, JFKL.
88. Theodore C. Sorenson, Oral History, p. 101, JFKL. Britain also had an asset that was important to the United States as a letter from the Minister of Defence to Macmillan reveals 'McNamara has formally

confirmed to me the position originally set out by General Twining, namely that the Americans attach far greater importance to Britain maintaining her position in S. E. Asia, the Indian Ocean, Aden and, so long as we can, East Africa, than to making a larger contribution to NATO . . .'. In the margin he wrote that McNamara did not want to be quoted on that. MoD to PM 19 December 1961, PREM 11/3782, PRO.

89. Kennedy to Macmillan, POF, Box 127, Countries, UK general 1/63, JFKL.

CHAPTER 2   THE ORIGINS OF A CRISIS

1. Blue Streak was regarded as having no military value by the Chiefs of Staff who recommended that it be cancelled in favour of Skybolt. Chiefs of Staff Committee, Confidential Annex to C.O.S. (60) 11th Meeting, 16 February 1960, DEFE 4/124, PRO.
2. Timothy J. Botti, *The Long Wait: The Forging of the Anglo-American Nuclear Alliance, 1945–1958* (Greenwood Press, Westport, CT, 1987), pp. 22–3. Martin S. Navias, *Nuclear Weapons and British Strategic Planning 1955–58* (Clarendon Press, Oxford 1990), p. 16.
3. Navias, *Nuclear Weapons*, p. 14.
4. Prime Minister Attlee said of the period before the setting up of NATO: 'At that time we had to bear in mind that there was always the possibility of [the United States] withdrawing and becoming isolationist again. The manufacture of a British atom bomb was therefore at that stage essential to our defence.' F. Williams, *A Prime Minister Remembers* (William Heineman: London, 1961), p. 119. See also Clark and Wheeler, *The British Origins of Nuclear Strategy 1945–55* (Clarendon Press: Oxford, 1989), p. 214.
5. Memorandum: 'Preliminary Political Considerations', Appendix 'B' (continued), undated, DEFE 4/127, PRO.
6. While there was concern about the United States withdrawing its protection, in some minds the fear was quite the opposite with some believing that it might drag Britain into a nuclear war over issues only peripheral to British interests.
7. Fear of nuclear proliferation was one reason why Britain chose to pursue a nuclear relationship with the United States and not any of her European allies. Jan Melissen, *The Struggle for Nuclear Partnership*, p. 54.
8. C. Gordon, 'Duncan Sandys and the Independent Nuclear Deterrent' in I. Beckett and J. Gooch (eds), *Politicians and Defence* (Manchester University Press, Manchester: 1981), p. 14.
9. According to Botti, it was around this time that a noticeable shift occurred in American objectives and policy as they began to consider seriously whether co-operation with Britain might accelerate the growth of their joint atomic strength vis-à-vis the Soviet Union. Botti, *The Long Wait*, p. 244.
10. Andreas Wenger, *Eisenhower, Kennedy and Nuclear Weapons* (Rowman

& Littlefield Publishers: Lanham, MD, 1997), p. 49. For an excellent account of Eisenhower's 'New Look', see Saki Dockrill, *Eisenhower's New Look National Security Policy 1953–1961* (Macmillan: London, 1996).

11. David N. Schwartz, *NATO's Nuclear Dilemmas* (Brookings Institute: Washington, 1983), p. 22.
12. Schlesinger, *A Thousand Days*, p. 261.
13. In addition, as Saki Dockrill points out, Eisenhower and his team might not have foreseen how expensive it would become to maintain a nuclear deterrence favourable to the West, nor the problems the effort would create. Dockrill, *Eisenhower's New Look National Security Policy*, p. 218.
14. Melissen, *The Struggle for Nuclear Partnership*, pp. 36–8. Botti, *The Long Wait*, pp. 171–4.
15. The late 1950s version of the later 'missile gap' was the 'bomber gap'. It was believed for a time that the Soviet Union had a much larger bomber capacity than the United States. Like the 'missile gap', this too turned out to be fictitious.
16. According to Melissen, cohesion within the Anglo-American nuclear alliance was considered of central importance for the achievement of an arms control agreement. Melissen, *The Struggle for Nuclear Partnership*, p. 128.
17. For a full account of the impact of the *Sputnik* satellites, see Robert A. Divine, *The Sputnik Challenge: Eisenhower's Response to the Soviet Satellite* (Oxford University Press: New York, 1993). See also Chester J. Pach and Elmo Richardson, *The Presidency of Dwight D. Eisenhower* (University Press of Kansas: Kansas, 1991), pp. 170–4.
18. Divine, *The Sputnik Challenge*, p. xviii.
19. Melissen, *The Struggle for Nuclear Partnership*, p. 77. Although Eisenhower was personally unpeturbed by *Sputnik* (US intelligence sources had known for some months that the Soviets possessed the capability of initiating ICBM flight testing) he was forced by the public reaction to take a number of steps to counter what he and many of his advisers considered to be little more than a propaganda victory. Dockrill, *Eisenhower's New Look National Security Policy*, p. 210. One of his first actions was to speed up earlier plans for the initial deployment of American IRBMs overseas, including the Thor negotiations with Britain. Divine, *The Sputnik Challenge*, pp. 34 and 205. The Allies were concerned about the implications of *Sputnik* because the launch of the satellite appeared to challenge the credibility of the US nuclear guarantee to Europe. See Andreas Wenger, *Living with Peril*, p. 154. According to Dockrill, the American scientists' estimates of Soviet ICBM capabilities turned out to be reasonably accurate! The SS–6 rocket, the first Soviet ICBM, which was used to launch *Sputnik*, was unsuitable for military purposes. Moscow possessed only four SS-6 first generation ICBMs and these would not become operational until 1960. Dockrill, *Eisenhower's New Look National Security Policy*, p. 212.
20. Wenger, *Living with Peril*, p. 166.
21. Botti, *The Long Wait*, pp. 246–7. Pierre, *Nuclear Politics*, p. 143.
22. Malone, *The British Nuclear Deterrent*, p. 13.

23. Harold Macmillan, *Riding the Storm 1956–1959* (Macmillan: London, 1971), p. 322; *New York Times*, 4 February 1960.
24. Dwight D. Eisenhower, *The White Years* (Heineman: London, 1965), p. 219. According to Melissen, 'only after the President had asserted his powers, did Macmillan get what he wanted'. Melissen, *The Struggle for Nuclear Partnership*, p. 50.
25. Navias, *Nuclear Weapons and British Strategic Planning*, pp. 216–19. Although the initial offer was made in January 1957 and had been agreed upon in principle (at Bermuda in March), negotiations quickly got bogged down and were only reactivated by the events of October 1957. Melissen, *The Struggle for Nuclear Partnership*, pp. 63–86. Botti, *The Long Wait*, pp. 180–97.
26. HMD, d. 30, 9 October 1957.
27. Melissen, *The Struggle for Nuclear Partnership*, p. 128.
28. HMD, d. 30, 23 October 1957.
29. Pierre, *Nuclear Politics*, p. 142. Botti, *The Long Wait*, p. 201.
30. First Sea Lord's Secret and Personal Bulletins, 29 September 1958, ADM 205/172, PRO. Baylis, *Anglo-American Defence Relations 1939–84*, p. 91. These changes in the law enabled Britain to develop technology that otherwise would have been out of reach. The sale of the nuclear propulsion plant in particular was instrumental in enabling her to construct the submarines needed to carry the Polaris missiles offered at Nassau.
31. Lawrence Freedman, *Evolution of Nuclear Strategy* (Macmillan: London, 1989), p. 317.
32. Indeed, as Melissen has pointed out, an important reason why Eisenhower and his Secretary of State wanted to help Britain in the nuclear field was that they thought they could thus save the British the necessity of cutting their conventional forces. Melissen, *The Struggle for Nuclear Partnership*, p. 44.
33. Schwartz, *NATO's Nuclear Dilemmas*, p. 179.
34. Brandon, *SKYBOLT* (*The Sunday Times*, 8 December 1963).
35. Richard E. Neustadt, *Alliance Politics* (Columbia University Press: London and New York, 1972).
36. CAB 133/243 Commonwealth & International Conferences, 1960 Washington Meeting, PRO.
37. The Blue Streak was powered by a licence-built version of the rocket motor developed for the USAF's Atlas ICBM. Its inertial guidance system was also of American origin.
38. Britain had already spent £65 million and was facing an estimated bill of £600 million. The British government's professional military advisers were unanimous in recommending that it was militarily unacceptable to them. See Clark, *Nuclear Diplomacy*, p. 185.
39. The Cabinet had taken the decision to abandon the project on 24 February 1960, but made no formal announcement until Macmillan had received the promise of Skybolt from Eisenhower. *The Times*, 14 April 1960.
40. Both the Royal Navy and the Air Force had been in contact with their American counterparts about the respective weapons for some

time. As early as February 1960 *before* the project had been officially approved by the Defense Department, representatives of the British Ministries of Air and Defence along with the RAF had been to Washington to discuss the use of the weapon on the British V-bombers. *Aviation Week*, 22 February 1960.

41. HMD, d. 38, 6 April 1960.
42. *New York Times*, 14 April 1960; 31 May 1960; 2 June 1960.
43. It is interesting to note that the policy of allowing Britain to become dependent on the United States was discussed by the British Nuclear Deterrent Study Group in 1959. In a report they considered this course of action and recommended that if Ministers acquiesced, a request for either a weapon such as the WS138 A (an early prototype of Skybolt) or Polaris should be drafted and put to the US government. Interim Report by the British Nuclear Deterrent Study Group BND (SG) (59) 19 (Final), 31 December 1959, DEFE 7/2301, PRO.
44. The decision was taken on the recommendation of the Defence Committee on 24 Feb. 1960. HMD, d. 38, 24 February 1960.
45. In 1958 it was thought that Polaris might not be suitable for UK requirements. Report of Visit to United States with Minister of Defence, 21 September 1958–5, October 1958, DEFE 11/360, PRO. However, by mid-March, neither Polaris nor Skybolt had been ruled out by the Eisenhower administration as possible alternatives to the British Blue Streak. Caccia to Prime Minister, 19 March 1960, AIR 2/15603, PRO.
46. The Ministry of Defence was under the impression that Polaris was the preferred vehicle not just of the US Navy but also of the Department of Defense which had expressed a desire to see Britain choose it instead of Skybolt. Memorandum from R. C. Chilver to Minister of Defence, 23 March 1960, DEFE 13/195, PRO.
47. According to an Air Ministry Minute Sheet, by the beginning of March 1960, a great deal of momentum had gathered behind the idea of a submarine-based deterrent. Air Ministry File No. AUS (A)/4031, Minute sheet by R. C. Kent, 1 March 1960, AIR 20/10697, PRO.
48. From Office of Deputy Chief of Naval Staff to First Sea Lord, 1 January 1958, ADM 205/179, PRO.
49. Vice Chief of the Air Staff Joint General War Committee, 16 October 1959, AIR 2/13707, PRO.
50. According to the First Sea Lord, Admiralty policy was 'not to bid for POLARIS as with our own present resources we just cannot afford the cost. We must wait for a Governmental direction that the Navy is to be armed with Polaris, whereupon we shall be able to put in for the necessary funds . . .'. First Sea Lord's Records, weekly meeting, 17 September 1958, ADM 205/72, PRO. Appendix to Newsletter, First Sea Lord's Records, 29 September 1958, ADM 205/72, PRO. Memorandum for Board by D.C.N.S. 3 March 1958, ADM 205/179, PRO.
51. The Americans were reluctant to consider a bilateral deal involving Polaris. In a memorandum Secretary of State Herter told President Eisenhower, 'A bilateral understanding with the British on Polaris would clearly be inappropriate so long as a NATO MRBM program is under

consideration . . .' Memorandum from Herter to Eisenhower, 27 March 1960, Document No. 369, Vol. VII, FRUS.

52. Mountbatten kept in close contact with the Polaris project and a considerable exchange of information flowed between the US Navy and the Royal Navy. Of great importance was the relationship he had with Admiral Arleigh Burke. Arleigh Burke to Lord Mountbatten, 29 November 1957, ADM 205/179, PRO. Lord Mountbatten to Arleigh Burke, 8 May 1958, ADM 205/179, PRO. John Simpson, *The Independent Nuclear State: The US, Britain and the Military Atom* (Macmillan: London, 1983), p. 117.
53. This was certainly the sentiment expressed by the RAF and the Air Ministry who were extremely for the Skybolt option. Minute No. 8110, 8 December 1960 signed by P. J. Hudson, AIR 2/13710, PRO. Memorandum by Group Captain D. S. Lindsay DD(ops), 20 December 1960, AIR 2/13710, PRO.
54. A memorandum for the Minister of Air reiterated this advantage Skybolt had over Polaris: 'the Minister should be reminded that Skybolt represents the only means of preserving a UK deterrent force during the period 1965–70 – Polaris submarines could not begin to be deployed in significant numbers until 1969 or 1970 at the earliest.' Memorandum from P. J. Hudson to the Minister of Air, 23 March 1960, AIR 2/13708, PRO. Such a force was also thought to be potentially very expensive and risked a large degree of dependence on the United States. Note by Minister of Defence, 29 August 1960, DEFE 13/113, PRO.
55. According to a memorandum from R. C. Chilver to Watkinson, the main reason why the US offered to sell the UK Skybolt was to clinch the government's decision to drop Blue Streak. Chilver to Watkinson, 29 August 1960, DEFE 13/113, PRO.
56. Memorandum for the Secretary of State for Air, 28 March 1960, AIR 20/10697, PRO.
57. Note of meeting, 20 February 1960, CAB 131/23, PRO.
58. Clark, *Nuclear Diplomacy*, p. 280.
59. Memorandum entitled: 'The Future of the Deterrent', 11 January 1961, AIR 2/13710, PRO. Clark, *Nuclear Diplomacy*, p. 284. Memorandum from E. W. Playfair to Minister of Defence, 17 June 1960, DEFE 13/195, PRO.
60. Watkinson to Macmillan, 22 July 1960, PREM 11/2940, PRO.
61. Facilities for American Polaris submarines was the only bargaining chip that Macmillan had at Camp David. Initially, from the American perspective, this was used to attempt to get guarantees on Skybolt and possibly also Polaris. When the Americans proved reluctant to consider a bilateral deal vis-à-vis Polaris, the natural exchange (at the suggestion, it seems, of the United States) came to involve Skybolt and Polaris facilities. Herter to Eisenhower, 27 March 1960, Document No. 369, Vol. VII, FRUS.
62. Text of Statement from Macmillan to Watkinson, 29 March 1960, PREM 11/2941, PRO.
63. Although neither document made reference to the other, Neustadt was convinced that in the prime minister's mind, the link was real.

64. In 1955 a report just recently partially declassified – the Strath Report – presented to the government a shocking study on the effects of a limited Soviet nuclear attack – now. Report by W. Strath, 8 December 1954, DEFE 13/11, PRO. See Navias, *Nuclear Weapons and British Nuclear Planning*, p. 23.
65. Letter from Prime Minister to President Eisenhower, 15 June 1960 Document No. 377, Vol. VII, FRUS. The State Department was well aware of Macmillan's tactics. In a telegram to the president who was on a state visit, Douglas Dillon advised that Eisenhower take a firm line by reminding the Prime Minister of the Camp David 'deal'. The result was the letter (see note 68) which prompted an angry response from Macmillan.
66. Letter from Eisenhower to Macmillan, 20 June 1960, DEFE 13/105, PRO.
67. Message from Eisenhower to Macmillan, 20 June 1960, PREM 11/ 2941, PRO.
68. Freedman, *Britain and Nuclear Weapons*, p. 7.
69. Memorandum of Understanding signed by Harold Watkinson and Thomas Gates, 6 June 1960, DEFE 13/195, PRO.
70. Dillon to Prime Minister, 29 March 1960, CAB 133/243, PRO London.
71. Clark, *Nuclear Diplomacy*, p. 292.
72. Brief for Meeting of Ministers, 14 June 1960, DEFE 13/195, PRO. This was not a new idea. According to American sources, the British had been considering this tactic at Camp David. Herter to Eisenhower 27 March 1960, Document No. 369, Vol. VII, FRUS.
73. Brief for Meeting of Ministers on 15 June, 14 June 1960, DEFE 13/ 195, PRO.
74. The British Embassy in Washington reported the general feeling in the US Government about Britain acquiring Polaris saying: 'it is clear that the Americans will insist on some mention of NATO if there is to be any public reference to the possibility of acquiring Polaris submarines . . .' Telegram to the Foreign Office from Washington, 28 August, 1960, DEFE 13/274, PRO. A few days later, in a discussion with the Chief of Defence Staff, the Civil Lord of the Admiralty and the First Sea Lord, the Minister of Defence outlined his thinking: 'The Minister said that we were years away from Polaris either for building or buying . . . He did not wish this weapon to tie in at all with NATO and he thought that the best thing to do was to drop the subject of Polaris for the time being . . .' Note for the Record, 31 August, 1960, DEFE 13/274, PRO. Eisenhower to Macmillan, 15 July 1960, PREM 11/2940, PRO. Eisenhower to Macmillan, 22 July 1960, DEFE 13/274, PRO.
75. Foreign Office to Washington, 27 July 1960, DEFE 13/274, PRO.
76. Draft telegram to Washington undated, PREM 11/2941, PRO. Hood (Foreign Office) to Caccia (Washington) 23 July 1960, DEFE 13/274, PRO.
77. *New York Times*, 2 June 1960.
78. Until now there existed no declassified evidence to corroborate Macmillan's assertion that Eisenhower did indeed offer him Polaris

(Harold Macmillan, *At The End of the Day*, p. 342). However, the recent opening of the Macmillan diaries reveals the prime minister's private account of the talks is in complete agreement with his other statements. For example, in his 29 March 1960 entry Macmillan writes: 'we have also got out of the Americans a very valuable exchange of notes about SKYBOLT and POLARIS. They undertake to let us have the *vehicles* (by sale or gift) . . .'. Copy of a Personal Minute from the Prime Minister to the Minister of Defence, 18 September 1960, DEFE 13/195, PRO. Moreover, another new piece of corroborative evidence has been uncovered in the form of a revealing document from the Ministry of Defence which states: 'The US government has just offered us for sale Skybolt and Polaris missiles (Washington telegram No. 689 of March 29).' Memorandum by B. H. Wilson (MoD), 1 April 1960, DEFE 13/195, PRO. Indeed, this is further confirmed by the revelation that the prime minister and the president had a private meeting on the afternoon of 28 March (without any aides) of which no record was kept. Memorandum for the Files, 29 March 1960, Document No. 370, Vol. VII, FRUS. It is quite conceivable, therefore, that the men did come to a private understanding about a future Polaris deal.

79. Underpinning the British government's willingness to 'give up' on actively acquiring Polaris in 1960 was the cost factor. In a memorandum (unsent), Harold Watkinson, the British Minister of Defence, confided his concerns to the prime minister: 'it is becoming increasingly plain that whatever we might wish to do in a perfect world about Polaris submarines, we just cannot afford to purchase outright or even build and purchase the equipment until the late 1960s or early 1970s . . .'. Memorandum from Watkinson to Macmillan (unsent), 29 August 1960, DEFE 13/274, PRO. Foreign Office to British Embassy Washington, 22 July 1960, DEFE 13/274, PRO. Copy of a Personal Minute from the Prime Minister to the Minister of Defence, 18 September 1960, DEFE 13/195, PRO.

80. This document links the Skybolt and Holy Loch deals and adds another dimension – a NATO MRBM force. Telegram from Washington to Foreign Office, 29 March 1960, PREM 11/2940, PRO. Memorandum from Eisenhower to Macmillan, 29 March 1960, Document No. 371, Vol. VII, FRUS.

81. In a letter to Eisenhower, Macmillan wrote: 'I was also grateful to you for expressing your willingness to help us when the time comes by enabling us to purchase supplies of Skybolt without warheads or to acquire in addition or substitution a mobile MRBM system *in the light of such decisions as may be reached in the discussions under way in NATO . . .*' (author's emphasis). Memorandum from Prime Minister to President Eisenhower, 29 March 1960, Document No. 372, Vol. VII, FRUS.

CHAPTER 3   CHAOS AND CONFUSION – ALLIES IN TROUBLE

1. Macmillan to Watkinson, 29 March 1960, CAB 133/243, PRO.
2. While the eventual agreement had no strings attached, British Ministers feared for a time that American officials were seeking to link the deal with British participation in the US MRBM scheme. Foreign Office to Washington, 24 February 1960, CAB 131/23, PRO.
3. Memorandum from Zuckerman to Watkinson, 7 February 1961, DEFE 13/408, PRO.
4. In a conversation with John Rubel, Watkinson learned in April 1961 that Skybolt might be even more prone to fatal complications than had first been thought. According to Rubel, Skybolt relied on celestial navigation for homing on to the target – i.e. it 'acquired' a star in order to navigate. Alarmingly, Watkinson informed the Minister of Aviation, this meant the probability that because 'the present day navigation equipment in British V-bombers is so markedly more inaccurate than the American counterpart that in certain circumstances SKYBOLT would be virtually unusable as a weapon...'. Harold Watkinson to Minister of Aviation, 12 September 1961, DEFE 13/408, PRO.
5. The Skybolt project started life in 1958 as the Bold Orion Rocket programme produced from a ALBM called WS-199B by the Martin Company.
6. Brandon, *SKYBOLT*.
7. See Peter Roman, 'Strategic Bombers over the Missile Horizon, 1957–1963' (*Journal for Strategic Studies*, Vol. 18, No. 1, 1995).
8. During the 1960s it was thought that anti-ballistic missile (ABM) systems could be developed which would track and destroy the incoming warheads of a nuclear attack. Although both the Russians and the Americans deployed such systems, they proved to be extravagantly expensive and essentially unworkable.
9. *The Times*, 9 June 1960.
10. Clark, *Nuclear Diplomacy*, pp. 281–4. See also *The Times*, 9 June 1960. Watkinson to Macmillan, 1 November 1960, DEFE 19/76, PRO.
11. Nunnerley, *President Kennedy and Britain*, p. 130.
12. Neustadt, *Report to the President*, p. 7.
13. Draft secret memorandum on Skybolt, PREM 11/3262, PRO.
14. Pentagon Background Briefing Paper, 17 December 1962, Richard E. Neustadt Papers, Governmental Consulting, Box 19, Skybolt/Atlantic Affairs, Statements and Clippings. NSF JFKL. See also Ward S. Just, 'The Scrapping of Skybolt' (*The Reporter*, 11 April 1963), p. 19. A further report by the Strategic Weapons Panel of the President's Science Advisory Committee in mid-July 1960 also admitted to having 'serious doubts' about the project. A third report came from the Pentagon's Weapons Systems Evaluation Group also recommended cancellation. *New York Times*, 17 December 1962.
15. The other missiles were Minuteman, Titan and Polaris.
16. It is interesting to note that Thomas Gates, far from being regarded by the British as a difficult American to deal with, was perceived as a

172   *Notes and References*

friend of Britain. In a confidential telegram from the British Ambassador to Selwyn Lloyd at the Foreign Office, Harold Caccia refers to him as a 'sincere believer in Anglo/American cooperation, and our relations with him have always been close and friendly . . .'. 8 December 1959, DEFE 13/126, PRO.
17. Record of Meeting, 21 October 1960, PREM 11/3261, MM46/60, PRO.
18. Brandon, *SKYBOLT*. Watkinson to Macmillan, 12 May 1960, DEFE 13/195, PRO.
19. Watkinson to Macmillan, 12 December 1960, DEFE 19/76, PRO.
20. The January budget did not include additional funds for Skybolt on the assumption that the $150 million available in fiscal year 1961 could be stretched out to support the project during the coming fiscal year.
21. Memorandum, December 1960, PREM 11/3261, PRO. Record of Meeting between Gates and Watkinson, 12 December 1960, PREM 11/3261, MM54/60, PRO. E. W. Playfair to Minister of Defence, DEFE 13/421, PRO. *The Christian Science Monitor* reported that the British government was more concerned about the USAF having second thoughts about the project than the funding cut authorised by Gates. *Christian Science Monitor*, 23 December 1960.
22. POF, Box 77, Depts. & Agencies 1/61–3/61 JFKL. See also B. D. S. Washington to MoD, Mills to Zuckerman, 14 February 1961, DEFE 19/77, PRO.
23. Roswell Gilpatric, Oral History, JFKL, p. 74. See also Richard E. Neustadt, *Alliance Politics* (Columbia University Press: New York, 1970), p. 37; George Ball, *The Past Has Another Pattern* (W.W. Norton & Co.: New York, 1982), pp. 229–30. According to Zuckerman, his sources were under the impression that Skybolt would survive the Defense Review 'if only on grounds of international politics and employment problems in Southern California . . .'. B. D. S. (Washington) to MoD, 7 February 1961, DEFE 13/408, PRO.
24. Memcon of US–UK defense talks, 28 March 1961, Box 3, Folder 'UK' Box 3, RG59, Records of State Department, Bureau of European Affairs, Office of Atlantic Political & Military Affairs, 1961–63, National Archives.
25. DoD appropriations for 1962, Senate Subcommittee for Appropriations (18 April 1961) Neustadt Papers, Box 19, Government Consulting, Statements and Clippings on Skybolt 1959–63, JFKL. Another reason why McNamara was reluctant to move against Skybolt was the revelation at the Tushino Air Show that the Russians had substantially augmented air defence capabilities than had been previously thought. *Denver Post*, 4 September 1962.
26. Brandon, *SKYBOLT*.
27. Brandon, *SKYBOLT*.
28. Nunnerley, *President Kennedy and Britain*, p. 134.
29. Having been alerted to McNamara's intentions, the weapon's supporters in Congress and the USAF had united to oppose cancellation. In the end, Kennedy himself was forced to intervene by formally impounding the funds allocated by Congress for the bombers.
30. Brandon, *SKYBOLT*. It is interesting to note that the British Liaison

Staff in Washington (in particular the Skybolt Progress Officer) were reporting around this time that McNamara was 'very taken with SKYBOLT ... much more so than his predecessors had been ...'. Note for the Record, 3 November 1961, DEFE 13/409, PRO.

31. Brandon, *SKYBOLT.*
32. Memorandum for President, 9 December 1961, Box 273A–274, Depts. and Agencies DoD McNamara group in Paris and London 7/61- McNamara speech 11/18/63, JFKL.
33. Ironically, MINUTEMAN was to enter its production phase on 11 December 1962 – the day the crisis broke in London.
34. Neustadt, *Report to the President*, p. 4.
35. Neustadt, *Report to the President.*
36. Neustadt, *Report to the President*, p. 9.
37. Neustadt, *Report to the President*, p. 10.
38. Thorneycroft, Oral History, p. 12, JFKL.
39. Thorneycroft appears to have ignored warnings from the Secretary of State for Air that the situation regarding Skybolt 'could not be more pregnant for a miscarriage'. Secretary of State for Air to Minister of Defence, 16 October 1962, DEFE 13/410, PRO.
40. Neustadt, *Report to the President*, p. 12.
41. Neustadt, *Report to the President.*
42. Neustadt, *Report to the President*, p. 13.
43. Thorneycroft to McNamara 5 November 1962, PREM 11/3706, PRO. Thorneycroft might also have been prompted by a message from the British liaison staff in Washington reporting that they had learned unofficially that the Department of Defense was considering cancelling Skybolt. British Defence Staff (B. D. S.) Washington to Ministry of Defence, 5 November 1962, DEFE 13/409, PRO.
44. Neustadt, *Report to the President*, p. 15.
45. Document No. 399, Vol. XIII, FRUS.
46. Neustadt, *Alliance Politics*, p. 42.
47. Arthur Schlesinger Jr, *A Thousand Days*, p. 371.
48. According to Neustadt, the telegram was so unusual that Bruce wondered what was going on in Washington. Neustadt, *Report to the President*, p. 55.
49. Box 275, Depts. & Agencies, Department of Defense Defense Budget FY1964 Vol. 1, misc, NSF, JFKL.
50. Kennedy had been asked by Macmillan (via Ormsby-Gore) for a number of assurances about the handling of the matter which included a commitment that no decision would be taken without consultation with the British. The President apparently thought that his staff were fully aware of this and did not need reminding of procedures they were following anyway and so did not bring Macmillan's requests up at the meeting. It is unclear as to whether or not Kennedy informed anyone of the British prime minister's request or his own promises. However, nothing more was said about the matter. Later, Macmillan was to wonder why Kennedy had broken his promise. In all likelihood, the president was under the impression that his staff had honoured his commitments. By the time he realised this was not the case, things had gone

badly wrong indeed. Neustadt, *Report to the President*, pp. 49, 52.
51. Richard E. Neustadt Papers Box 19, Government consulting, Skybolt/ Atlantic Affairs 12/62, Skybolt-Nassau (classified) Folder 2, JFKL.
52. Memcon 10 December 1962, NSF Meetings and Memos, meetings with the President 6/62–12/62, Box 317, JFKL.
53. Dean Rusk, *As I Saw It*, p. 266.
54. Neustadt Papers Box 19, Government Consulting, Skybolt/Atlantic Affairs, Statements and Clippings, 17 December Pentagon Background Briefing Paper, JFKL.
55. Neustadt, *Report to the President*, p. 48.
56. This paper was prepared by Yarmolinsky and had been passed by George Ball and approved by the president.
57. Roswell Gilpatric offers an explanation as to why Thorneycroft was so reluctant to negotiate with McNamara at this juncture. He believes that the British Minister felt that he could not afford to be seen to be asking for Polaris especially in front of the British staff who were present at the meeting. Gilpatric, Oral History, p. 63, JFKL.
58. While McNamara certainly believed that Thorneycroft had deliberately whipped up the press, others are not so sure and argue that the press had already received enough to go on from the Secretary's press statement, see Neustadt, *Report to the President*, pp. 68–9.

CHAPTER 4 A CRISIS EXPLAINED

1. Theodore C. Sorenson, *Kennedy* (Hodder & Stoughton: London, 1965), p. 558.
2. Neustadt, *Alliance Politics*, p. 72.
3. This is clearly appreciated in a brief for the Minister of Defence: 'The Americans have the money and resources in research and development and production of modern weapons that we cannot match and it is clear we must rely more and more on them in this field. On our side, we can bargain only on our reliability as an ally and our geographical position . . .'. Brief for Minister of Defence, 1 February 1961, DEFE 13/11, PRO.
4. Bundy, Oral History, p. 2, JFKL.
5. Zuckerman, *Monkeys, Men and Missiles 1946–88: An Autobiography* (Collins: London, 1988), p. 235. In a memorandum, Air Commodore S. W. R. Hughes told Zuckerman that the two Air Forces were 'very much in each other's pocket'. Hughes (D.R.P.S.) (Air) to Zuckerman, 16 June 1960, DEFE 19/75, PRO.
6. Navias, *Nuclear Weapons and British Strategic Planning*, p. 86.
7. In fact, the original suggestion that Britain send a Royal Navy Liaison Officer to participate in the US Polaris programme came from Arleigh Burke and not Lord Mountbatten.
8. Memorandum for the Minister of Defence, 15 January 1963, AIR 20/11169, PRO. The British government's chief liaison officer was Group Captain. G. B. Fryer (Skybolt Progress Officer) appointed 1 September 1960. S. W. R. Hughes to E. W. Playfair, 30 August 1960,

DEFE 13/195, PRO. A joint Air Ministry and Ministry of Aviation Skybolt Management Board was also formed to liaise with the staff in the USA. Brief of Skybolt, January 1961, AIR 20/10830, PRO.

9. Group Captain Fryer sent back six progress reports and numerous memoranda about the development of Skybolt. For examples see: 'Status of Skybolt', 28 December 1960, DEFE 13/408, PRO; 'Skybolt Progress Report', 31 May 1961, DEFE 13/408, PRO; Memorandum from Fryer to Air Minister, 9 November 1962, DEFE 13/409, PRO. The British government was also in direct contact with the Douglas Corporation. Memorandum for Minister of Defence, 12 December 1960, DEFE 13/408, PRO.

10. John Newhouse, *De Gaulle and the Anglo-Saxons* (André Deutsch: London, 1970), p. 199.

11. Memcon US–UK Defence Talks, 28 March 1961, Box 3, Folder 'UK', National Archives Washington DC. Zuckerman to Watkinson, 7 February 1961, DEFE 13/408, PRO.

12. Watkinson, *Turning Points*, p. 128.

13. Watkinson to Macmillan, 7 June 1960, PREM 11/2940, PRO. He was also keeping his options open on Polaris. Watkinson to Chief of Defence Staff, 31 October 1960, DEFE 7/2064, PRO.

14. Watkinson to Macmillan, 12 May 1960, DEFE 13/195, PRO.

15. In a memorandum to Duncan Sandys he spelt out his concerns sayings: 'It is certain that we shall have to defend ourselves against a lot of criticism in the years ahead. We must make sure that we have full knowledge of developments at all levels in the United States . . .'. Watkinson to Sandys, 6 July 1960, DEFE 13/195, PRO. Extract from Minutes of Meeting of the Minister of Defence and the Chiefs of Staff, 17 June 1960, DEFE 13/195, PRO.

16. Memcon US–UK Defence Talks, 28 March 1961, Box 3, Folder 'UK', National Archives.

17. Watkinson to Macmillan, 4 November 1960, PREM 11/3261, PRO.

18. Horne, *Macmillan*, p. 276.

19. Macmillan to Watkinson, 19 November 1960, PREM 11/3261, PRO.

20. These alternatives were 1) V-bombers with a US substitution for Skybolt; 2) Polaris missiles in US-built or British-built submarines; 3) The T.S.R.2 could be used in the strategic role; 4) V-bombers with a British cruise-type missile, superior in performance to Blue Steel. See: Watkinson to Macmillan, 23 November 1960, PREM 11/3261, PRO.

21. Watkinson to Macmillan, 23 November 1960, PREM 11/3261, PRO.

22. Sir Solly Zuckerman to Hugh Fraser, 30 October 1962, AIR 19/1036, PRO.

23. Sir Solly Zuckerman, *Monkeys, Men and Missiles*, p. 237.

24. Zuckerman was widely known to be a critic of the Skybolt programme as well as the British liaison staff in the US whom he felt were consistently over-optimistic. On one occasion, Air Vice-Marshall Emson accused him of seriously damaging British interests by giving the impression to the Americans that Britain would 'not oppose too strongly a decision to cancel'. Air Vice-Marshall Emson, Commander and Air

Attaché, British Embassy, 2 November 1962, AIR 19/1036, PRO. A few weeks later, in an angry letter to the Minister of Defence, the Minister of Aviation made his feelings clear: 'your Chief Scientific Adviser questioned the competence of my staff to have an independent view on the state of Skybolt development ... I conclude that your Chief Scientific Adviser's doubts of our ability to judge Skybolt developments are ill-based ...'. Minister of Aviation to Minister of Defence, 17 December 1962, DEFE 13/410, PRO.

25. According to Air Commodore Hughes (D.R.P.S. in Washington), the British staff liaising with the Skybolt project had excellent sources. Hughes to Watkinson, 15 March 1961, DEFE 13/408, PRO.

26. McNamara had sworn his staff to secrecy. Neustadt, *Report to the President*, p. 20.

27. Neustadt reports that Hawthorne's source was McGeorge Bundy although Zuckerman was unaware of this at the time.

28. Neustadt, *Report to the President*, p. 43.

29. Thorneycroft to Macmillan, 7 December 1962, PREM 11/3716, PRO. In this document Thorneycroft even suggests *borrowing* a number of American Polarises to cover the gap whist they waited for delivery of their own.

30. de Zulueta to Ormsby-Gore, 11 December 1962, PREM 11/3779, PRO.

31. Ormsby-Gore to Foreign Office, 18 November 1962, DEFE 13/409, PRO. Ormsby-Gore to Foreign Office, 21 November 1962, DEFE 19/78, PRO.

32. Bruce to State Department, 21 November 1962: 'if a decision to discontinue ... the SKYBOLT program is taken ... or seems likely, I believe the government here should be afforded maximum amount of time possible to make its own consequent decisions and to prepare its plans and their presentation ... [SKYBOLT] abandonment now could have the most fundamental consequences ...' Neustadt, *Report to the President*, p. 55.

33. Neustadt, *Report to the President*, p. 16.

34. McGeorge Bundy, Oral History, p. 4, JFKL.

35. Sorenson, *Kennedy*, p. 566.

36. Zuckerman to Thorneycroft, 9 December 1962, PREM, 11/3716, PRO.

37. Incidentally, the British were under the impression that *all* of the American Chiefs of Staff had voted to continue with the project. This (incorrect) information was passed to them from the liaison staff in Washington. Air Ministry to Ministry of Defence, 29 November 1962, DEFE 19/78, PRO.

38. McNamara was aware that no leaks could occur before he had negotiated alternative arrangements with Britain. To ensure this, he ordered that the Douglas Corporation should be paid as usual for the month of December. Discussing the matter with Ormsby-Gore, the Secretary of Defense referred to the $20 million involved as 'peanuts' compared with the important decisions at stake. Note of conversation between Ormsby-Gore and McNamara, 29 November 1962, DEFE 19/78, PRO.

39. Memorandum, 23 November 1962, Box 275 Depts. & Agencies DoD Defense Budget FY 1964 Vol. 1 misc. NSF, JFKL.

40. After all, this was not an inter-governmental agreement but an agreement between the US Department of the Air Force and the UK Ministry of Aviation relating only to research and development. Telegram from Foreign Office to Washington, 5 April 1963, DEFE 13/736, PRO. Ormsby-Gore made this point in a telegram to the Foreign Office when he warned that 'those responsible for the project in the Department of Defense, both military and scientific, are not interested in the political aspect . . .'. Ormsby-Gore to the Foreign Office, 18 November 1962, DEFE 13/409, PRO.
41. Nunnerley, *President Kennedy and Britain*, p. 132.
42. Full-page advertisements placed in *Time*, *Newsweek* and *Fortune Magazine* by the Douglas Corporation suggested that the completed operational weapon would not only form an important and useful contribution to defence strategy, but it would save taxpayers billions of dollars by extending the useful life of the B-52 and British Vulcan II bombers. The *Washington Post* also reported that it was suspected that the company had something to do with stirring up British political repercussions in England. *Washington Post*, 21 December 1962 and 3 January 1963.
43. Yarmolinsky, Oral History, p. 62, JFKL.
44. Eugene Zuckert, the Secretary of the Airforce believed that McNamara had been swayed by 'the technical people downstairs' who had convinced him and the president of the 'technical infeasibility' of the project by making 'dampening comments' about its chances of ever becoming operational. Zuckert Oral History p. 89, JFKL.
45. There was some speculation in the United States and in Britain that the administration was attempting to get rid of the manned bomber as quickly as possible believing it to be increasingly obsolescent in the missile age. *The Times*, 27 December 1962.
46. *Washington Post*, 21 December 1962.
47. McNamara to the House Committee on Armed Services, US Defense Policies in 1962: A compilation of material relating to US Defense Policies in 1962, US Library of Congress, 10 June 1963, London School of Economics and Political Science.
48. Zuckert, Oral History, p. 82, JFKL. Roswell Gilpatric, Oral History, p. 87, JFKL.
49. *The Washington Star*, 16 December 1962, *Philadelphia Inquirer*, 28 December 1962, *Chicago Tribune*, 28 December 1962.
50. *The Washington Star* reported that Kennedy wanted to hold down defense costs in order to persuade Congress to pass the personal and corporate tax cuts he was proposing. *Washington Star*, 16 December 1962.
51. Peter Thorneycroft, Oral History, p. 17, JFKL.
52. Ormsby-Gore to Foreign Office, (undated) PREM 11/4229, PRO.
53. Neustadt, *Report to the President*, p. 61.
54. George Ball, *The Past Has Another Pattern*, p. 264.
55. Neustadt, *Report to the President*, p. 78; Adam Yarmolinsky, Oral History, pp. 61, 64, JFKL.
56. Adam Yarmolinsky, Oral History, p. 62, JFKL.

57. Hockaday to Samuel, 9 November 1962, PREM 11/3716, PRO.
58. Nunnerley, *President Kennedy and Britain*, p. 130.
59. Neustadt, *Report to the President*, p. 37.
60. Neustadt, *Report to the President*, p. 25.
61. Draft cable from Weiss to Secretary 12/13/62, Neustadt Papers, Government consulting, Box 19 Folder 3, JFKL.
62. The State Department got a window of opportunity to influence the final recommendations via Harry Rowen, who was eventually entrusted with pulling all the alternatives together in a report.
63. Neustadt, *Report to the President*, p. 28.
64. Neustadt, *Report to the President*, p. 28.
65. Neustadt, *Report to the President*, pp. 31, 32.
66. This was much exaggerated and did not accurately reflect the position of Department of Defense.
67. Neustadt, *Report to the President*, p. 57.
68. Neustadt, *Report to the President*, p. 58.
69. Neustadt, *Report to the President*, p. 70.
70. Neustadt, *Report to the President*, p. 74.
71. The intervention of Kitchen's Office of Politico-Military Affairs managed to reduce this to a mere lecture.
72. Neustadt, *Report to the President*, p. 23.
73. According to Bundy, Kennedy had little enthusiasm for the British deterrent which he called 'a political necessity, but a piece of military foolishness'. Bundy, Oral History, p. 3, JFKL.
74. Ormsby-Gore to Macmillan, 13 April 1962, PREM 11/3783, PRO.
75. Macmillan was personally unconcerned about Acheson's remarks. HMD, d. 48, 7 December 1962.
76. In private, McNamara told George Brown of the Labour Party that he had in fact been talking about Britain when he condemned independent deterrents. Neustadt, *Report to the President*, pp. 39–40. What is interesting about the general uproar that surrounded McNamara's speeches is the fact that, in private, the British government appeared to have no great problem with the content of his remarks. Memorandum from Watkinson to Ormsby-Gore, 10 May 1962, DEFE 13/355, PRO.
77. *The Manchester Guardian*, 10 December 1962.
78. For example, in early 1961, Zuckerman advised the Minister of Defence that Skybolt's position was very tenuous and was currently surviving only because of the British factor. Zuckerman to Watkinson, 7 February 1961, DEFE 13/408, PRO.
79. Harold Macmillan, *At the End of the Day*, p. 343.
80. Dean Rusk, *As I Saw It*, p. 266.
81. The Air Ministry was certain that the Kennedy administration was not speaking with one voice. Air Ministry File No. F/24/8, 14 December 1962, AIR 19/1036, PRO.
82. George Ball, *The Past Has Another Pattern*, pp. 299–30.
83. Neustadt, *Alliance Politics*, p. 41.
84. Pierre, *Nuclear Politics*, p. 93. See also Groom, *British Thinking about Nuclear Weapons*, p. 209.

85. *The Times,* 24 February 1958.
86. Neustadt, *Report to the President*, p. 37.
87. Zuckerman, Oral History, p. 28, JFKL.
88. According to Thorneycroft, during the course of that telephone conversation McNamara assured the Minister of Defence that no firm recommendations would be made for several weeks ...'. Notes for Talk with Professor Neustadt (undated), DEFE 13/411, PRO.
89. Brief for Prime Minister by Minister of Defence, December 1962, AIR 19/1036, PRO.
90. Memorandum on Skybolt by Arthur Hockaday, 15 November 1962, DEFE 13/409, PRO.
91. Memorandum for Minister of Defence, 3 December 1962, DEFE 13/410, PRO.
92. Thorneycroft himself had long since set his sights and was against continuing to press the Americans for Skybolt. Thorneycroft, Oral History, p. 19, JFKL.
93. Neustadt, *Report to the President*, p. 34.
94. Neustadt, *Report to the President*, p. 35.
95. Horne, *Macmillan*, p. 433.
96. Bundy, Oral History, p. 4, JFKL. Macmillan to Watkinson, 3 December 1962, DEFE 19/78, PRO. According to Group Captain Fryer the USAF was aware in early November that Skybolt was close to being cancelled. This may have reassured Macmillan and his Ministers and contributed to their early optimism about the future of the project. Judging, however, by the lack of activity on the part of the USAF, it would seem that Fryer was incorrect in his analysis. Fryer to the Air Ministry, 9 November 1962, DEFE 13/409, PRO.
97. Gilpatric, Oral History, pp. 87–8, JFKL. The British liaison staff in Washington (and especially Fryer) must take some share in the blame. Fryer's reports are consistently over-optimistic and misleading. For example, in his sixth progress report, Fryer mentions that while Skybolt would appear to be a prime candidate for cancellation, in his opinion (and according to his contacts) this would be 'extremely unlikely'. Fryer Progress Report No. 6, 22 August 1962, DEFE 19/77, PRO.
98. Telegram from Ormsby-Gore to Macmillan, PREM 11/4229, PRO. Watkinson to Macmillan, 23 September 1960, PREM 11/2941, PRO. Brandon, Oral History, p. 3, JFKL. Macmillan was convinced that nothing had been finalised, noting in his dairy: 'The President has stated that no decision will be taken definitely until after our talks in the Bahamas next week ...'. HMD, d. 48, 13 December 1962.
99. Memorandum from E. W. Playfair to Minister of Defence, 17 June 1960, DEFE 13/195, PRO.
100. Neustadt, *Report to the President*, p. 42.
101. Neustadt, *Report to the President*, p. 44. A letter from US Embassy to State indicated that at working level, the Foreign Office had very little information concerning the Prime Minister's plans. Neustadt Papers Government Consulting, Skybolt/Atlantic Affairs Folder 3, 13 December 1962, JFKL.
102. Neustadt, *Report to the President*, p. 46.

103. Clark, *Nuclear Diplomacy*, p. 349.
104. Note for Record by Bligh, 9 December 1962, PREM 11/3716, PRO.
105. Extract of Private Meeting between the Minister of Defence and the US Secretary of Defense, 15 December 1962, DEFE 13/619, PRO. During this secret lunch meeting, Thorneycroft and McNamara discussed Polaris as an alternative to Skybolt. It is almost certain; given the details of the conversation that Thorneycroft was presenting his government's position – i.e. that Polaris was the only possible weapons system that Britain would accept.
106. Nunnerley, *President Kennedy and Britain*, p. 137.
107. *Christian Science Monitor*, 17 December 1962.
108. Whatever was said in public about the lack of consultation, Macmillan was content that he had played a constructive role in the crisis. According to Macmillan's diary of appointments, the prime minister and President Kennedy spoke a total of four times (officially) during the crisis. HMD Typescript Narrative of Daily Events.
109. HMD, d. 48, 16 December 1962.

CHAPTER 5   FINDING A SOLUTION: THE NASSAU COMPROMISE

1. Brandon, *SKYBOLT*.
2. Jan Melissen, Pre-Summit Diplomacy: Britain, the US and the Nassau Conference, December 1962 (*Diplomacy & Statecraft*, November 1996, Vol. 7, No. 3, pp. 652–87). Unless otherwise stated, all references in this chapter are from Record of Meeting, 19 December 1962, PREM 11/4229, PRO.
3. Record of Conversation at Rambouillet, 15 December 1962, PREM 11/4230, PRO.
4. Sir Alec Douglas Home, *When the Wind Blows* (Collins: Glasgow, 1976), p. 432.
5. Transcript of Interview with the President, 16 December 1962, Box 20, NSF, Skybolt/Atlantic Affairs, NATO Defense Policy Conference (Legere) 11/62, JFKL.
6. The British delegation consisted of Macmillan, Lord Home, Peter Thorneycroft, Commonwealth Secretary Duncan Sandys, Sir David Ormsby-Gore, Lord Hood, Deputy Under-Secretary at the Foreign Office, Sir Robert Scott, Permanent Secretary at the Ministry of Defence and Sir Solly Zuckerman, Thorneycroft's Chief Scientific Adviser. Also included were Macmillan's Private Secretaries Philip de Zulueta and Tim Bligh along with Harold Evans, the Prime Minister's Public Relations Adviser. Notable by their absence were Sir William Penny, Deputy Chairman of the UK Atomic Energy Authority and the Chief of Defence Staff, Earl Mountbatten. The lack of military opinion clearly made this a *political* team. The American team was also curiously without a key member, the Secretary of State Dean Rusk, who had decided to remain in Washington. Instead, Rusk had appointed George Ball, his strongly pro-European Deputy to take his place. Also accompanying

Kennedy was Secretary of Defense McNamara (who had changed his mind at the last minute and decided to go), McGeorge Bundy, the President's National Security Adviser, Ambassadors Bruce and Llewelyn and Assistant Secretary of State William Tyler. Also notable for his absence was the Chairman of the Joint Chiefs of Staff, General Maxwell Taylor.

7. Neustadt, *Report to the President*, p. 87.
8. David Ormsby-Gore, Suez SNAFU, Skybolt SABU (*Foreign Policy* 2, Spring, 1971), pp. 46–7.
9. Schlesinger, *A Thousand Days*, p. 737.
10. David Ormsby-Gore, Suez SNAFU, pp. 46–7.
11. Schlesinger, *A Thousand Days*, p. 737.
12. Neustadt, *Report to the President*, p. 88.
13. Neustadt, *Report to the President*.
14. Neustadt, *Report to the President*.
15. See Memorandum Cabinet Office, 10 January 1963, CAB 128/37, PRO. Memorandum from Sir Solly Zuckerman to Minister of Defence, 1 January 1963, DEFE 13/619, PRO.
16. Nunnerley, *President Kennedy and Britain*, p. 153.
17. Brandon, *Special Relationships*, p. 165.
18. The American Hound Dog was also offered.
19. William Tyler had proposed this idea. George Ball got to hear of it and on the way to Nassau suggested it as a possible alternative to Kennedy.
20. Macmillan rejected it because the missile would need highly complex technical adjustments in order to fit the Vulcan bomber. In addition, the British press had ridiculed the weapon saying that the public could never have any confidence in a missile named Hound Dog. See Unsigned Memorandum, 23 July 1963, PREM 11/4737, PRO.
21. Neustadt, *Report to the President*, p. 90.
22. Rostow, Oral History, p. 102, JFKL.
23. Neustadt, *Report to the President*, p. 91.
24. Kennedy, McNamara and Rusk had discussed the possibility of giving Britain Polaris as early as 10 December, when they had a meeting prior to McNamara's London trip. Polaris was again mentioned as a probable solution six days later during the administration's last meeting before Nassau. Neustadt, *Report to the President*, p. 60 and Memorandum of Conversation, 16 December 1962, NSF, Box 317, Meetings and Memos, meetings with president, general, 1/1/63–2/17/63, JFKL.
25. Statement on Nuclear Defense Systems, 21 December 1962: Appendix II, Problems and Trends in Atlantic Partnership, Committee on Foreign Relations, US Senate, 17 June 1963, London School of Economics and Political Science.
26. Neustadt, *Report to the President*, p. 96.
27. The idea to extend the Polaris offer to France is certainly a curious one. Some months later Kennedy mentioned that the idea had come from Macmillan.
28. HMD, d. 48, 23 December 1962.
29. Horne, *Macmillan*, p. 442.

30. Changes in British strategic targeting in early 1962 reduced the total number of Russian cities targeted from 40 to 15. This brought British targeting into line with McNamara's new thinking on nuclear warfare and defence and, ironically, paved the way for the Polaris deal. In short, these changes were not only helpful, but also really necessary for Britain to be in a position to make use of Polaris. See Clark, *Nuclear Diplomacy*, p. 394 and Baylis, *Ambiguity and Deterrence*, p. 342.

31. Horne, *Macmillan*, p. 443. It is interesting that at the same time as Macmillan was praising Kennedy, he was also questioning the president's integrity, confiding in his diary: 'McNamara strikes me as a man of integrity – much more . . . than President Kennedy who makes the facts fit his arguments – or so often it seems . . .'. HMD, d. 48, 23 December 1962.

32. House of Commons Debates, 30 January 1963, col. 975, Hansard.

33. Although, in effect, Britain had to face a deterrent gap, the British suggestion that the US could loan Britain a couple of Polaris submarines until the British force was ready was not pursued at Nassau.

34. Nunnerley, *President Kennedy and Britain*, p. 161.

35. Nunnerley, *President Kennedy and Britain*, p. 160. Macmillan recorded in his diary: 'No one will find it profitable to take a fair or balanced view . . .'. HMD, d. 48, 23 December 1962.

36. London to Secretary of State, 22 December 1962, RG 59, Box 1236, General Records of the State Department, Central Decimal File, 611.41\12–22–62, National Archives.

37. Rostow, Oral History, p. 102, JFKL.

38. House of Commons Debates, 30 January 1963, col. 975, Hansard.

39. House of Commons Debates, 30 January 1963, col. 979, Hansard.

40. Kennedy was furious. The test had been scheduled for some months as the last in a series. Gilpatric (McNamara's deputy) had given the go-ahead (with McNamara's knowledge) to avoid criticism that the missile was being scrapped for non-technical reasons. Making a last-ditch attempt to have the cancellation reversed, the Air Force announced the test to be a complete success – thus vindicating their backing of the project. The Department of Defense was forced to publish a retraction and a statement explaining that although some success could be measured, on the whole, the test had not been successful. Gilpatric, Oral History, p. 89, JKFL.

41. Macmillan was deeply concerned about the implications of the 'successful' test for the deal struck 'and *published*' at Nassau. HMD, d. 48, 23 December 1962.

42. Telegram from Ormsby-Gore to Macmillan, PREM 11/4229, PRO.

43. Brandon, *SKYBOLT*.

44. Brandon, *SKYBOLT*.

45. According to Neustadt, it was at this point that Ormsby-Gore opened Kennedy's mind to Macmillan problem and encouraged the President to empathise with the Prime Minister. Correspondence between R. E. Neustadt and the author.

46. *The Times*, 13 December 1962.

47. Neustadt is certain that the 'unexpectedness' of the crisis added to the pressures on Kennedy. Correspondence between Neustadt and the author.
48. Although Kennedy was personally fond of the British prime minister, there is no evidence to suggest that he acted out of fear that the Skybolt crisis might cause Macmillan's government to fall. According to Arthur Schlesinger Jr, Kennedy would not have been upset by a Labour victory in an election. Correspondence between Schlesinger and the author.
49. Rostow, Oral History, p. 102, JFKL. Carl Kaysen confirmed this to the author adding that Macmillan 'skilfully exploited Kennedy's embarrassment at all this' during their meeting. Correspondence between Kaysen and the author.
50. Brandon, Oral History, p. 7, JFKL.
51. Brandon.
52. Horne, *Macmillan*, p. 439.
53. *Washington Post,* 15 December 1962.
54. According to Neustadt, the *Washington Post* article had a deep impact on Kennedy's thinking about the crisis. Correspondence between Neustadt and the author.
55. According to Schlesinger this was entirely possible, for, 'instead of pleading that his government would fall', Macmillan 'seemed to be saying that his party would accept anti-Americanism to keep itself in power . . .' Schlesinger, *A Thousand Days*, p. 737.
56. Neustadt, *Report to the President*, p. 77.
57. Macmillan later claimed that this proposal had not been very serious.
58. A US position prepared in April 1962 stated: 'we do not agree to the US and UK providing nuclear assistance to the French national program. Such action would in the long run stimulate a German aspiration for comparable treatment; it would tend to fragment the nuclear deterrent and would almost certainly not divert de Gaulle from his basic policies or national nuclear effort . . . *We believe that the nuclear problem of the Alliance must be met through a multilateral, rather than bilateral, approach. Initial French participation in a multilateral approach is not essential and would be self-defeating if secured through bilateral nuclear aid. Such bilateral aid would whet German appetites for comparable treatment. It would thus prevent the multilateral approach from achieving one of its basic purposes: weakening and diverting German pressures for a nuclear program*' (author's emphasis). Position paper for Macmillan Visit, 21 April 1962, RG 59, Box 3, General Records of the State Department, Bureau of European Affairs Office of the British Commonwealth and N. European Affairs, Alpha-Numeric Files relating to the UK, 22-B travel from UK to 22-B Lord Atlee Visit, Folder: PM's visit April, 1962, National Archives.
59. Record of Meeting, 19 December 1962, PREM 11/4229, PRO.
60. Neustadt, *Report to the President*, p. 98.
61. Although not stated explicitly, the implication was that the United States would provide France with all the help necessary for the latter to make use of the Polaris offer. Telegram, from the State Department

to the Embassy in Paris, 1 January 1963, Document No. 262, Vol. XIII, FRUS.

62. Neustadt told the author that Kennedy was 'always intrigued by possibilities (even slight ones) of rapprochement with de Gaulle'. Correspondence between Neustadt and the author.

63. Home, *When The Wind Blows*, pp. 152–3. Harold Watkinson (now a backbencher) was certain that the government had mishandled the whole Skybolt affair. See Watkinson, *Turning Points*, pp. 170–1.

64. Sir Edward Playfair described it as 'ludicrous' that the government pinned all its hopes on such a complicated weapon. Correspondence between Sir Edward and the author.

65. Macmillan did not like the study group idea because it would have done away with the advantageous crisis atmosphere, and his personal powers of persuasion.

66. Many Cabinet members were quite surprised (and not very pleased) about Macmillan's 'success' in Nassau. Rostow, Oral History, p. 102, JFKL. According to Macmillan himself: 'the Cabinet (which met on the Friday night and was kept fully informed throughout) did not much like it, although they backed us up loyally . . .'. HMD, d. 48, 23 December 1962.

67. Neustadt, *Report to the President*, p. 91.

68. Gilpatric, Oral History, p. 88, JFKL.

69. Nunnerley, *President Kennedy and Britain*, p. 157.

70. Macmillan, it would appear, was aided by the fact that Kennedy and McNamara seemed 'strangely ignorant of the immediate past', and according to Bundy the Kennedy team was not as well versed in the details of the issues at hand as they might have been. See McGeorge Bundy, *Danger and Survival*, p. 491.

71. Author's conversation with Sir Nicholas Henderson.

72. Neustadt, *Report to the President*, p. 92.

73. Macmillan's statement to the House of Commons, 30 January 1963, col. 962, Hansard.

74. Sir Frederick Bishop is not so sure that the deal was good for Britain. He told the author 'one can only go by the outcome – which was that Macmillan could not in the end find the solution. And so we were left with a wasting asset in our doubtfully independent nuclear deterrent, a nominal but declining special relationship with the US, and failure to enter the European Union at the crucial moment'. Correspondence between Sir Frederick and the author.

75. Newhouse, *De Gaulle and the Anglo-Saxons*, p. 213.

76. Record of Meeting (Nassau Talks, 18–21 December 1962), PREM 11/4229, PRO.

77. Neither party had brought along any military staff nor technical advisers equipped to deal with the complex matters being discussed. One wonders if this was an oversight (the original meeting was to centre on mainly foreign affairs issues) or a deliberate move by one or both sides. Macmillan certainly benefited from having left behind his military men whom he knew would have seriously complicated matters and possibly prevented him from concluding the deal that *he* wanted.

On the American side, negotiations were no doubt complicated by the absence of any personnel (besides McNamara) familiar with the Skybolt problem. Ball had only been briefed on the matter the previous week and, while Tyler had been involved, he was then sent away in the crucial weeks before the conference and had only returned the day before. See Jan Melissen, *Summit Diplomacy and Alliance Politics: The Road to Nassau, December 1962* (Diplomatic Studies Programme, University of Leicester Discussion Paper, No. 12, 1995).

78. Sorenson, *Kennedy*, p. 567.
79. Schwartz, *NATO's Nuclear Dilemmas*, p. 102.
80. Neustadt, *Report to the President*, p. 100.
81. Schlesinger, *A Thousand Days*, p. 738.
82. Memorandum from Rostow to Secretary of State, 21 December 1962, Box 19, Neustadt Papers, Government Consulting, Skybolt/Atlantic Affairs 12/62, Skybolt-Nassau (classified) Folder 1, JFKL.
83. Neustadt, *Report to the President*, p. 100.
84. According to Neustadt, for some of the most zealous multilateralists the whole idea of giving Britain Polaris 'risked the whole of European policy for nothing but fidelity to a declining ally whose defence posture was silly on its face . . .' Neustadt, *Report to the President*, p. 28.

CHAPTER 6   A NEW FOREIGN POLICY INITIATIVE – ARE THERE ANY TAKERS?

1. President Kennedy's State of the Union Address, 14 January 1963.
2. Pierre, *Nuclear Politics*, p. 251.
3. Kissinger, *A Troubled Partnership*, p. 131.
4. Telegram from the Embassy in Germany to the Department of State, Bonn, 14 January 1963, Document No. 166, FRUS. Haftendorn, *NATO and the Nuclear Revolution: A Crisis of Credibility, 1966–1967* (Oxford: Clarendon Press, 1996), p. 120.
5. Carl Kaysen called it a 'fundamentally silly idea' which was, in his eyes, 'an unworkable solution to a problem more imagined than real'. Correspondence between Kaysen and the author.
6. Pierre, *Nuclear Politics*, p. 244.
7. Pascaline Winand, *Eisenhower, Kennedy and the United States of Europe* (Macmillan: London, 1993), p. 342.
8. According to Haftendorn, the MLF was something of a 'panacea – a means for accentuating US leadership while eliminating the effects of nuclear inequality and their detrimental impact on Alliance cohesion'. Haftendorn, *NATO and the Nuclear Revolution*, p. 121. Hanrieder, however, claims that: 'American support for the MLF was designed not to satisfy West Germany's alleged desire to become a nuclear power but to forestall it . . .'. Wolfram F. Hanrieder, *Germany, America, Europe: Forty Years of German Foreign Policy* (Yale University Press: New Haven and London, 1989), p. 46.
9. NATO Polaris Force Document, 17 January 1963, General Records

of the Department of State, Deputy Assistant Secretary for Politico-Military Affairs, subject files 61–63, INAF to Rostow Strategy Papers, Box 4, Folder 'Polaris', National Archives.

10. In a perceptive article, Walter Lippman of the *New York Herald Tribune* claimed that the purpose of the MLF was to 'vaccinate the Germans against wanting a nuclear force of their own'. *New York Herald Tribune* (European Edition), 10 May 1963.

11. Schlesinger, *A Thousand Days*, p. 745.

12. After all, it was widely accepted that any conflict in the core area of NATO would take place on German soil, making deterrence through threat of rapid nuclear escalation the central aim of German defence policy. Haftendorn, *NATO and the Nuclear Revolution*, p. 35.

13. Catherine McArdle Kelleher, *Germany and the Politics of Nuclear Weapons* (Columbia University Press: New York and London 1975), p. 4.

14. Germany's perceived demand for nuclear status was reinforced for the United States by statements made by senior ministers about the deployment and use of such weapons. For example, in April 1962, Defence Minister Franz-Josef Strauss laid down three requirements in a debate in the Bundestag: 1) information on the type and location of American nuclear weapons in Europe; 2) a guarantee that these would not be withdrawn against the will of the countries affected; 3) positive as well as negative co-determination concerning nuclear weapons based on national territory. H. Haftendorn: *NATO and the Nuclear Revolution*, p. 34.

15. Memorandum from Rostow to the President, 19 February 1963, POF, staff memorandum, Rostow, 1/61–7/63, Box 65, JFKL.

16. Adenauer retired on 11 October 1963.

17. This belief in the existence of a German thirst for nuclear parity was not universal in the Kennedy administration. As the year wore on, figures like Henry Kissinger (an official government consultant) and Arthur Schlesinger expressed doubts about this. See *Washington Post*, 1 June 1963, Arthur Schlesinger Jr, Oral History, p. 2, JFKL, McGeorge Bundy, Oral History, p. 5, JFKL and author's conversation with Arthur Schlesinger Jr.

18. *New York Times*, 12 April 1963.

19. Yarmolinsky Papers, Box 32, Ditchley Conference, p. 41, JFKL.

20. Theodore C. Sorenson, Oral History, p. 106, JFKL. Incidentally, nothing more ever came of this and Sorenson assumes that the report was false.

21. McGeorge Bundy, Oral History, p. 5, JFKL. Ball had not always been a supporter of the MLF proposal. He apparently changed his mind at the Nassau Conference in December 1962.

22. Henry Brandon, Oral History, p. 10, JFKL.

23. As Secretary of Defense, McNamara had the primary responsibility of working out details of the MLF. According to Rusk, 'it seemed to be a workable plan from McNamara's point of view. But he was not wholeheartedly committed to it in any way that went beyond the attitude of the President.' Rusk, Oral History, p. 182, JFKL. His deputy, Gilpatric claims that the Secretary's main concern at the time was to engage the Europeans in a form of exercise that would cure their

desire for nuclear participation. Gilpatric, Oral History, pp. 82, 84, JFKL. According to Kaysen, the DoD never did believe in the proposal. Correspondence between Kaysen and the author. I.N.N.A (W.G.)/M (63) 5 Ministry of Defence Working Group on the Implementation of the Nassau Nuclear Agreement, 5 March 1963, DEFE 10/548, PRO.

24. Summary Record of NSC Executive Committee Meeting, No. 41, Washington, 12 February 1963, Document No. 173, Vol. XIII, FRUS. He was also concerned about potential targeting problems that would be created by the force. Haftendorn, *NATO and the Nuclear Revolution*, p. 118.

25. Memorandum of Conversation, 18 February 1963, Document No. 174, Vol. XIII, FRUS.

26. Memorandum for the Record, Washington, 14 March 1963, Document No. 181, Vol. XIII, FRUS. The *Washington Post*, 31 May 1963. Rusk himself claimed in later life that he had been more 'cool' than some of his subordinates and that there had been some division between himself and the proponents of the MLF because he generally took the view of the president that it was a proposal made in the interests of America's allies. Rusk, Oral History, p. 182, JFKL.

27. Schlesinger, *A Thousand Days*, p. 746.

28. National Security Council Executive Meeting on MLF, 12 February 1963, Document No. 173, Vol. XIII, FRUS.

29. Summary Record of NSC Executive Committee Meeting, No. 41, Washington, 12 February 1963, Document No. 173, Vol. XIII, FRUS. During the course of this meeting one official made a revealing comment which received no criticism or rebuke. He told the gathering that 'we are committed to discuss a multilateral force with the Europeans, *even if our hope is that the Europeans would not accept it*' (author's emphasis).

30. According to Schlesinger, Kennedy was not 'doctrinaire' on European matters and was 'skeptical' about 'gimmicks' like the multilateral force. He regarded the MLF as an idea worth exploring rather than one worth fighting for. Correspondence between Arthur Schlesinger and the author.

31. Charles E. Bohlen observed that Kennedy 'had a certain reservation as to the German future and the danger of German militarism ... [he] was very conscious of the possibility that given a few turns or twists of events, you could be headed back to another situation where Germany again could become a menace'. Bohlen, Oral History, p. 37, JFKL.

32. At this meeting Kennedy emphasised his belief that the control issue was going to be a major, if not fatally damaging factor in the MLF negotiations. He felt that it was worth a shot, but did not appear even partially convinced that this would turn out to be a winning policy. Memorandum of Conversation, Washington, 18 February 1963, Document No. 174, Vol. XIII, FRUS.

33. Kennedy was concerned that such a force, especially if it involved West Germany would undermine the test ban negotiations with the Soviet Union who was not likely to be happy about the idea of her traditional enemy participating in a nuclear force. Kennedy was not

far off the mark here. In October, after the initial treaty had been agreed, the USSR again began linking the MLF with a further agreement to prevent the dissemination of nuclear weapons and knowledge.
34. The Merchant team's mission lasted from 22 February to 17 March.
35. Memorandum from President Kennedy to the Members of the MLF Negotiating Delegation, Washington, 21 February 1963, Document No. 176, Vol. XIII, FRUS.
36. Memorandum for the Record, Washington, 21 February 1963, Document No. 175, Vol. XIII, FRUS.
37. Nitze's proposal eventually was embodied in the Nuclear Planning Group (NPG) which was formed in December 1966.
38. Memorandum of Conversation, 18 February 1963, Document No. 174, Vol. XIII, FRUS.
39. Ibid.
40. Memorandum of a telephone conversation, 26 February, Department of State, Central Files, Defense (MLF), National Archives. (Quoted in footnote, FRUS, Vol. XIII, p. 508).
41. This was pointed out to the president for the first time in the course of a meeting on 21 February. See Memorandum for the Record, Washington, 21 February 1963, Document No. 175, Vol. XIII, FRUS.
42. The *New York Times* reported that the committee's opposition was so 'overwhelming' that it apparently 'doomed any hopes for implementing the Administration's proposal'. Some members were reported to have dismissed the whole 'scheme' as 'nutty'. *New York Times*, 23 February 1963.
43. *New York Times*, 23 February 1963.
44. According to Ball: 'The multilateral force was conceived as an educational instrument and a healing ointment to relieve the pressures for proliferation; it was also – and this was perhaps the crucial consideration in most of our minds – a means of strengthening Western cohesion in a testing time for our common civilization and political purpose'. George Ball, *The Discipline of Power* (The Bodley Head: London, 1968), p. 206.
45. Memorandum of Conversation NSC Executive Meeting No. 38, 25 January 1963, Document No. 169, Vol. XIII, FRUS.
46. Nitze recalls that Kennedy was concerned about the ongoing test ban treaty negotiations. The Soviet Union had complained that the MLF would violate the non-proliferation aspect that was an important part of the proposed treaty. Paul H. Nitze, *From Hiroshima to Glasnost: At the Centre of Decision: A Memoir* (Weidenfeld & Nicolson: London, 1989), p. 212.
47. Memorandum of Conversation, 18 February 1963, Document No. 174, Vol. XIII, FRUS.
48. According to Haftendorn, Germany welcomed proposals for the MLF because nuclear sharing might lead to nuclear co-determination, but for the long-term Bonn wanted to see the Alliance maintain the option of a European nuclear force operating independently of a US veto. Haftendorn, *NATO and the Nuclear Revolution*, p. 113.
49. Memorandum from Merchant to Rusk, Washington, 20 March 1963, Document No. 183, Vol. XIII, FRUS.

50. I.N.N.A. (W.G.) P (63) 20, Working Group on the Implementation of the Nassau Nuclear Agreement, conversation between Foreign Secretary and Merchant, 26 March 1963, DEFE 10/548, PRO.
51. Morris in Bonn to Secretary of State, 18 March 1963, Box 218, MLF cables 3/16/63–3/31/63, JFKL.
52. Ibid.
53. Winand, *Eisenhower, Kennedy and the United States of Europe*, p. 343.
54. Macarthur to Secretary of State, 8 March 1963, Box 216, MLF, general, 3.1.63–3.10.63, NSF, JFKL.
55. Telegram from Brussels to State about conversation with Spaak, 6 March 1963, Box 218, MLF cables 3/1/63–3/10/63, NSF, JFKL.
56. Memorandum of Meeting, Washington, 22 March 1963, Document No. 184, Vol. XIII, FRUS.
57. Although the reception was cold in Paris, Merchant was sure that France would not block the discussions between the interested parties in NATO. He told the British Foreign Secretary that he had also received information suggestive of the fact that de Gaulle was not as implacably opposed as commonly thought. I.N.N.A. (W.G.) P (63) 20, Working Group on the Implementation of the Nassau Nuclear Agreement, conversation between the British Foreign Secretary and Merchant, 26 March 1963, DEFE 10/548, PRO.
58. Memorandum from Merchant to Rusk, Washington, 20 March 1963, Document No. 183, Vol. XIII, FRUS.
59. Merchant to Secretary of State, 1 March 1963, Box 218, MLF cables 3/1/63–3/10/63, NSF, JFKL.
60. Finletter, Paris to Secretary of State, 16 March 1963. Boxes 211–220, Regional Security, Anzus, NATO, 6/1/63–6/30/63, Box 218, MLF cables 3/16/63–3/31/63, NSF, JFKL.
61. Telegram from Secretary of State to Embassy in London, 14 March 1963, Document No. 182, Vol. XIII, FRUS.
62. The British government regarded Merchant as an 'old friend'. According to the Prime Minister: 'there could not be a better person for the job as he understands us and our problems . . .'. Foreign Office to Washington, 29 January 1963, DEFE 13/734, PRO.
63. State Department to Paris, London and Bonn, 5 March 1963, NSF, Box 218, MLF general, cables 3/1/63–3/10/63, JFKL.
64. Telegram from Brussels to State, 7 March 1963, Box 218, MLF, general, 3/1/63–3/10/63, NSF, JFKL.
65. Memorandum from Merchant to Rusk, 20 March 1963, Document No. 183, Vol. XIII, FRUS.
66. Ibid.
67. Memorandum from Merchant to Rusk, 20 March 1963, Document No. 183, Vol. XIII, FRUS.
68. Communiqué on US–UK Talks on MLF, 13 March 1963, Boxes 211–220, MLF, general, Merchant, 3/9/63–3/28/63, NSF, JFKL.
69. Telegram from Merchant to Furnas, 10 March 1963, Box 218, MLF cables 3/1/63–3/10/63, NSF, JFKL.
70. Memorandum from Schlesinger to the President, 25 March 1963, NSF, Box 71, countries, UK, general, 3/25/63–3/31/63, folder 6, JFKL.

CHAPTER 7   DO OR DIE: THE MAKING AND BREAKING OF
THE MLF

1. I.N.N.A. (W.G.) / P (63) 18 Working Group on the Implementation of the Nassau Nuclear Agreement, Note by the Secretary, 8 March 1963, DEFE 10/548, PRO.
2. Sir Pierson Dixon to the Foreign Office, 7 January 1963, PREM 11/4151, PRO.
3. Baylis, *Ambiguity and Deterrence*, p. 328.
4. Memorandum on Mixed Manned Force of Surface Ships, 6 June 1963, PREM 11/4162, PRO.
5. Neither was the press for that matter. The *New York Times* (5 June 1963) noted that 'editorial opinion in Britain has been almost unanimous in condemning the proposal, and it has become a cartoonist's delight'.
6. Thorneycroft believed that one of the reasons why the Americans had come up with the proposal was to engage Britain in sufficiently heavy expenditure in order to prevent the maintenance of the national deterrent. He saw no reason to have Britain saddled with these 'white sea-elephants'. Thorneycroft to Macmillan, 4 October 1963, DEFE 11/314, PRO.
7. Annex A: Views of the Chiefs of Staff: Cabinet Document C.(68) 103, 21 June 1963, CAB 129/114, PRO. According to the Chiefs of Staff: 'the formation of such a force would almost certainly lead to increased Soviet activity at sea, and therefore, *increase the chances of war by miscalculation* . . .'. (author's emphasis). Chiefs of Staff 38th meeting, 13 June 1963, DEFE 4/155, PRO.
8. Horne, *Macmillan*, p. 437.
9. Memorandum from R. H. Scott to Hood at Foreign Office, 11 March 1963, FO 371/173439, PRO.
10. Figures as high as 15–20 million pounds were also mentioned. See Memorandum, 21 June 1963, Annex B CAB 129/114. R. H. Scott (MoD) to Hood (FO), 11 March 1963, Western Organisations & Planning Dept., NATO, FO 371/173439, PRO.
11. The United States was also urging NATO to buy American MRBMs to replace obsolete bomber aircraft.
12. Cabinet Minute, 25 March 1963, CAB 128/37, PRO.
13. Memorandum by H. T. A. Overton, 23 May 1963: UK Contribution to Western Defence, FO 371/173439, PRO.
14. Message from Kennedy to Macmillan, 29 May 1963, PREM 11/4162, PRO.
15. Memorandum from Burke Trend to Prime Minister, 29 May 1963, PREM 11/4162, PRO.
16. There is some evidence to suggest that Macmillan had some private doubts and concerns about German nuclear aspirations. He confided in his diary: 'my fear is that unless we can satisfy them by a general Test Ban Treaty with a treaty against the spreading of nuclear weapons . . . the Germans are bound to become a nuclear power sooner or later. The "multilateral force" agreed at Nassau will perhaps do

something to satisfy them. Or may it merely whet their appetite?' HMD, d. 49, 24 March 1963.

17. Minutes of Cabinet Meeting, 25 June 1963, CAB 128/37, PRO.

18. This argument has been refuted by those who claimed that Germany's commercial nuclear development had enabled the country to have the capacity to build a bomb in a very short time and at little cost. See W. B. Bader, 'Nuclear Weapons Sharing and "The German Problem"' (*Foreign Affairs*, July 1966, Vol. 44, No. 4), p. 697.

19. Alistair Buchan, 'Europe and the Atlantic Alliance: Two Strategies or One?' (*Journal of Common Market Studies*, Spring 1963, Vol. 1, No. 3), pp. 231–2.

20. A. Duff (British Embassy, Bonn) to E. J. W. Barnes (Foreign Office), 21 March 1963, Western Organisations & Planning Dept., NATO, FO 371/173431, PRO.

21. On 7 July 1963 an article appeared in *The Observer* claiming that France had asked Germany officially for help with her nuclear weapons programme and that Germany had refused citing treaty obligations. Notations by British officials reveal that they regarded the story as 'quite plausible' and 'intelligent speculation?' Perhaps it was not considered 'beyond the pale' for de Gaulle to make a highly improbable request in order to simply 'test the water'. Newspaper cutting: *The Observer*, 7 July 1963, FO 371/173432, PRO.

22. Memorandum: Summary of NATO Nuclear Force Memoranda from Burke Trend to Macmillan, 29 May 1963, PREM 11/4162, PRO.

23. Memorandum by A. M. Warburton (British Embassy, Bonn) to Foreign Office, 28 May 1963, FO 371/173432, PRO.

24. Memorandum by Minister of Defence, 13 September 1963, C.(63) 153, 16 September 1963, CAB 129/114, PRO.

25. British Embassy, Bonn to Foreign Office, 10 August 1963, FO 371/ 173432, PRO.

26. Sir Alec Douglas-Home, Oral History, p. 9, JFKL.

27. Yarmolinsky Papers, Box 32, Ditchley Foundation Record, p. 33, JFKL.

28. Quoted in McGeorge Bundy, *Danger and Survival*, p. 495. Indeed, by March 1963, officials in Bonn were suggesting that American behaviour vis-à-vis the MLF, rather than responding to an existing or potential German demand for nuclear status, had instead precipitated German aspirations in this direction. Frank Roberts (British Embassy in Bonn) to Harold Caccia (Foreign Office), 21 March 1963, Western Organisations & Planning Dept., NATO, FO 371/173431, PRO. J. A. Thomson (British Embassy, Washington) to E. J. W. Barnes (Foreign Office), 25 March 1963, Western Organisations & Planning Dept., NATO, FO 371/173431, PRO.

29. Minutes of Cabinet Meeting, 25 June 1963, C.C.42 (63), CAB 128/ 37, PRO.

30. Minister of Defence to Foreign Secretary, 10 December 1963, DEFE 13/411, PRO.

31. Memorandum: NATO Nuclear Force: the Merchant Mission by R. H. Scott, 11 March 1963, FO 371/173439, PRO. I. N. N. A. (W. G)/M (63) 5 Ministry of Defence Working Group on the Implementation

of the Nassau Agreement, 5 March 1963, DEFE 10/548, PRO.
32. Minutes of Cabinet Meeting, 25 March 1963, C.C.18 (63), CAB 128/37, PRO. HMD, d. 49, 1 April 1963.
33. *Washington Daily News*, 30 May 1963.
34. Minutes of Cabinet Meeting, 25 March 1963, C.C.18 (63), CAB 128/37, PRO.
35. With this in mind, Macmillan records in his diary that the Defence Committee decided on 1 April to support the proposal 'while secretly hoping the scheme will fall through!' HMD, d., 49, 1 April 1963. This tacit support without commitment appears to have been the strategy maintained by the government for some months in an effort not to alienate the Americans. As Macmillan admitted in an entry a few weeks later when Britain was being asked to contribute financially to the force: 'We agreed, at Nassau, to this plan in principle. But I never intended to contribute to it'. HMD, d. 49, 9 May 1963.
36. Cabinet Memorandum by Secretary of State for Foreign Affairs, 27 May 1963, C.(63) 95, CAB 129/113, PRO.
37. Message from Kennedy to Macmillan, 29 May 1963, PREM 11/4162, PRO.
38. Memorandum of Conversation, 8 May 1963, FO 371/173439, PRO.
39. Ibid.
40. Telegram from Ormsby-Gore to Foreign Office, 9 May 1963, FO 371/173439, PRO.
41. Memorandum from T. A. K. Elliott to Carless about conclusions of talks about the MLF at Chequers last week, 22 May 1963, FO 371/173439, PRO.
42. In contrast to their attitude to the MLF proposal, the British government was enthusiastic about the implementation of the Inter-Allied Nuclear Force as identified in paragraph 6 of the Nassau Agreement. This was to consist of American Polaris submarines and British V-bombers, along with contributions from other interested NATO partners. The various elements comprising the force were to remain in national hands and therefore no additional control mechanism was needed or additional costs involved. The final agreement was reached at Ottawa on 22 May. This force, along with the MLF was to form a NATO Nuclear Force (NNF).
43. Macmillan to Home in Ottawa for NATO Council Meeting, 22 May 1963, FO 371/173439, PRO.
44. Ormsby-Gore to Macmillan, 23 May 1963, FO 371/173439, PRO.
45. Ibid.
46. Cabinet Memorandum by the Secretary of State for Foreign Affairs, 28 May 1963, C.(63) 95, CAB 129/113, PRO.
47. It would appear that the Foreign Office was subjected to 'unusually heavy pressure' from the State Department, according to Pierre, which eventually persuaded them to come out in favour of the proposal. Pierre, *Nuclear Politics*, p. 247.
48. Home also suggested that the United States was willing to offer a number of incentives. These included: contracts for shipbuilding and

repairing, the establishment of a new base in the UK; and if Britain were to supply the warheads, contracts for making, servicing and replacing the warheads and the provision for the warheads of Uranium–235 on generous terms.

49. Memorandum by Minister of Defence, 28 May 1963, C.(63) 96, CAB 129/113, PRO.
50. Summary of NATO Nuclear Force Memoranda from Burke Trend to Macmillan, 29 May 1963, PREM 11/4162, PRO.
51. *New York Times,* 28 May 1963.
52. Memorandum from the Head of the MLF Negotiating Delegation (Merchant) to Secretary of State Rusk, Washington, 20 March 1963, Document No. 183, Vol. XIII, FRUS.
53. Ibid.
54. Memorandum of Meeting, Washington, 22 March 1963, Document No. 184, Vol. XIII, FRUS.
55. Memorandum for the Record by David Klein, Discussion with President about MLF and IANF, 5 April 1963, Box 317 meetings and memoranda, meetings with the President, general, 4/63 NSF, JFKL.
56. Memorandum of Meeting, Washington, 22 March 1963, Document No. 184, Vol. XIII, FRUS.
57. Telegram from the Department of State to Embassy in Germany, Kennedy to Adenauer, Washington, 29 March 1963, Document No. 185, Vol. XIII, FRUS. Telegram from the Department of State to the Embassy in Germany, Washington, 5 April 1963, the text of an unofficial translation of text of letter from Adenauer to Kennedy, Document No. 187, Vol. XIII, FRUS.
58. Draft letter (undated) to Prime Minister Fanfani from Kennedy, RG 59, General Records of the Department of State, Deputy Assistant Secretary for Politico-Military Affairs, subject files 1961–63, Multilateral force December 1962 to December 1963 to Steering Cmttee, folder 'MLF December 1962–December 1963', National Archives.
59. This intimation was deemed necessary to get the Germans to agree to the surface mode for the time being. Kennedy was very concerned, however, that even this was perhaps going too far, virtually promising something that the United States had neither studied nor intended to pursue in order to get consensus. See Memorandum for the Record, Washington, 24 April 1963, Document No. 191, Vol. XIII, FRUS.
60. Ibid.
61. Telegram from the Department of State to the Embassy in Germany, Washington, 2 May 1963, unofficial Germany Embassy translation of letter from Chancellor to President Kennedy, Document No. 192, Vol. XIII, FRUS. The German Cabinet had taken the decision formally on 24 April to enter into negotiations on German participation in the MLF scheme. Haftendorn, *NATO and the Nuclear Revolution*, p. 123.
62. Macmillan wrote in his diary: 'They are trying to force us to contribute to the "multilateral" force of surface ships . . .'. HMD, d. 49, 9 May 1963.
63. Memorandum from Kitchen to G. Smith, 16 April 1963, RG 59,

General Records of the Department of State, Deputy Assistant Secretary for Politico-Military Affairs, subject files 1961–63, Multilateral Force, December 1962–December 1963, folder MLF December 1962–1963, National Archives.

64. Memorandum on MLF Alternatives from Kitchen, undated, RG 59, General Records of the Department of State, Assistant Secretary for Politico-Military Affairs, subject files 1961–63, folder MLF December 1962–December 1963, National Archives.

65. The Cabinet was divided. According to Macmillan, the Foreign Secretary was 'mildly in favour', the Lord Privy Seal was 'strongly in favour', while the Minister of Defence and the Chancellor of the Exchequer were 'strongly against'. As for the Prime Minister himself, he had decided to 'play for time'. HMD, d. 49, 20 May 1963.

66. Luncheon Conversation between Ball, Tyler and Ormsby-Gore, 3 May 1963. Box 171, countries, UK, general, 4/19/63–5/14/63, Folder 8, NSF, JFKL.

67. Ibid.

68. Draft letter from Kennedy to Macmillan, Box 174 countries, UK, subjects, Macmillan correspondence, 4/29/63–5/7/63 (Tab 1–2), NSF, JFKL. (It is unclear whether or not this letter was actually sent.)

69. Message from the president's Special Assistant for National Security Affairs (Bundy) to Macmillan's Private Secretary (de Zulueta), Washington, 10 May 1963, Document No. 195, FRUS. Kennedy admitted to the Canadian Prime Minister on 15 May that although earlier he had been 'rather lukewarm' about the MLF, he now felt 'very strongly in its favour'. Meetings between John F. Kennedy and Prime Minister Lester B. Pearson, Summary Report, 15 May 1963, DEFE 13/126, PRO.

70. Ormsby-Gore's meeting with Kennedy 22 May produced the suggestion that Admiral Ricketts should go to Britain to explain the technical aspects of the proposed force. Ormsby-Gore to Foreign Office, 23 May 1963, FO 371/173439, PRO.

71. Memorandum from Rusk to Kennedy: proposed reply to PM Macmillan, 27 May 1963, NSF, Box 174, countries, UK, subjects, Macmillan correspondence, 5/29/63 Tab 15, JFKL.

72. Ibid.

73. A message sent on 10 May stated that the British government needed to hold Cabinet meetings before a decision could be taken on the MLF. On 30 May, Macmillan recorded in his diary that the ministers were still equally divided and so he had sent another message to Kennedy telling the President that the British government needed more information about the proposal before a decision could be made. HMD, d. 49, 30 May 1963.

74. Memorandum for President: Procedure for getting on with the MLF by Rusk, 6 June 1963, RG 59, General Records of the Department of State, Deputy Assistant Secretary for Politico-Military Affairs, subject files 1961–63, Multilateral Force December 62–December 63, folder MLF December 1962–1963, National Archives.

75. Memorandum of Conversation, Washington, 6 May 1963, Document No. 194, Vol. XIII, FRUS.

76. Memorandum from Weiss to Kitchen about the MLF fall-back exercise, 5 June 1963, RG 59, Records of the Department of State, Deputy Assistant Secretary for Politico-Military Affairs, subject files, folder MLF December 1962–1963, National Archives.
77. Ibid.
78. Schlesinger, *A Thousand Days*, p. 747.
79. Schlesinger, Oral History, p. 2, JFKL.
80. According to Schlesinger in 1962 Bundy was for it, 1963 he was agnostic, and by 1964 he was very much in his mind against it. Oral History, p. 2, JFKL.
81. Memorandum from Bundy to Kennedy, 15 June 1963, Document No. 201, Vol. XIII, FRUS.
82. Telegram from Secretary of State Rusk to Department of State, Wiesbaden, 25 June 1963, Document No. 203, Vol. XIII, FRUS. See also *New York Times*, 29 June 1963.
83. Memorandum from Bundy to Secretary of State Rusk, Washington, 11 July 1963, Document No. 206, Vol. XIII, FRUS.
84. Ibid.
85. The American press became increasingly derisive. The *Washington Post* likened the American approach to the 'persistence of a door-to-door brush salesman' and warned that it was dangerous to get bogged down with one idea. The *Washington Post,* 23 July 1963.
86. Memorandum for the Record by Carl Kaysen, 10 July 1963 – An account of a presidential meeting with Ambassador Harriman, Box 265, Departments and Agencies, arms control and Disarmament Agency, NSF, JFKL. One account of this meeting has the president admitting in response to Harriman's suggestion that the MLF could be offered as a 'sweetener' that 'it would be a great relief to get rid of that'. Reeves, *The Kennedy Presidency*, p. 546.
87. Carl Kaysen told the author that had Kennedy faced a decision about the MLF he would 'probably have been negative'. Correspondence between Kaysen and the author.
88. Information reaching the Foreign Office suggested that Kennedy was not now as committed to the MLF proposal as were some of his advisers. Frank Roberts (British Embassy, Bonn) to Hood (Foreign Office), 3 July 1963, Western Organisations & Planning Dept., NATO, FO 371/173432, PRO.
89. HMD, d. 49, 7 July 1963.
90. Telegram from Shuckburgh to Home (UK Delegation to NATO), 2 July 1963, Western Organisations & Planning Dept., NATO, FO 371/173430, PRO.
91. NSAM No. 253, memorandum from Bundy to Secretary of Defense, 13 July 1963, Boxes 340–341, NSF, JFKL. According to Rostow, this was one of the only two policy ideas ever to have directly originated from a president of the United States. This idea was 'planted' in the course of the discussions so that it would not be seen as another American initiative, diversion or gimmick.
92. In August and early September the Ministry of Defence and the Foreign Office were still debating the official government line vis-à-vis possible

British participation in the MLF talks. Minister of Defence to Foreign Secretary, 2 September 1963, DEFE 11/314, PRO.

93. A. Buchan, 'The MLF: A Historical Perspective' (*The Institute for Strategic Studies*, Adelphi Papers, No. 13, October 1964), p. 9.

94. Weiss to Furnas, 3 September 1963, Memorandum from Weiss to Kitchen, 3 September 1963, RG 59 General records of the State Department, Office of the Deputy Assistant Secretary for Politico-Military Affairs, Folder MLF December 1962–December 1963, National Archives.

95. Ibid.

96. Postscript to Memorandum reporting Furnas' view of White House support for the MLF, 6 September 1963, Weiss to Kitchen, RG 59, General Records of the Department of State, Deputy Assistant Secretary for Politico-Military Affairs, subject files 1961–63, folder MLF December 1962–1963, National Archives.

97. Ibid.

98. Memoranda by the Minister of Defence and the Foreign Secretary, 16 September 1963 C.(63) 153, CAB 129/114, and 16 September 1963 C. (63) 151 CAB 129/114, PRO. See also Draft Cabinet Paper, Memorandum by Minister of Defence, 11 September 1963, DEFE 11/314, PRO. The Chief of Defence Staff also shared this opposition to the proposal. Memorandum by Assistant Chief of Defence Staff, 12 September 1963, DEFE 11/314, PRO. Macmillan confirms this Cabinet division in his diaries. See HMD, d. 49, 19 September 1963. On 23 September the Cabinet appears to have reached a general agreement about participation (without any commitment) in the MLF talks. HMD, d. 49, 23 September 1963. The *New York Times*, 20 September 1963. (As yet, the author has been unable to locate any useful material in either DEFE 4 or 5 (COS memoranda and meetings) or in the Foreign Office Planner's Papers as a considerable amount of the documentation relating to the MLF project still remain closed to the public.)

99. Although they had decided to participate, general sentiment within the government remained negative. Shuckburgh (UK Delegation to NATO, Paris) to Caccia (FO), 17 October 1963, Western Organisation & Planning Dept., NATO, FO 371/173462, PRO. According to Sir Nicholas Henderson, it had become an 'obsession' for the government. Conversation between Sir Nicholas and the author.

100. Note by the Secretary of the Cabinet: Statement on NATO Multilateral Nuclear Force, 30 September 1963, CAB 129/114, PRO. The Foreign Office and the Ministry of Defence had only decided on an agreed recommendation to the Prime Minister (concerning the instructions to the talks team) around 8 October. As late as 4 October, important differences had still existed between the two departments. Minister of Defence to Prime Minister, 4 October 1963, DEFE 11/314, PRO. Minister of Defence to Foreign Secretary, 8 October 1963, DEFE 11/314, PRO.

101. Memcon US–UK discussions on the MLF, 4 October 1963, POF Box 127, UK general, 7/63–11/63, folder 10, JFKL.

102. The British Chiefs of Staff were unhappy with the idea of experimental ship believing it to be an expensive, time-wasting exercise of limited value. Chiefs of Staff Committee, 6 November 1963, DEFE 11/314, PRO.

CONCLUSION

1. Richard Lamb, *The Macmillan Years 1957–63: The Emerging Truth* (John Murray: London, 1995).
2. See chapter 2.
3. See chapter 4.
4. Between 8 November (when Ormsby-Gore was notified about Skybolt's imminent demise) and 17 December when he went to Nassau, Macmillan and Thorneycroft met (with top aides) a total of *11 times* (not including regular Cabinet meetings). Prime Minister's Diary – Typescript narrative of daily events, appointments, dep.c.30 vols. 1–88.
5. Roswell Gilpatric to John Rubel, 28 December 1964, Roswell Gilpatric Papers, Box 10, President's Task Force on Nuclear Proliferation, Correspondence, November 1964–March 1965, JFKL.
6. Baylis, *Ambiguity and Deterrence*, p. 331. McGeorge Bundy, *Danger and Survival*, p. 494.

Glossary of Names

Acheson, Dean	Former US Secretary of State, 1949–53.
Amery, Julian	Secretary of State for Air, 1960–2; Minister for Aviation, 1962–4.
Ball, George	US Under-Secretary of State, 1961–6.
Bishop, Frederick	Principal Private Secretary to PM, 1956–9, Deputy Secretary of Cabinet, 1959–61.
Bligh, Timothy	Principal Private Secretary to PM, 1959–64.
Bohlen, Charles E.	US Ambassador to Paris, 1962–8.
Bowie, Robert R.	US Assistant Secretary of State for Policy Planning, 1955–7; Director, Centre for International Affairs, Harvard, 1957–72.
Boyle, Sir D. A.	Air Marshall, Chief of Air Staff, 1957–9.
Brook, Sir Norman	Secretary of the Cabinet, 1947–62.
Brown, George	Deputy Leader Labour Party, 1960–70.
Brown, Harold	Director, Lawrence Livermore Laboratory, 1960–1; Director of Research and Engineering, US Dept. of Defense, 1961–5.
Bruce, David	US Ambassador to London, 1961–9.
Brundrett, Sir Frederick	Scientific Adviser, MOD and Chairman, DRPC, 1954–9.
Bundy, McGeorge	US Special Assistant to the President for National Security Affairs, 1961–6.
Burke, Admiral Arleigh	US Chief of Naval Operations, 1955–61.
Butler, Richard A.	Lord Privy Seal, 1955–9; Home Secretary, 1957–62.
Brandon, Henry	*Times* Washington Correspondant.
Caccia, Sir Harold	British Ambassador to Washington, 1956–61; Permanent Under-Secretary of State, Foreign Office, 1962–5.
Cary, Michael	Deputy Secretary of the Cabinet, 1961–4.
Chauvel, Jean	French Ambassador to London, 1958–62.
Courcel, Geoffroy de	French Ambassador to London, 1962–72.
Couve de Murville, M.	French Minister for Foreign Affairs, 1958–68.
Dean, Sir Maurice J.	Permanent Under-Secretary, Air Ministry, 1955–63.
Dean, Sir Patrick	Deputy Under-Secretary of State, Foreign Office, 1956–60.
Dillon, C. Douglas	US Ambassador to Paris, 1953–7.
Dixon, Sir Pierson	British Ambassador to Paris, 1960–4.
Douglas, James H.	US Secretary of Air Force, 1957–9; Deputy Secretary of Defense, 1959–61.
Dulles, John Foster	US Secretary of State, 1953–9.
Earle, Sir A.	Air Vice-Marshal, Assistant Chief of Air Staff, 1955–7; Deputy Chief of Defence Staff, 1960–2.

Eden, Sir Anthony — Prime Minister, 1955–7.
Eisenhower, Dwight D. — US President, 1953–61.
Fessenden, Russel — European Desk, US State Department, 1959–62.
Finletter, Thomas K. — US Ambassador to NATO, 1961–5.
Fraser, Hugh — Under-Secretary of State, War Office, 1958–60; Secretary of State for Air, 1962–4.
Gaitskell, Hugh — Leader of the Labour Party, 1955–63.
Gates, Thomas G. — US Secretary of the Navy, 1957–9; Deputy Secretary of Defense, 1959–60; Secretary of Defense, 1960.
Gaulle, Charles de — French President, 1958–69.
Gavin, James M. — US Ambassador to Paris, 1961–2.
Geraghty, William — Assistant Under-Secretary of State, War Office, 1958–60; Under-Secretary, Cabinet Office, 1960–2.
Gilpatric, Roswell L. — US Deputy-Secretary of Defense, 1961–4.
Goodpaster, General A. — Staff Secretary to US President, 1954–61.
Hailsham, Lord — First Lord of the Admiralty, 1956–7; Lord Privy Seal, 1959–60; Lord President of the Council, 1957–9; 1960–4.
Head, Sir Anthony — Secretary of State for War, 1951–6; Minister of Defence, 1956–7.
Healey, Denis — Shadow Cabinet, 1959–64.
Heath, Edward — Lord Privy Seal, 1960–3.
Herter, Christian A. — US Under-Secretary of State, 1957–9; Secretary of State, 1959–61.
Hockaday, Arthur — Private Secretary to Minister of Defence, 1962–5.
Home, Lord — Commonwealth Secretary, 1955–60; Foreign Secretary, 1960–3; Prime Minister, 1963–4.
Hood, Viscount — British Minister, Washington, 1957–62.
Kaysen, Carl — US Deputy Assistant to the President for National Security Affairs, 1961–3.
Kennedy, John F. — US President, 1961–3.
Killian, James R. — US Special Assistant to the President for Science and Technology, 1957–9.
Kitchen, Jeffrey C. — US Head, Bureau of Political and Military Affairs, Department of State, 1962.
Kohler, Foy D. — US Deputy Assistant and Assistant Secretary of State for European Affairs, 1958–62; Ambassador to Moscow, 1962–6.
Komer, Robert W. — Senior Staff Member, US National Security Council, 1961–5.
LeMay, General Curtis — Commander US SAC, 1948–57; Air Force Vice-Chief of Staff, 1955–61; Chief of Staff, 1961–5.
Lemnitzer, General L. — Chairman, USJCS, 1960–2; SACEUR, 1963–9.
Lloyd, Selwyn — Minister of Defence, 1955; Foreign Secretary, 1955–60; Chancellor of Exchequer, 1961.

McCone, John A.	Chairman USAEC, 1958–61.
Macleod, Iain N.	Leader of House of Commons, 1961–3.
Macmillan, Harold	Minister of Defence, 1954–5; Foreign Secretary, 1955; Chancellor of Exchequer, 1955–7; Prime Minister, 1957–63.
McNamara, Robert S.	US Secretary of Defense, 1961–8.
Makins, Sir Roger	British Ambassador to Washington, 1953–6; Chairman, UKAEA, 1960–4.
Mason, Sir Paul	UK Permanent Representative to North Atlantic Council, 1960–2.
Maudling, Reginald	Minister of Supply, 1955–7; Paymaster General, 1957–9; Chancellor of Exchequer, 1962–4.
Merchant, Livingston T.	US Assistant Secretary of State for European Affairs, 1953–6; 1958–9; Under-Secretary of State for Political Affairs, 1959–61.
Messmer, Pierre	French Armed Forces Minister, 1960–9.
Monckton, Sir Walter	Minister of Defence, 1955–6; Paymaster General, 1956–7.
Mottershead, Frank W.	Ministry of Defence, 1956; Deputy Secretary, 1958.
Mountbatten, Earl	First Sea Lord and Chief of Naval Staff, 1955–9; Chief of Defence Staff, 1959–65.
Murphy, Robert D.	US Deputy Under-Secretary of State, 1953–9; Under-Secretary of State for Political Affairs, 1959.
Neustadt, Richard E.	Professor of Government, Harvard and Consultant to President Kennedy.
Nitze, Paul	US Assistant Secretary of Defense for International Security Affairs, 1961–3.
Norstad, General Lauris	SACUER, 1956–63.
Ormsby-Gore, David	Minister of State for Foreign Affairs, 1957– 62; British Ambassador to Washington, 1961–5.
Owen, Henry	Policy Planning Staff, US State Department, 1955–62.
Penny, Sir William	Member for Weapons R & D, UKAEA, 1954–9; Member for Research, 1959–61; Deputy Chairman, UKAEA, 1961–4.
Playfair, Sir Edward	Permanent Under-Secretary of State for War, 1956–9; Permanent Secretary, Ministry of Defence, 1960–1.
Plowden, Sir Edwin	Chairman, UKAEA, 1954–9.
Powell, Sir Richard	Permanent Secretary, Ministry of Defence, 1956–9.
Quarles, Donald	US Secretary of Air Force, 1955–7; Deputy Secretary of Defense, 1957–9.
Ramsbotham, Peter E.	Foreign Office, 1957; Counsellor, Head of Western Organisations and Planning Dept., 1961–3.
Rickover, Admiral H. G.	Chief, Bureau for Nuclear Propulsion, US

	Bureau of Ships; Chief, Naval Reactors Branch, USAEC.
Rostow, Walter W.	US Deputy Special Assistant to President for National Security Affairs, 1961; Chairman, Policy Planning Council, State Department, 1961–6.
Rowen, Henry S.	US Deputy Assistant Secretary of Defense for International Security Affairs, 1961–4.
Rubel, John	US Deputy, R & D, Dept. of Defense, 1961–2.
Rusk, Dean	US Secretary of State, 1961–9.
Salinger, Pierre	Press Secretary to President Kennedy.
Samuel, Adrian C.	Principal Private Secretary to Secretary of State for Foreign Affairs, 1959–63.
Sandys, Duncan	Minister of Supply, 1951–4; Minister of Defence, 1957–9; Minister of Aviation, 1959–63.
Schaetzel, J. Robert	US Office of Special Assistant for Atomic Energy Affairs; European Desk, Department of State.
Schlesinger, A. M. Jr,	Special Assistant to the President.
Scott, Sir Robert	Permanent Secretary, MOD, 1961–3.
Seaborg, Glenn T.	Chairman, USAEC, 1961–71.
Shuckburgh, Sir C. A. E.	Assistant Under-Secretary, Foreign Office, 1954–6; Deputy Under-Secretary, Foreign Office, 1960–2.
Slessor, Marshal Sir John	Chief of Air Staff, 1950–2.
Smith, Gerard	US Special Assistant to Secretary of State for Atomic Energy Affairs; Director, Policy Planning Council; Consultant to State Department, 1962–3.
Soames, Christoper	Under-Secretary of State for Air, 1955–7; Secretary for Admiralty, 1957–8; Secretary of State for War, 1958–60.
Sorenson, Theodore C.	US Special Counsel to the President, 1961–3.
Strath, Sir William	UKAEA, 1955–9; Permanent Secretary, Ministry of Supply, 1959; Ministry of Aviation, 1959–60.
Strauss, Rear Admiral L.	Chairman, USAEC, 1953–8.
Taylor, General M. D.	Chairman, USJCS, 1962–4.
Thorneycroft, Peter	Chancellor of Exchequer, 1957–8; Minister of Aviation, 1960–2; Minister of Defence, 1962–4.
Trend, Burke St J.	Deputy Secretary of the Cabinet, 1956–9; Third and Second Secretary of the Treasury, 1959–62.
Twining, General N. F.	Chairman, USJCS, 1957–60.
Tyler, William R.	US Assistant Secretary of State for European Affairs, 1962.
Watkinson, Harold	Minister of Defence, 1959–62.
Weiss, Seymour	US Department of State, and ICA, 1955–60; State Department, Bureau of Political and Military Affairs, 1960–7.

Whitney, John Hay	US Ambassador to London, 1956–61.
Weisner, Jerome	US Special Assistant to President for Science and Technology, 1961–4.
Wilson, Harold	Labour Leader, 1963–4.
Yarmolinsky, Adam	Special Assistant to the Secretary of Defense, 1961–5.
York, Herbert	Director, Lawrence Livermore Laboratory, 1952–8; Director, Defence Research and Engineering, Office of US Secretary of Defense, 1958–61.
Zuckerman, Sir Solly	Chief Scientific Adviser, Ministry of Defence, 1960–6.
Zuckert, Eugene	Secretary of the Air Force, 1961–5.
Zulueta, Philip de	Private Secretary to PM, 1955–64.

Select Bibliography

ARCHIVE AND MANUSCRIPT COLLECTIONS

Britain

Public Record Office, Kew

CAB 128	These files contain records of Cabinet Minutes and Memoranda
CAB 129	Defence Committees and Cabinet Committees
CAB 131	Defence Committee Minutes & Papers
CAB 133	Commonwealth & International Conferences Minutes & Papers
CAB 134	Miscellaneous Committees – Minutes & Papers
CAB 139	Central Statistical Office Correspondence & Papers

DEFE 4	Meetings of the Chiefs of Staff
DEFE 5	Chiefs of Staff Memoranda
DEFE 6	Reports of the Joint Planning Staff
DEFE 7	Ministry of Defence Registered Files, General
DEFE 10	Major Defence Committee Working Parties Papers
DEFE 11	Chief of Staff Committees Registered Files
DEFE 13	Private Office MoD Registered Files
DEFE 19	Central Scientific Defence Staff Files
DEFE 25	Chief of Defence Staff Registered Files

FO 371	Foreign Office Files. This grouping includes documents, memoranda, telegrams, Western Organisation and general Foreign Office correspondence

PREM 11	Prime Minister's Office. This record grouping contains all documents relating to the Prime Minister, including private memoranda, letters and notes

AIR 2	Research and Development
AIR 8	Chief of the Air Staff Files
AIR 19	Private Office Papers
AIR 20	Air Ministry Unregistered Papers

ADM 205	Private Papers of the First Sea Lord

Bodleian Library, Oxford
Harold Macmillan Diaries

Published Official Documents, Britain

Command Papers
Defence: Outline of Future Policy, Cmnd. 124 (HMSO, 1957)
Agreement for Co-operation on the Uses of Atomic Energy for Mutual Defence Purposes, Cmnd. 537 (HMSO, 1958)
Amendment to Agreement for Co-operation on the Uses of Atomic Energy for Mutual Defence Purposes, Cmnd. 733 (HMSO, 1969)
Statement on Defence 1962: The Next Five Years, Cmnd. 1639 (HMSO, 1962)
Bahamas Meetings: Texts of Joint Communiques, Cmnd. 1915 (HMSO, 1962)

Parliamentary Debates
Hansard, *House of Commons Debates, Vols. 568–670, 1957–January 1963*

United States

John F. Kennedy Presidential Library, Boston, Mass.

Pre-Presidential Papers, 1946–1960	This subcollection of papers reflects Representative and Senator Kennedy's major official activities
Presidential Papers, 1961–1963	This is a large collection containing the working files of President Kennedy and his presidential staff. It contains a number of subcollections including:
National Security Files	These are documents constituting the working files of McGeorge Bundy, Special Assistant to the president for National Security issues. It is the primary foreign policy file of the Kennedy White House and consists of the following series: countries, regional security, trips and conferences, departments and agencies, subjects, meetings and memoranda and staff files
President's Office Files	This subfile consists of the working files of President Kennedy as maintained by his personal secretary, Mrs Evelyn Lincoln, in the Oval Office of the White House. Series includes: general correspondence, special correspondence, speech files, legislative files, press conferences, staff memoranda, departments and agencies, subjects and countries
White House Central Files	Designed as a reference service for the president and his staff and to

<table>
<tr><td></td><td>document White House activities, the Central Files consist of four major subdivisions: White House central subject file, White House central name file, chronological file and over-size materials</td></tr>
<tr><td>White House Staff Files</td><td>This contains the files of the White House Staff during the Kennedy presidency</td></tr>
<tr><td>Presidential Recordings</td><td>This subcollection contains audiotapes of White House meetings and dictabelt recordings of telephone conversations. Topics include the Cuban Missile Crisis and winning Senate support for the Nuclear Test Ban Treaty, 1963</td></tr>
<tr><td>Private Papers</td><td>Papers of McGeorge Bundy
Papers of Robert Estabrook
Papers of Roswell Gilpatric
Papers of Robert F. Kennedy
Papers of Richard E. Neustadt
Papers of Arthur M. Schlesinger Jr
Papers of Theodore C. Sorenson
Papers of Dean Rusk
Papers of Adam Yarmolinsky</td></tr>
<tr><td>Oral History Programme</td><td>These are interviews conducted with individuals who have recollections of events and people associated with John F. Kennedy:
Richard Bissell
Charles E. Bohlen
Henry Brandon
Henry Brandon (David Nunnerley interview)
McGeorge Bundy (Nunnerley interview)
Couve de Murville
Sir Alec Douglas-Home
Hugh Fraser
William J. Fulbright
Roswell Gilpatric
Foy Kohler
Lyman L. Lemnitzer (Nunnerley interview)
Livingston T. Merchant
Robert S. McNamara
Robert S. McNamara (Nunnerley interview)</td></tr>
</table>

James   Reston   (Nunnerley
    interview)
Walt W. Rostow
Dean Rusk
Arthur Schlesinger Jr. (Nunnerley
    interview)
Theodore C. Sorenson
Peter Thorneycroft (Nunnerley
    interview)
Peter Thorneycroft
William R. Tyler
Adam Yarmolinsky
Sir Solly Zuckerman
Eugene Zuckert

National Archives, Washington, DC.
Record Group 59 Department of State

London School of Economics and Political Science
Papers of the United States Congress and Senate

Published Official Documents, USA

Foreign Relations of the United States:
1961–1963 Vol. XIII: Western Europe and Canada (1993)
1958–1960 Vol. VII: Western European Integration & Security (1993)
    (Washington DC: United States Government Printing Office)

Printed Sources, USA and Britain

Newspapers
Aviation Week
Baltimore Sun
Chicago Sun Times
Chicago Tribune
Christian Science Monitor
Daily Telegraph
Economist
The Times
Observer
Philadelphia Inquirer
Sunday Times Magazine
Manchester Guardian
Missiles and Rockets
New York Herald Tribune
New York Times
Newport News Press
Newsweek
Wall Street Journal

Washington Post
Washington Daily News
Washington Star
Space Business Daily

Interviews/Correspondence

Sir Frederick Bishop
Sir Nicholas Henderson
Karl Kaysen
Keith Kyle
Richard E. Neustadt
Sir Edward Playfair
Arthur M. Schlesinger Jr.

A number of figures from the Kennedy and Macmillan governments were also approached but declined to answer the author's questions.

Memoirs and Autobiographies

Ball, George, W., *The Discipline of Power* (Bodley Head: London, 1968).
—— *The Past Has Another Pattern: Memoirs* (W. W. Norton and Co.: New York, 1982).
Brandon, Henry, *Special Relationships: A Foreign Correspondent's Memoirs from Roosevelt to Reagan* (Atheneum: New York, 1988).
Bundy, McGeorge, *Danger and Survival: Choices about the Bomb in the First Fifty Years* (Schwartz & Wilkinson: Melbourne, 1990).
De Gaulle, Charles, *Memoirs of Hope, Renewal and Endeavor* (Weidenfeld & Nicolson: London, 1971).
Eisenhower, Dwight, D., *The White House Years* (Heinemann: London, 1965).
Evans, H., *Downing Street Diary: The Macmillan Years 1957-63* (Hodder and Stoughton: London, 1981).
Home, Alec, Douglas, *The Way The Wind Blows* (Collins: London & Glasgow, 1976).
Kennedy, Robert, *Thirteen Days* (W. W. Norton: New York, 1969).
Khrushchev, Nikita, *Khrushchev Remembers, Vols. 1 & 2* (André Deutsch: London, 1974).
Macmillan, Harold (Earl of Stockton, OM), Autobiography: Vol. IV: *Riding The Storm 1956-1959* (Macmillan: London, 1971); Vol. V: *Pointing The Way 1959-1961* (Macmillan: London, 1972); Vol. VI: *At The End Of The Day 1961-1963* (Macmillan: London, 1973)
Major Addresses, Statements, and Press Conferences of General Charles de Gaulle, 19 May 1958-31 January 1964 (French Embassy, Press and Information Division, New York, 1964).
Neustadt, Richard, E, *Alliance Politics* (Columbia University Press: London & New York, 1970).
McNamara, Robert, S., *The Essence of Security* (Hodder & Stoughton: London, 1968).

208   *Select Bibliography*

Nitze, Paul, *From Hiroshima to Glasnost: At the Centre of Decision – A Memoir* (Weidenfeld & Nicolson: London, 1989).
O'Donnell, Kenneth, P & Powers, David F., *'Johnny We Hardly Knew Ye'*: *Memories of John Fitzgerald Kennedy* (Little, Brown & Co.: Boston & Toronto, 1972).
Rostow, W. W., *The Diffusion of Power* (Macmillan: New York and London, 1972).
Rusk, Dean, *As I Saw It* (W. W. Norton & Co.: New York, 1990).
Salinger, Pierre, *With Kennedy* (Trinity Press: London, 1967).
Schlesinger, Arthur, M., Jr, *A Thousand Days* (André Deutsch: London, 1965).
Schaetzel, Robert, J., *The Unhinged Alliance* (Harper and Row: New York, 1975).
Sorenson, Theodore, C., *Kennedy* (Hodder and Stoughton: London, 1965).
Taylor, Maxwell, D., *The Uncertain Trumpet* (Atlantic Books, Stevens & Sons: London, 1960).
—— *Swords and Plowshares* (W. W. Norton: New York, 1972).
Watkinson, Harold, *Turning Points: A Record of our Times* (Michael Russel: Salisbury, 1986).
Wofford, Harris, *Of Kennedy's and Kings* (Farrar, Straus & Giroux: New York, 1980).
White, Theodore, H., *The Making of a President* (Jonathan Cape: London, 1969).
Zuckerman, S., *Monkeys, Men and Missiles 1946–88: An Autobiography* (Collins: London, 1988).

SECONDARY SOURCES

Books

Aldous, R. and Lee, Sabine, (eds), *Harold Macmillan and Britain's World Role* (Macmillan: London 1996).
Ambrose, Stephen, E., *Eisenhower the President 1952–1969, Vol. 2* (George Allen & Unwin: London, 1984)
Ball, Desmond, *Politics and Force Levels: The Strategic Missile Program of the Kennedy Administration* (University of California Press: Berkeley, 1980).
Baylis, John, *Ambiguity and Deterrence: British Nuclear Strategy* (Oxford University Press: New York, 1995).
—— *Anglo-American Defence Relations 1939–1980: The Special Relationship* (Macmillan: London, 1984 second edition).
Bell, Coral, *The Conventions of Crisis: A Study in Diplomatic Management* (Oxford, 1971).
—— *The Debatable Alliance: An Essay in Anglo-American Relations* (Oxford University Press: London, 1964).
Beschloss, M. R., *Kennedy v Khrushchev: The Crisis Years 1960–63* (Faber & Faber: New York, 1991).
Beloff, Nora, *The General Says No* (Penguin: Middlesex, 1963).

Botti, Timothy, J., *The Long Wait: Forging the Anglo-American Nuclear Alliance 1945–1958* (Greenwood Press: Connecticut, 1987).

Bowie, Robert, R., *Shaping the Future Foreign Policy in an Age of Transition* (Columbia University Press: New York, 1964).

Brodie, Bernard, *The American Scientific Strategists* (RAND Corporation, Santa Monica, 1964).

Buchan, Alastair, *The Multilateral Force: An Historical Perspective* (Institute for Strategic Studies, Adelphi Papers, Oct. 1964).

—— *NATO in the 1960s* (Weidenfeld & Nicolson: London, 1960).

Bull, Hedley, *Strategy and the Atlantic Alliance: A Critique of United States Doctrine* (Center of International Studies, Woodrow Wilson Hall: Princeton University, 1964).

Chichester, Michael and Wilkinson, J., *The Uncertain Ally: British Defence Policy 1960–1990* (Gower: Aldershot, 1982).

Clark, Ian, *Nuclear Diplomacy and the Special Relationship* (Clarendon Press: Oxford, 1994).

I. Clark and N. J. Wheller, *The Origins of Nuclear Strategy 1945–55* (Clarendon Press: Oxford, 1989).

Crawley, Aidan, *De Gaulle* (Collins: London, 1969).

Crockatt, Richard, *The Fifty Years War: The United States and the Soviet Union in World Politics, 1941–1991* (Routledge: London, 1995).

De Kadt, Emanual, *British Defence Policy and Nuclear War* (Frank Cass: London, 1964).

De Weerd, H. A., *Britain's Defence New Look Five Years Later* (RAND, March 1962).

—— *British Defence Policy: An American View* (RAND, Aug. 1961).

Dickie, John, *'Special' No More: Anglo-American Relations: Rhetoric and Reality* (Weidenfeld & Nicolson, London, 1994).

Dillon, G. M., *Dependence and Deterrence* (Gower: London, 1983).

Divine, Robert, A., *The Sputnik Challange: Eisenhower's Response to the Sputnik Satellite* (Oxford University Press: New York, 1993).

Dockrill, M., *British Defence since 1945* (Blackwell: Oxford, 1988).

Dockrill, S., *Eisenhower's New Look National Security Policy, 1953–61* (Macmillan: London, 1996).

Freedman, Lawrence, *Britain and Nuclear Weapons* (Macmillan: London, 1980).

—— *The Evolution of Nuclear Strategy* (Macmillan: London, 1989).

Furniss, Edgar, S., *France, Troubled Ally: De Gaulle's Heritage and Prospects* (Heritage & Prospects, Greenwood Press: Westport, CT, 1960).

Garnett, John (ed.), *Theories of Peace and Security: A Reader in Contemporary Strategic Thought* (Macmillan: London, 1970).

Gowing, Margaret, *Britain and Atomic Energy, 1939–1945* (Macmillan: London, 1964).

—— *Independence and Deterrence: Britain and Atomic Energy 1945–52, Vol. 1* (Macmillan: London, 1974).

—— *Independence and Deterrence: Britain and Atomic Energy, Vol. 2* (Macmillan: London, 1974).

Groom. A. J. R., *British Thinking about Nuclear Weapons* (Pinter: London, 1974).

Haftendorn, H., *NATO and the Nuclear Revolution: A Crisis of Credibility, 1966–67* (Clarendon Press: Oxford, 1996).

Halberstam, David, *The Best and the Brightest* (Random House: New York, 1969).

Hanrieder, W. F., *Germany, America, Europe: Forty Years of German Foreign Policy* (Yale University Press: New Haven & London, 1989).

Hershberg, James G., *James B. Conant: Harvard to Hiroshima and the Making of the Nuclear Age* (Stanford University Press: Stanford, California, 1993).

Hitch, Charles, J., *Decision-Making for Defense* (University of California Press: Berkeley and Los Angeles, 1965).

Horne, Alistair, *Macmillan 1957–1986*, vol. II of the *Official Biography* (Macmillan: London, 1989).

Jones, Roy, E., *Nuclear Deterrence: A Short Political Analysis* (Routledge & Kegan Paul: London, 1968).

Kahan, Jerome, H., *Security in the Nuclear Age: Developing US Strategic Arms Policy* (Brookings Institution: Washington DC, 1975).

Kaufmann, William, *The McNamara Strategy* (Harper and Row: New York, 1964).

Kelleher, Catherine, McArdle, *Germany and the Politics of Nuclear Weapons* (Columbia University Press: New York & London, 1975).

Kissinger, Henry, *The Troubled Partnership* (McGraw-Hill: New York, 1965).

—— *The White House Years* (Weidenfeld & Nicolson: London, 1979).

Kirkpatrick, Lyman, B. Jr, *The Real CIA* (Macmillan: New York, 1968).

Kleiman, R. *Atlantic Crisis: American Diplomacy Confronts a Resurgent Europe* (W. W. Norton and Co.: New York, 1964).

Kraft, Joseph, *The Grand Design* (Harper: New York, 1962).

Kyle, Keith, *Suez* (Weidenfeld & Nicolson: London, 1991).

Lamb, Richard, *The Macmillan Years 1957–1963: The Emerging Truth* (John Murray: London, 1995).

Lankford, Nelson, D., *The Last American Aristocrat: The Biography of Ambassador David K. E. Bruce* (Little, Brown and Co: Toronto, 1996).

Leifer, M., *Constraints and Adjustments in British Foreign Policy* (Allen & Unwin: London, 1972).

Louis, W. R. & Bull, H. (eds.), *The Special Relationship: Anglo-American Relations since 1945* (Oxford University Press: Oxford, 1986).

Lucas, Scott, *Divided We Stand: Britain, the US and the Suez Crisis* (Hodder and Stoughton: London, 1991).

Mako, William, P., *US Ground Forces and the Defence of Central Europe* (Brookings Institution: Washington, 1983).

Malone, Peter, *The British Nuclear Deterrent: A History* (Croom Helm: London, 1984).

Mander, John, *Great Britain or Little England?* (Penguin: London, 1963).

Melissen, Jan, *The Struggle for Nuclear Partnership: Britain, the United States and the Making of an Ambiguous Alliance, 1952–1959* (Styx Publications: Netherlands, Groningen, 1993).

Nailor, Peter, *The Nassau Connection: The Organisation and Management of the British Polaris Project* (HMSO: London, 1988).

Navias, Martin, S., *Nuclear Weapons and British Strategic Planning 1955–1958* (Clarendon Press: Oxford, 1991).

Newhouse, John, *De Gaulle and the Anglo-Saxons* (André Deutsch: London, 1970).

Nicholas, H. G., *Britain in the World Today: Britain and the United States* (Chatto & Windus: London, 1963).

Nieburg, H. L., *Nuclear Secrecy and Nuclear Policy* (Public Affairs Press: Washington, D.C., 1964).

Northedge, F. S., *British Foreign Policy* (Minerva series George Allen & Unwin: London, 1962).

Nunnerley, David, *President Kennedy and Britain* (Bodley Head: London, 1972).

Osgood, Robert, E., *NATO: The Entangling Alliance* (University of Chicago Press: Chicago 1966).

—— *The Case for the MLF: A Critical Evaluation* (Washington Centre of Foreign Policy Research, 1964).

Pach, Chester J. and Richardson, E., *The Presidency of Dwight D. Eisenhower* (University Press of Kansas: Kansas, 1991).

Patterson, Thomas, G. (ed.), *Kennedy's Quest for Victory* (Oxford University Press: New York and London, 1989).

Pierre, Andrew, J., *Nuclear Politics: The British Experience with an Independent Strategic Force, 1939–1970* (Oxford University Press: London, 1972).

McCloy, John, J., *The Atlantic Alliance: Its Origins and Future* (Carnegie-Mellon University Press: Pittsburgh, Pennsylvania, 1969).

Ranelagh, J., *The Agency: The Rise and Decline of the CIA from Wild Bill Donovan to William Casey* (Simon & Schuster: New York, 1986).

Reeves, Richard, *The Kennedy Presidency* (Papermac: London, 1994).

Reynolds, David, J., *Britannia Overruled: British Policy and World Power in the Twentieth Century* (Longman: London & New York, 1991).

Rostow, Eugene, V., *Toward Managed Peace* (Yale University Press: Yale, 1993).

Sampson, Anthony, *Macmillan: A Study in Ambiguity* (Allen Lane the Penguin Press: London, 1967).

Sanders, D., *Losing an Empire, Finding a Role: British Foreign Policy since 1945* (Macmillan: London, 1990).

Sapolsky, H. M., *The Polaris System Development: Bureaucratic and Programmatic Success in Government* (Harvard University Press: Cambridge, MA, 1972).

Schwartz, David, N., *NATO's Nuclear Dilemmas* (Brookings Institution: Washington, 1983).

Seaborg, Glen, *Kennedy, Khrushchev and the Test Ban* (University of California Press: Berkeley, 1981).

Serfaty, Simon, *France, de Gaulle and Europe* (Johns Hopkins University Press: Baltimore, MD, 1968).

Sidey, H., *John F. Kennedy: Portrait of a President* (Readers Union André Deutsch: London, 1965).

Simpson, John, *The Independent Nuclear State: The US, Britain and the Military Atom* (Macmillan: London, 1983).

Smith, M. E. and Johns, J., *American Defense Policy*, 2nd edition (The Johns Hopkins University Press: Baltimore, MD, 1968).

Snyder, William, P., *The Politics of British Defense Policy 1945–1962* (Ernest Benn Limited/Ohio State University Press: Ohio, 1964).

Spanier, John, *American Foreign Policy Since World War Two* (Holt, Rinehart and Winston: New York, 1985).

Steinbruner, John, D., *The Cybernetic Theory of Decision* (Princeton University Press: Princeton, NJ, 1974).

Steinbruner, J. D. and Sigal, Leon, V, *Alliance Security: NATO and the No-First-Use Question* (Brookings Institution: Washington, 1983).

Taber, George, M., *John F. Kennedy and a Uniting Europe* (College of Europe Press: Bruges, 1969).

Tanter, Raymond and Ullman, R. H. (eds), *Theory and Policy in International Relations* (Princeton University Press: Princeton, NJ, 1972).

Thompson, Kenneth, W. (ed.), *The Kennedy Presidency: Seventeen Intimate Perspectives of John F. Kennedy* (University Press of America: Lanham, MD, 1985).

Turner, A. C., *The Unique Partnership: Britain and the United States* (Pegasus: New York, 1963).

Warshaw, Shirley Ann (ed.), *The Eisenhower Legacy: Discussions of Presidential Leadership* (Bartleby Press: Silver Spring, MD, 1992).

Wenger, Andreas, *Living with Peril: Eisenhower, Kennedy and Nuclear Weapons* (Rowman & Littlefield: Lanham, MD, 1997).

Williams, F., *A Prime Minister Remembers* (William Heinemann: London, 1961).

Winand, Pascaline, *Eisenhower, Kennedy and the United States of Europe* (Macmillan: London, 1983).

Articles

Alderman, K., Harold Macmillan's 'Night of the Long Knives' (*Contemporary Record* 6:2, Autumn 1992).

Ball, George, W., 'The Nuclear Deterrent and the Atlantic Alliance' (*Atlantic Community Quarterly*).

Ball, Simon, J., 'Military Nuclear Relations Between The United States and Great Britain under the Terms of the McMahon Act, 1946–1958' (*The Historical Journal*, 38, 2, 1995).

Beaton, Leonard, 'The Facts About Skybolt' (*New Scientist*, No. 275, 22 February 1962).

Bowie, Robert, R., 'Strategy and the Atlantic Alliance' (*International Organization*, 1963, Vol. XVII).

Boyle, Peter G., 'The British Government's View of the Cuban Missile Crisis' (*Contemporary Record*, (10) 3 Autumn 1996).

Brandon, Henry, 'SKYBOLT: The Full Inside Story of How a Missile Nearly Split the West' (*The London Times*, 8 December 1963).

Brown, Nevile, 'Britain's Strategic Weapons II: The Polaris A-3' (*The World Today*, August 1964, Vol. XX).

Buchan, Alastair, 'Europe and the Atlantic Alliance: Two Strategies or One?' (*Journal of Common Market Studies*, 1963, Vol. 1, No. 3, Spring).

—— 'Partners and *Allies*' (*Foreign Affairs*, July 1963, Vol. XLI, No. 4).

—— 'The Choices For British Defence Policy' (*International Journal*, Summer 1963, Vol. XVIII, No. 3).

Bundy, McGeorge, 'The Presidency and the *Peace*' (*Foreign Affairs*, April 1964, Vol. 42, No. 3).

Rear Admiral Sir Anthony Buzzard, 'The H-Bomb: Massive Retaliation or Graduated Deterrence?' (*International Affairs*, 1956, Vol. XXXII, No. 2, April).

Costigliola, Frank, 'The Failed Design: Kennedy, de Gaulle and the Struggle for Europe' (*Diplomatic History*, Vol. 8, No. 3 Summer 1984).

Crossman, R. H. S., 'The Nuclear Obsession' (*Encounter*, 1958, Vol. XI, No. 1, July).

Dawson, R. and Rosecrance, R., 'Theory and Reality in the Anglo-American Alliance' (*World Politics*, October 1966).

Edmonds, Martin, 'International Collaboration in Weapons Procurement: The Implications of the Anglo-French *Case*' (*International Affairs*, April 1967, Vol. XLIII, No. 2).

Goldberg, Alfred, 'The Atomic Origins of the British Nuclear Deterrent' (*International Affairs*, July 1964, Vol. XL, No. 2).

Gott, Richard, 'The Evolution of the British Deterrent' (*International Affairs*, April 1963, Vol. XXXIX, No. 2).

Lord Harlech, 'Suez SNAFU, Skybolt SABU' (*Foreign Policy 2*, Spring 1971).

Healy, D., 'Sputnik and Western Defence' (*International Affairs*, April 1958).

—— 'Interdependence' (*Political Quarterly*, Jan.–March 1960 Vol. XXXI).

Hollis, Martin and Smith, Steve, 'Roles and Reasons in Foreign Policy Decision Making' (*British Journal of Political Science*).

Just, Ward S., The Scrapping of Skybolt (*The Reporter*, 11 April 1963).

Kaufman, B. I., 'John F. Kennedy as World Leader – A Perspective on the Literature' (*Diplomatic History* Vol. 17, No. 3, 1993).

Kennan, George, F., 'Polycentrism and Western Policy' (*Foreign Affairs*, January 1964, Vol. 42, No. 2).

Kennedy, P., 'The Continental Commitment and the Special Relationship in Twentieth Century British Foreign Policy' (*Journal of the Royal United Services Institute*, September 1983).

Kissinger, Henry A., 'Coalition Diplomacy in a Nuclear Age' (*Foreign Affairs*, July 1964, Vol. 42, No. 4).

Kopkind, Andrew, 'The "Special Relationship"' (*The New Left Review*, October 1968, Vol. 1).

Krozewski, G., 'Finance and Empire: The Dilemma Facing Great Britain in the 1950s' (*Review of International History* 1996, Vol. 18, No. 1).

Mayer, F. A., 'Adenauer and Kennedy: An Era of Distrust in German–American Relations' (*German Studies Review* 1994, Vol. 17, No. 1).

Melissen, Jan, 'Summit Diplomacy and Alliance Politics: The Road to Nassau, December 1962' (*Diplomatic Studies Programme Discussion Papers*, Leicester University, No. 12, December 1995).

—— 'Pre-Summit Diplomacy: Britain, the US and the Nassau Conference December 1962' (*Diplomacy & Statecraft*, November 1996, Vol. 7, No. 3).

Nash, P., 'Jumping Jupiters: The US Search for IRBM Host Countries in NATO 1957–59' (*Diplomacy & Statecraft*, November 1995, Vol. 6, No. 3).

Neustadt, Richard E., 'Memorandum on The British Labour Party and the MLF' (*New York Review of Books*, 5 December 1968, Vol. XI, Part 10).

Owen, L., 'Nuclear Engineering and the United Kingdom' (*Journal of the British Nuclear Society*, 1963).

Pierre, Andrew J., 'Britain's Defence Dilemmas' (*Proceedings of the Academy of Political Sciences*, November 1968, Vol. XXIX).

—— 'Nuclear Diplomacy: Britain, France and *America*' (*Foreign Affairs*, January 1971).

Rabe, S. G., 'Eisenhower Revisionism – A Decade of Scholarship' (*Diplomatic History*, 1993, Vol. 17, No. 1).

Rawnsley, Gary D., 'How Special is Special? The Anglo-American Alliance during the Cuban Missile Crisis (*Contemporary Record*, Winter 1995, Vol. 9, No. 3).

Roman, P. J., 'Strategic Bombers over the Missile Horizon, 1957–1963' (*Journal for Strategic Studies*, 1995, Vol. 18, No. 1).

Rusk, Dean, 'The State of the North Atlantic Alliance' (*Department of State Bulletin*, 5 August, 1963, Vol. 49).

Scott, Len, 'Back from the Brink: The Cuban Missile Crisis Revisited' (*Modern History Review*, 1995, Vol. 9, No. 3).

—— 'Close to the Brink: Britain and the Cuban Missile Crisis' (*Contemporary Record*, Winter 1991, Vol. 5).

Smith, Steve and Scott, Len, 'Lessons of October: Historians, Political Scientists, Policy-Makers and the Cuban Missile Crisis' (*International Affairs*, 1994, Vol. 40, No. 4).

Spaak, Paul-Henri, 'Hold Fast' (*Foreign Affairs*, July 1963, Vol. 41, No. 4).

Twigge, S. and Macmillan, A., 'Britain, the US and the Development of NATO Strategy, 1950–64' (*Journal for Strategic Studies*, 1996, pp. 260–81, Vol. 19, No. 2).

Verrier, A., 'Defence and Politics After Nassau' (*Political Quarterly*, July–September 1963).

Warner, Geoffrey, 'The Nassau Agreement and NATO' (*The World Today*, February 1963).

Williams, P., 'The United States and Western Europe: A Conditional Commitment' (*Interstate*, 1978, Vol. 3, No. 2).

Index

Acheson, Dean, 73–4, 152
Adenauer, Conrad, 85, 97, 106, 110, 116, 135–6, 140
air-launched ballistic missile, 1
Anglo-American relations, 1–3, 6, 8, 11–13, 19, 30–1, 84, 87, 89, 107, 130, 132–3, 145–6, 152–5
armed services, 7, 16, 76
Atlantic Alliance, 1, 111, 113, 118
Atlas, 38, 46, 66
atomic energy, 15
  weapons, 7, 15, 17, 33–4, 108
atomic research, 14
  see also United States

Ball, George, 68, 72, 85–6, 103, 109, 111, 137, 144
ballistic missiles, 1, 19, 35, 37–8, 45, 84, 86
Belgium, 117
Berlin, 22, 30, 58
Blair, Tony, 7
Blue Steel, 60
Blue Streak, 31, 36, 38–9, 41
bombers
  B-29, 17
  B-52, 50
  B-70, 48–50
  Canberra, 17
Britain
  alienation from US, 33
  atomic device, 16
  bid for EEC entry, 10, 30, 70–1, 78, 85, 100, 106, 111, 152
  Chiefs of Staff, 124
  defence policy, 20, 33, 37, 39, 53, 89
  dependence on US, 37, 84, 145
  economy, 5
  foreign policy, 89
  hydrogen device, 19
  independent deterrent, 10, 18, 32, 52, 70, 73–5, 77–8, 81, 89–92,

98, 101, 104, 145, 149, 152, 158
  military co-operation with US, 16
  McMahon Act, 15, 17
  nuclear co-operation with US, 15, 17–19, 31–2, 36
  nuclear independence, 8, 10, 15–17, 32, 70
  nuclear strategy, 3–4, 10, 32, 33
  nuclear technology, 34–5
  relations with France, 19
  relations with Western Europe, 21
  views on Multilateral Nuclear Force see MLF
British Army of the Rhine (BAOR), 125
British Government
  Communications Headquarters (GCHQ), 19
Brown, George, 92
Bruce, David, 3, 18, 54, 59, 63–4, 112–13, 144
Bundestag, 116–17
Bundy, McGeorge, 51, 64, 139–40, 142, 150

cabal, 109
Caccia, Lord Harold, 23, 131
Camp David, 3–4, 9, 36–9, 41, 45, 99, 145, 153
China, 21
Churchill, Winston, 23, 37
Clinton, William, J., 7
Cold War, 7, 16, 19, 158
Congress, 49, 60, 64, 68, 94, 112, 114–15, 135, 138, 150
Conservative Party, 2, 52, 64, 76
Cuba, 158
Cuban Missile Crisis, 10, 28, 51, 79–80, 152
Cabinet see Macmillan

De Gaulle, Charles, 30, 81, 85–6, 93–4, 97–8, 100, 103, 106–7,

215

De Gaulle – *continued*
    109, 111–12, 115–16, 127,
    131–2, 138, 140, 154, 155
De Murville, Couve, 111, 118
détente, 21, 86
Douglas Corporation, 46, 62, 65, 77
Douglas, James, 46–7, 146
Douglas-Home, Sir Alec, 29, 59, 83,
    90, 139, 156
Dulles, John Foster, 33

East–West relations, 17, 34, 36, 86
Eden, Sir Anthony, 2, 17
Egypt, 18
Eisenhower, Dwight, D., 3, 33, 88,
    144
    administration, 17, 33, 58
    defence policy, 33
    Holy Loch deal, 42, 84
    multilateral nuclear force, 105
    New Look, 33, 37, 58
    Skybolt offer to Britain, 41, 95,
        145
    Suez crisis, 18, 34
    relations with Britain after Suez,
        18, 35, 145
    relations with Macmillan, 18, 21,
        23, 58, 84
European
    Economic Community, 30, 70–1,
        80–1, 106
    deterrent, 92
    sixes and sevens divide, 2
Europeanists, 67, 72, 93, 103, 109, 139

fission, 14–15
Fletcher Committee, 46
flexible response, 37
Force de Frappe, 94, 127–8, 131
Ford Motor Company, 48
Foreign Office, 123, 133, 140, 142,
    146
France, 17, 59, 70, 85, 87, 90, 92–4,
    98, 100, 103, 111, 115–16, 118
Franco-German Treaty, 107
Frisch, Otto, 15

Gaitskell, Hugh, 92
Gaither Report, 33

Gates, Thomas, 33, 42, 46–8, 69,
    146
Gilpatric, Roswell, 51, 99
Greece, 118
GAM-87A *see* Skybolt
Gareloch *see* Holy Loch
Germany *see* West Germany

Harriman, Averell, 141, 156
Holland, 118
Holy Loch
    Agreement, 35, 41, 78, 146
    link with Skybolt deal, 4, 8–9, 42,
        43
    attempts to disassociate from
        Skybolt deal, 43
hydrogen bombs, 17, 19

Italy, 119, 120, 156
intelligence, 7, 59
intermediate range ballistic missiles
    see ballistic missiles

Johnson, Lyndon B., 2, 143, 158
Joint Chiefs of Staff (US), 53–4, 64
Joint Congressional Committee on
    Atomic Energy, 114

Katanga crisis, 79
Kennedy, Jacqueline, 25, 28
Kennedy, John F., 1
    administration, 9, 11–13, 23, 29,
        37, 47, 53, 58, 60, 62, 70, 73,
        76, 79, 93–4, 103–4, 112, 125,
        129, 131, 136, 139, 144, 147,
        150–4, 158
    assassination, 143, 158
    background, 23
    briefings on Skybolt, 9, 53, 55, 64,
        82, 89, 94, 151
    character, 23–4, 158
    concerns about Anglo-French
        nuclear collaboration, 94,
        100, 154
    concerns about West German
        nuclear ambitions, 85, 94,
        100, 109–11, 126, 128, 132
    Cuban Missile Crisis, 29
    decision to cancel Skybolt, 54, 65

decision to sell Britain Polaris, 11
fears about nuclear war, 20
feeling about MLF, 11–12, 108,
   113–14, 119–22, 132, 135,
   138–41, 143, 155, 156
Grand Design, 106, 111
links to aristocracy, 27
presidency, 2, 6, 11, 96, 158
pressures on, 11, 93–5, 153
reaction to Skybolt partial test
   flight success, 92
relations with France, 97, 100,
   103, 115, 154
relations with Macmillan, 7, 21–2,
   25, 26, 28–9, 58, 91, 95, 121,
   144, 154, 158
remarks about Skybolt, 81
sense of humour, 25
service record, 25
U-turn in foreign policy, 11, 93–5,
   153
views on nuclear proliferation, 73,
   93
views on small, independent
   nuclear forces, 93
see also Special Relationship
see also Skybolt
Khrushchev, Nikita, 111
Kissinger, Henry, 14
Korean War, 5, 16–17
Kennedy, Joseph P., 22

Laos, 25
Labour Party, 92

Macmillan, Harold
   Bermuda meeting, 18
   Cabinet, 78, 80, 90, 99, 128–9,
      131, 133, 136, 138, 141, 149
   Conservative government, 38–9,
      64, 70, 76, 82, 96, 99–100,
      103, 122, 152, 154
   Cuban Missile Crisis, 29, 152
   desire for an independent British
      nuclear deterrent, 78, 104
   links to aristocracy, 27
   meeting with de Gaulle, 81, 85,
      100
   Nassau, 80–104, 139, 154

nuclear testing, 78
pay-pause, 79, 152
policy of co-operation with US,
   18–19, 34–5, 38, 58, 104, 158
political career, 27, 81
relations with Eisenhower, 3–4, 9,
   21, 23, 43, 58
relations with Kennedy, 7, 21,
   24–6, 28–9, 58, 82, 91, 104,
   144, 158
service record, 25, 88
Skybolt, 9, 39, 61–3, 74–5, 77–8,
   80–81, 83, 87, 88, 99
views on Europe, 78–9
views on West German nuclear
   ambitions, 126–9, 156
views on MLF, 122, 124, 130–1,
   137, 142, 156, 157
views on Polaris, 39, 78, 83–5, 89,
   145, 154
Manhattan Project, 15, 85
Massive Retaliation, 33
Maud Committee, 15
medium range ballistic missile force
   (MRBM), 4, 43, 70, 117
see also ballistic missiles
Merchant, Livingstone, 107, 113–14,
   116–20, 134–6, 140
see also Multilateral Nuclear
   Force
Military Assistance Program, 17
Ministry of Defence, 76, 123, 133,
   142
Minuteman, 50, 67, 81, 87
Missile Development Programme,
   17, 38
missile gap theory, 50
Mountbatten, Lord Louis, 40, 78
Multilateral (Nuclear) Force (MLF)
   analysis of, 5
   background, 1, 3, 11, 70, 96
   British views on, 12, 120–2, 124,
      129, 131–4, 136, 140–2, 156,
      157
   costs, 107, 118, 124–5, 129, 135
   debate over, 2, 4, 12, 105, 113,
      115, 128, 137
   discussed at Nassau, 85, 94, 96,
      101–3, 106, 130

Multilateral – *continued*
  Merchant Mission, 116, 120, 122,
    134
  mixed-manned concept, 97, 104,
    123, 129, 135, 139, 142–3, 156
  multilateral component, 102, 104,
    119, 122, 123, 130
  multinational component, 102,
    104, 119, 122, 130
  proponents of, 107, 109–11, 117,
    125, 138, 140, 142, 154
  proposal, 10–12, 107–8, 112–14,
    117–18, 122–5, 129–30, 135,
    139, 142, 154, 158
  Sales Agreement, 129
  thrust in 1963, 11, 113, 131, 135
  under Lyndon Johnson, 158
  views of European countries,
    115–19, 134, 139, 140
  West German support for, 116–17,
    135–6, 140, 142–3, 156
Mutual Assured Destruction, 33
McMahon Act, 15–16, 19, 31, 35, 87
  see also United States
McNamara, Robert
  reform of Department of
    Defense, 48, 66, 147
  relations with Thorneycroft, 5, 10,
    59, 65
  meetings with Thorneycroft, 5,
    10, 50–1, 55–6, 65, 68, 72, 76,
    99, 153
  Skybolt, 9, 49–50, 53–5, 63–4,
    67–72, 146–7, 150
  views on British independent
    nuclear deterrent, 73
  views on MLF, 112, 136

Nassau
  Agreement, 4, 11, 90–1, 93, 98,
    102, 105, 111, 123, 129, 139,
    146, 154, 158
  background, 12
  British press reaction to, 91
  Communiqué, 4, 90, 92–3, 122,
    156
  Conference, 1, 3–4, 10, 11, 56,
    63–4, 79–104, 106, 115, 131,
    133–4, 151, 153, 154

  controversy surrounding, 101–3
  negotiations, 81–104
  Polaris offer to France, 19, 90, 93,
    103
  political reaction to, 91–2
  vagueness of, 12, 92, 101, 102–3,
    154
National Security Agency (NSA), 19
North Atlantic Treaty Organisation
  (NATO), 1, 8, 12, 16, 20, 33–4,
  40, 43–4, 56, 71–4, 85, 87,
  89–90, 97–8, 101, 103, 105, 107,
  111, 113, 117, 119, 124–6, 130,
  133, 154–5, 158
New Frontier, 1, 144
Neustadt, Richard, E., 6, 54, 57, 58,
  69
Nitze, Paul, 52, 64, 72, 103, 112
Nixon, Richard, 21
nuclear proliferation, 11, 15, 37, 73,
  93, 112, 137
nuclear test ban negotiations, 35,
  141, 155
Nuclear Test Ban Treaty, 30, 142,
  155
nuclear testing, 28, 34, 78
nuclear war, fears of, 5, 22, 28
nuclear weapons, 12, 17, 19, 32–4,
  109, 127

Ormsby-Gore, Sir David, 3, 11, 23,
  26–9, 53–4, 59, 62–4, 67, 82–3,
  94, 137–8, 144, 150–1, 153

Parliament, 91
Pearl Harbor, 36
Peierls, Rudol, 15
Pentagon, 46, 66, 70, 74
Polaris, 3–5, 36, 39, 41–2, 44, 47, 67,
  81, 87
  Agreement, 122
  as an alternative to Skybolt, 9, 11,
    40–1, 43, 55–6, 66, 71–2, 79,
    83–6, 88, 93, 145, 150–1,
    153–4
  costs, 90
  design, 45, 67
  offer to Britain at Nassau, 96,
    103–4, 122, 130, 157

offer to France at Nassau, 97
source of clash between
    McNamara and
    Thorneycroft, 10, 69, 147
see also MLF and NATO
Profumo Affair, 152

Reagan, Ronald, 7
Rhodesia, 79
Roosevelt, F, D, 23
Royal Air Force, 40, 46, 62, 76
    Relations with USAF, 16–17, 20,
    51, 59, 148
Royal Navy, 17, 40, 59, 76
Rubel, John, 50, 52–3, 62
Rusk, Dean, 9, 53, 55, 59, 63–5, 96,
    102, 112, 119–20, 135, 147,
    150–1

Sandys, Duncan, 83, 90
Schaetzel, Robert, 70, 72, 144
Schlesinger, Arthur, M., Jr, 1, 24
sea-launched ballistic missile *see*
    ballistic missiles
Second World War, 5, 7, 13–14, 19,
    145
Secretary of Defense *see* Robert
    McNamara and US
    Department of Defense
Secretary of State *see* Dean Rusk
    and US State Department
Sino-Indian dispute, 79
Skybolt, 1–2, 8, 53
    Agreement between US and
        Britain, 3, 42, 45, 69, 77, 86,
        96, 146, 153
    as a defence suppression weapon,
        49, 66
    as alternative to Blue Streak, 41
    American development of, 41, 46,
        48–9, 66
    analysis, 4–5, 8, 93
    background, 31, 39, 145–6
    British government's views on, 10,
        31, 40–1, 74, 86, 148–9
    British personnel involved in, 59,
        61, 65, 148–9
    cancellation of, 3, 8, 53–4, 62, 65,
        77, 84, 93, 146, 148–9

costs, 40, 45, 49, 53, 65, 67, 81, 83
crisis, 1–2, 5, 8, 9–12, 31, 55, 57,
    60, 80–2, 95, 106, 130, 146,
    158, 150, 152, 154
decision to sell to Britain, 19
design, 45, 49, 65–6, 146–7
Eisenhower administration, 58, 145
links to Holy Loch *see* Holy Loch
leaking of cancellation plans, 55,
    66, 148
McNamara's understanding of
    Agreement, 68–70, 150, 151
recommendations to cancel
    project, 50, 53, 147
report into, 6, 57
rumours about cancellation, 52
suggested alternatives to, 71, 82,
    85
see also Hound Dog
supporters of, 46, 49, 60, 64, 92
termination clause, 46, 69, 151
test flights, 51, 92
views of US administration, 70–1,
    79, 147
warnings about problems, 47,
    61–2, 75, 146, 148
Soreson, Theodore, 1, 58, 112
South East Asia Treaty
    Organisation (SEATO), 26
Soviet Union, 5, 13, 20–1, 26, 28,
    33–5, 41, 46, 115, 127–8
Spaak, Paul-Henri, 117
special relationship, 6–7, 12–14,
    18–20, 29–31, 34, 37, 57–8, 70,
    73, 76, 94, 100, 103–4, 111,
    129–30, 144, 151, 154, 157, 158
Sputnik, 19, 34–6
Suez Canal, 18
Suez Crisis, 6, 8, 10, 18, 34–6, 38
summitry, 21
Supreme Allied Commander,
    Europe (SACEUR), 43

Taylor, Maxwell, D., 64
technology, 5–6
Thatcher, Margaret, 7
theologians, 104, 109
Thermonuclear bomb *see* Hydrogen
    bomb

Thor intermediate range ballistic
    missiles, 19, 35, 37
Thorneycroft, Peter
    at Nassau, 83, 104
    relations with Macmillan, 62, 77,
        90, 149
    meetings about Skybolt, 5, 10,
        55–6, 65, 68, 72, 76, 99, 153
    political ambitions, 75
    relations with McNamara, 5, 10,
        50, 53–4, 65, 153
    Skybolt, 9, 52, 62, 75–6, 149
    views on MLF, 124, 133
Titan, 50–1
Tory Party *see* Conservative Party
Turkey, 118
Tyler, William, 52, 70, 137

United Nations, 16
United States, 1, 4
    Air Force, 16–17, 20, 39, 46, 48–9,
        51, 59–2, 64–5, 68, 77, 92, 99,
        147, 148
    anti-Americanism, 88, 131
    as a superpower, 5
    atomic co-operation, 7, 15, 36
    atomic legislation, 7, 145,
        Atomic Energy Act, 17, 19,
            36, 108, 114,
        McMahon Act, 15–17, 19, 31,
            35–7, 87,
        modus vivendi, 16
    atomic research, 15
    co-operation in intelligence, 13,
        17, 19
    co-operation in military defence,
        13, 17
    co-operation in Project E and X,
        17, 19–20
    defence policy, 33

Department of Defense, 59, 62,
    66, 71, 103
    see also Robert McNamara
Department of State, 12, 53–4,
    65–7, 70–1, 74, 94, 96, 107,
    129, 138, 147
    see also Rusk, Dean
    fear of West German nuclear
        ambitions, 86, 131
    see also West Germany
    foreign policy, 12, 21, 103, 109,
        111
    interdependence with Britain, 8,
        31
    isolationism, 13
    Navy, 39, 59, 124
    relations with Britain, 6, 10,
        13–14, 16–17, 20, 154
    relations with Europe, 34, 154
    relations with France, 93

Vassal scandal, 79, 152
V-bombers, 17, 38, 40–1, 43, 45–6,
    70, 89, 97–8, 101, 145–6

Watkinson, Harold, 39, 41, 59, 60,
    76, 148
Western Defence, 12
Western Europe, 11, 111
West Germany, 11, 15, 85, 113, 116,
    117, 119, 125, 135, 142–3, 155–6
    nuclear ambitions, 11, 71, 86, 94,
        109–10, 126–8, 157
Whitney, Jock, 25
Wilson, Harold, 128

Zuckerman, Sir Solly, 47, 59, 62, 64,
    76, 148
Zuckert, Eugene, 49, 67